Advance Praise for

THE LAST SUPPER

"More than any other recent book, this work sets out with absolute clarity and sometimes uncomfortable honesty the intolerable reality of life for Christians in the Middle East today ... a deeply intelligent picture of the situation, without cheap polemic or axe-grinding, this is a very important survey indeed."

—Former Archbishop of Canterbury Rowan Williams, Master of Magdalene College, Cambridge University

"This timely, unflinching and necessary book about the plight of Christians in the lands where Christianity first arose reminds us that we are all complicit, whether through indifference or ignorance. Klaus Wivel deprives us of any alibi for our silence."

—Professor Valentina Izmirlieva, Columbia University and author of *All the Names of the Lord: Lists, Mysticism, and Magic*

"A convincing and upsetting account of the systematic discrimination and persecution faced by Christians in the Middle East. We Jews have a special obligation to speak out and *The Last Supper* provides us with the information we need to take this challenge seriously."

—Rabbi Michael Lerner, editor of *Tikkun Magazine*

"An excellent, important and sad book ... Klaus Wivel provides a voice to a forgotten and oppressed minority in the Arab Middle East."

—Flemming Rose, author of *The Tyranny of Silence* and former foreign editor of *Jyllands-Posten*

"A sobering account with real life stories that detail the systemic targeting of ancient communities in the Middle East. By exposing such atrocities the hope is that people of all faiths can awaken and cleanse their societies of hate and intolerance."

—Professor Alexander Dawoody,
Marywood University and President of the Association
for Middle Eastern Public Policy and Administration

"A central question that animates Wivel is why those in the West, who profess a belief in such universal values as freedom and equality, have not done more to defend the human rights of this severely beleaguered minority."

—Eamon Moynihan, *The University Bookman*

"Revealing, shocking, and well-researched reading."

—*Jyllands-Posten*

"Wivel journeys to the West Bank, Gaza, Egypt, Lebanon and Iraq to investigate for himself the conditions of the Christian minority in this part of the Islamic world. The reality Wivel confronts … illustrates one of our time's greatest human rights violations."

—*Berlingske Tidende*

"Klaus Wivel has written an essential book about the Christians in a hot Arab Spring."

—*Information*

"With *The Last Supper*, Klaus Wivel has delivered a quite simply overwhelmingly pertinent book … *The Last Supper* should lead to a larger debate and self-reflection … over the neglect of a contemporary persecution that hasn't yet been given a name."

—*Weekendavisen*

THE LAST SUPPER

The Plight of Christians in Arab Lands

KLAUS WIVEL

Translated by Mark Kline

NEW VESSEL PRESS
NEW YORK

THE LAST SUPPER

 New Vessel Press

www.newvesselpress.com

First published in Danish in 2013 as *Den sidste nadver*
Copyright © 2013 Klaus Wivel and Kristeligt Dagblads Forlag A/S
Translation Copyright © 2016 Mark Kline

DANISH ARTS FOUNDATION

Cover photo: A blood-spattered poster of Jesus inside the Coptic Christian Saints Church in Alexandria, Egypt in 2011 after a car bomb. (Associated Press/Ben Curtis)

Library of Congress Cataloging-in-Publication Data
Wivel, Klaus
[Den sidste nadver. English]
The Last Supper/ Klaus Wivel; translation by Mark Kline.
p. cm.
ISBN 978-1-939931-344
Library of Congress Control Number 2015950562
I. Denmark – Nonfiction

CONTENTS

THE LAST SUPPER

PROLOGUE

We don't know much about the last days of Mahmoud Al-Asali, though a few details have emerged. He came from a highly regarded Muslim family, and he was a law professor in Mosul, Iraq's second largest city, which has been inhabited by Assyrians, Chaldeans, and Christians for nearly two millennia.

Prior to the Iraqi war in 2003, the city was home to fifty thousand Christians. But kidnappings, liquidations of priests, murders, and the burning of churches since then have thinned out their numbers; on the June day in 2014 when ISIS captured Mosul, it is believed that fewer than ten thousand Christians were living there. In a sense, that day was the culmination of a decade of persecution by Islamists. The Christians' days were numbered once the ISIS fighters took over.

They went to work with meticulous precision. On the walls of Christian homes they painted the Arabic letter *n*, nun, ن, which represents Nasara, Nazarenes. In Muslim countries, this word is a denigrating way to refer to people from Nazareth. It originates from the Koran.

ISIS gave the Christians an ultimatum: If they wanted to stay in Mosul, they must either convert to Islam or pay a head tax, the so-called *jizya*. If they refused, ISIS said, they would be executed. Their final option was to leave the city immediately, abandoning everything they owned, to be plundered by the new rulers; naturally most Christians chose to do that.

A seventy-five-year-old Christian woman (for her protection, I won't reveal her name) lived in Dindan, a Christian section of Mosul on the west bank of the Tigris River where ISIS fighters began their campaign of expulsion. She had no intention of converting or being killed, and the fighters demanded that she leave the city at once. Professor Al-Asali, who lived close to the woman, heard of this and asked them to give her time to get ready to leave, and also to find someone to take care of her house while she was gone.

We are only now beginning to realize the extent of the expulsions during the summer of 2014. Mosul and the plains of Nineveh are the traditional home of Christians, but outside of three or four families who chose to convert to Islam, there are virtually no Christians in Mosul today, or in the surrounding areas. All of them, approximately 110,000, have in all likelihood fled the sections of the Nineveh plains invaded by ISIS. The Islamic fighters are "waging war on history," as the Lebanese journalist Hisham Melhem, a correspondent for the Al-Arabiya network and *An-Nahar* newspaper, writes in a moving obituary for a lost culture. "The tragedy that befell the native Christians of the Fertile Crescent, Arabs and non-Arabs, since the American invasion of Iraq in 2003 ... has raised for the first time the specter of the possible end of Christianity in the Fertile Crescent."

The inability of the Western world to react to these recent events is also shocking. Very few are willing to emulate Professor Mahmoud Al-Asali in trying to protect an ancient culture that essentially is our own.

This book is not about what ISIS has done in Syria and Iraq. I traveled in four Arab countries from the autumn of 2012 to the summer of 2013, and this book was finished before ISIS appeared seemingly out of thin air and conquered an enormous area in Syria and Iraq.

Neither did I witness the drastic consequences for Egyptian Christians following the military intervention of July 3, 2013 that removed the Muslim Brotherhood from power. On August 14, 2013, a few days after I had handed in the manuscript of this book, Islamists took revenge on the new military regime that had brutally killed almost a thousand Brotherhood demonstrators. The vendetta was aimed at Copts, the Christian group whose situation in Egypt is becoming more precarious as their numbers dwindle. The Brotherhood justified their attack by claiming that the Copts' newly elected Egyptian pope, Tawadros II, had supported the coup and declared "war against Islam and Muslims," according to a statement by the Islamist movement. This statement was an open invitation to go amok. Copts were made the scapegoats for the clashes in Egypt between the old military regimes and the Islamists, which echoed what has happened to Christians all over the Middle East. In places such as Syria and Iraq, Christians are paying the price for their alliance with *l'ancien régime*.

The supporters of the Brotherhood knew where to vent their anger on that August day in 2013. According to an Egyptian human rights organization, the Egyptian Initiative for Personal Rights, at least forty-six churches and monasteries all across Egypt were plundered, destroyed, or set fire to. Many of them burned to the ground. The same happened to dozens of Christian parish halls, libraries, shops, homes, schools, and social centers. Even a Coptic children's orphanage was the victim of arson. The police and security forces, which also were under attack that day, provided no protection; it was up to Christians to defend themselves as best they could. Samuel Tadros, an Egyptian researcher at the Hudson Institute whom I interviewed at length for this book, believes it was the worst attack on Egyptian Christians since the fourteenth century. A *Kristallnacht* for the Copts.

Two stories illustrate the horrors of these historic attacks in Egypt and link them to what would happen in Mosul a year later. A thirty-three-year-old Christian businessman from Minya told the following story:

"A neighbor called me and said the store was on fire. When I arrived, three extremists with knives approached me menacingly when they realized I was the owner."

He was fortunate to escape when the arsonists discovered a Christian boy filming the episode with his cell phone. They began chasing after the boy instead, the man explained, while shouting "Nusrani, Nusrani,"—the same denigrating Arab word that the walls of houses in Mosul were marked with. "On our Mustafa Fahmy Street, the Islamists had earlier painted a red *X* on Muslim stores and a black *X* on Christian stores," he told the Associated Press. "You can be sure that the ones with a red *X* are intact." Then there's the second story: A forty-seven-year-old nun ran a Catholic school in Bani Suef, less than a hundred miles south of Cairo. She said the school had been attacked by a group of Islamists who tore down the cross visible from the street and replaced it with a black banner resembling that of Al Qaeda. They plundered the school, taking away its computers, furniture, and other contents, and then set it on fire. The nuns called the police, but to no avail. She and two other nuns were then taken as hostages and led out onto the street.

"At the end, they paraded us like prisoners of war and hurled abuse at us as they led us from one alley to another without telling us where they were taking us," she said.

A Muslim woman who once taught at the school spotted her and the two other nuns as they walked past her home.

"I remembered her, her name is Saadiyah," said the nun. "She offered to take us in and said she can protect us since her son-in-law was a policeman. We accepted her offer."

The nuns had to fight their way over to the woman while demonstrators molested and beat them. They were saved by an act of mercy. Muslims of the same cloth as the Mosul professor are also found in Egypt.

This book is in itself a prologue. It's an investigation of the festering that led to the outbreak of violence in Egypt and Iraq; it shows that the persecution of the past few years didn't appear out of the blue. Christians have been emigrating from Muslim countries for decades, but in the new millennium the violence and urge to leave have increased. I sensed it most clearly in Iraq, but not only there. The mood among many Christians in the Palestinian Territories, Egypt, and Lebanon was also bleak.

I had one question for all the people I met in these four places: Why were Christians fleeing, leaving the areas where Christianity was born? Christianity has spread across the globe, but here at its source the percentage of Christians was shrinking. No place in the world has such a small Christian population as in North Africa and the Middle East. Only about 4 percent.

What has happened?

Presumably Professor Al-Asali knew the possible consequences for helping the elderly Christian woman in Mosul. It was no secret at the time how Islamists had treated the aid workers they captured in Syria, and what was being done to the Christians there.

The complicity of the Sunni locals in Mosul was evident, too. When the professor decided to intervene on the woman's behalf, he might have known that others in Mosul had pointed out which walls the new rulers should mark with ن. There was a reason why Islamists took over the city so easily: they were welcomed with open arms.

Christians were painfully aware of this. They witnessed how

suddenly their neighbor, their old school classmate, the corner grocer, or their coworker, "joined with the young jihadists to steal, plunder our homes, and kidnap women and children," according to a thirty-seven-year-old Christian refugee in the Kurdish capital Erbil. For the same reason, it might be a long time before Christians, Yezidis (the religious group whose suffering at the hands of ISIS has been even worse than that of Christians), and other minorities return to their old homes in and around Mosul, even should ISIS one day be defeated. Most likely they will never come back. As a Christian refugee in Erbil told *The Washington Post*, "We wanted Iraq. Iraq doesn't want us."

Some did want the Christians, and they went to great lengths to show it. This book is dedicated to people like Saadiyah, the Egyptian teacher in Bani Suef, and Professor Al-Asali in Mosul. His concern for the elderly Christian lady cost him dearly. The ISIS warriors ignored his appeal of mercy and instead sent the woman out of Mosul into the burning summer sun, without any of her possessions. They took the professor to some unknown location. Later his family was told to pick him up at the morgue. When they arrived, they saw he had been shot in the head.

I didn't travel throughout the Arab countries to promote Christianity. If you are looking for a comprehensive survey of Christian Arab theology, liturgy, diversity, and tradition in this book, you have come to the wrong place. I traveled to meet Christians (and a few Muslims). Whether they were Greek Orthodox, Catholic, Protestant, Copt, Maronite, Chaldean, believers, doubters, or atheists, was of little importance. I was interested in their stories. I wanted to hear why so many of them yearned to leave the region.

This book is about those people.

And actually I should thank a former Danish politician, Villy Søvndal, for my journey. In October 2011, I wrote an open letter to him in the Danish newspaper I work for, *Weekendavisen*, shortly after he had become foreign minister. I wanted to hear what he was planning to do about the thousands of Copts in Egypt leaving the home of one of the world's oldest Christian populations, driven away by countless attacks and church burnings, the perpetrators of which were seldom brought to justice. Surely one of his first acts as minister would be to call in the Egyptian ambassador for a serious meeting, to make him aware that the Danish government frowned upon the crimes being committed against Christians. He was going to do something, right?

But the foreign minister never answered me, nor did he publicly protest the killing of Copts, which I assumed meant that he simply didn't share my concern. And that's why I went to the Middle East—to gain insight into what was happening. I have also tried to understand why Søvndal and so many of his Western colleagues, including in the United States, didn't seem all that worried. Many of the Christians I met in Arab lands also sensed a lack of interest from the West in their troubled circumstances. Why the silence, why no sense of empathy and alarm? One elderly Catholic gentleman in Bethlehem explained it in a way that has stuck with me: "The West considers us to be Arabs; the Arabs consider us to be Christians. We lose either way."

There is an astonishing breadth to the outrages Christians are being subjected to, from judicial and social discrimination to harassment and persecution and, in some instances, to expulsion. It has become more difficult for Christians to live in many Arab countries in the new millennium. But the discrimination against Christians has gone on for centuries.

Klaus Wivel
Copenhagen, March 11, 2016

CHAPTER 1

The West Bank and Gaza

I gaze out over southern Jerusalem as the Catholic priest places the wafer on my tongue. Behind me Beit Jala covers the top of this steep hillside leading down to the Cremisan Valley. We stand among the old olive trees on the slope, six hundred feet below the town.

The sun is about to set behind the hill on this late afternoon in October, 2012. We have driven here from Bethlehem in the West Bank, ten minutes to the west. The Catholic priest stands beside a small table covered by a white tablecloth in this no-man's-land between Israel and the Palestinian Territories. He has taken a small round piece of unleavened bread out of a gold cup and dipped it in sweet wine.

My host, an influential man in Bethlehem, has invited me to receive Communion even though I am not a Catholic. I'm not even a believer, nor have I been baptized. Of course I know the liturgy, but I'm a stranger in an unfamiliar world, in a brotherhood where I don't belong. I follow my host out of courtesy, but I feel like an anthropologist who for the sake of research blends into a local tribe and takes part in their cultural rituals.

Only once before have I received Communion. That happened about ten years prior in a small church in the flatlands of Nebraska. The church was half full of well-off, aged, sullen Scandinavian immigrant farmers with rough, large hands and leathery faces. Their children and grandchildren had long since moved away to cities. There, too, was a dying culture. I might as well have been on another planet. Back then I felt like a blasphemer on the road to perdition, as if the church would collapse around me if I received the wafer.

A circle of thirty people have gathered here on the hillside, half of them elderly, the other half young Western Christians in the country to aid the Palestinian cause. It seems as though these two categories of people—those too old to seek asylum and the young idealists—are the only Christians here. More Palestinian Christians now live outside Palestine than within. Many more.

About seven thousand Christians reside in Beit Jala, the Palestinian town behind us. About one hundred thousand immigrants or descendants of the town's residents today live in Central and South America and in the United States. In Latin America alone, Christian Palestinians make up approximately 85 percent of all Palestinian immigrants.

I'm not standing here with my tongue sticking out because I want to describe one more battle in the endless conflict over land and justice between two nations, even though this idyllic valley was a battlefield a little over ten years ago. Back then, Palestinian militias fired across the valley at Israeli civilians in the southernmost quarter of Israeli Jerusalem, and the Israeli military answered with heavy artillery that destroyed entire buildings.

I'm here because of the Christian Palestinians assembled on the slope. I want to write about them while they still live here. Palestinian militias from outside, not Christians, shot from the houses and yards of this primarily Christian town. At that time some of the citizens of Beit Jala sent a message to Yasser Arafat, president of the Palestinian Authority, pleading with him to stop the militias.

Other townsfolk simply emigrated, following the hundreds of thousands of other Christian Palestinians throughout the years.

The numbers speak for themselves. In 1922, 10 percent of the population in what was then officially known as Palestine were Christians. Today, according to the Palestinian Central Bureau of Statistics, there are forty thousand Christians in the West Bank (excluding East Jerusalem) out of a Palestinian population of two million. Two percent. And that percentage is dwindling.

Because of this, a sense of panic has been steadily growing among Christian Palestinians. Many of them talk about how the old churches—for example, the Church of the Nativity in Bethlehem and the Church of the Holy Sepulchre in Jerusalem—soon will be mere tourist attractions, ruins of a two-thousand-year-old vanished civilization kept open for visitors, their congregations on the brink of extinction.

One of the reasons for this is easy to understand. Christians have emigrated to countries where they can live under better conditions. Integration has gradually become easier for new Palestinian Christian immigrants in places such as those South American cities where their numbers have increased.

But the why cannot be ascribed to a single reason. Significant events include the Ottoman Empire's attempt to recruit non-Muslims for its army in 1909; the establishment of Israel and the expulsion of Palestinians in 1948; the Six Day War and the Israeli occupation of the West Bank and Gaza in 1967; the Palestinian rebellion, the First Intifada, from 1987 to 1993; the Second Intifada from 2000 to 2005. Each uprising or war has proven more damaging to Christians than to Muslims or Jews.

In addition, the Christians who have stayed behind make up a dwindling part of the population. The birth rate among Muslims has been much higher than that of Christians. No population in the world has grown as rapidly as that of the Palestinians—30 percent from 1998 to 2008. The average age on the West Bank is twenty-one.

What is causing the Christians to leave this land where they have lived for two thousand years? That question concerns not only the Palestinian Territories, but several Muslim countries as well. Our Western habit of referring to this region as Muslim has always been considered an insult by the Christians living there. Christianity was Middle Eastern not only before it spread throughout the rest of the world, but several centuries before Islam even existed. Various colonial powers have ruled this region, and the Christians have always found ways to adapt. That's no longer the case.

Christians are leaving the West Bank in droves. Leaving the land that has been Christian since Jesus was taken down from the cross. The old Western prejudice about the region being Muslim is perhaps about to become true.

• • •

After receiving Communion in the Cremisan Valley, my host takes me to the man who is perhaps Bethlehem's internationally best-known clergyman. He lives and works in the narrow alleyways of old Bethlehem. His full name is Mitri Bishara Mitri Konstantin Al-Raheb—Mitri Raheb for short. In the winter of 2012 he visited Germany to receive the prestigious German Media Prize for his humanitarian efforts. The prize was presented by the former German president, Roman Herzog. In May of the same year Raheb participated in a hearing in the Danish Parliament. He has the ear of Europe. He has been featured on the CBS news program *60 Minutes*, and he's received attention from other major American media outlets.

Christians haven't always been a minority in Bethlehem. In

1920 the small town had three thousand Christian citizens, a majority, but this changed dramatically during the war in 1948. The stream of refugees from Israel, most of whom were Muslim, settled in the area. Today the population of Bethlehem is twenty-five thousand, but only seven thousand of them are Christians.

Thus Christians are now a minority in the town said to be Jesus's birthplace. The Christian birth rate of about twenty-two per one thousand since 1960 should have resulted in a population of approximately twenty thousand Christians, but most of them have left Bethlehem. Four thousand Christians left the Bethlehem area during the Second Intifada alone.

I walk up to the first floor of the Evangelical Lutheran Christmas Church, built and established by Pastor Raheb. It looks empty, exquisite, renovated. He has also founded a health clinic and a college for "tomorrow's leaders," as he puts it, which look every bit as fashionable and lavish. He definitely has a talent for fund-raising.

Mitri Raheb's demeanor is slightly aloof, sophisticated, cool, perhaps the result of many years of theological study in Germany. He seems mildly irritated at being disturbed; obviously he is a busy man.

Before I say a word, Raheb hands a newly published report across the desk. The report, prepared by his own Diyar Consortium, concerns the Palestinian Christians. He leafs through the pages to a diagram which shows "Reasons for Emigration."

"Only point three percent of those questioned say that they have emigrated because of 'religious extremism'," he says.

This is a startling result. Later I take time to study the diagram. The three most important reasons are "Political Instability" (19.7 percent), "Worsening Economy" (26.4 percent), and

"Lack of Freedom and Security" (32.6 percent). The last number can be attributed to pressure from both Israelis and militant Islamists.

But the Lutheran pastor's most surprising piece of information, which he has traveled extensively to disseminate, is that Christians in the Arab world are neither a "minority" nor "persecuted." I want to hear more about this, as it directly contradicts the many reports on the situation of Christians in the Middle East.

"I am not persecuted because of my faith," he explains. "The Israelis are after us because we are Palestinians, not because we are Christians."

He points out that Christians in the West Bank can do whatever they please. They can build sports facilities, health clinics, and other amenities. Christians can do the same in Jordan and Syria—"At least until recently," he adds. No discrimination is taking place because of their religion.

"The situation is different in Egypt," he says. "Should you wish to build a church there, you must apply for permission fifty years in advance. It's not difficult to build churches in Israel. The problem is houses—Israeli settlers may build them, Palestinians may not. In this way, the Israelis resemble the Egyptians."

I ask him what he means when he claims that Christians aren't a minority in the Middle East. It's obvious to everyone that the percentage of Christians in the population is shrinking. If, for example, the number of Christians grew according to their birthrate, three times as many would be living in the West Bank and Gaza. One line on the graph, the Muslim line, shoots straight up, while the Christian line is flat because of massive emigration. In a few years it will be pointing downward.

"In Europe, a minority is considered to be an ethnic group from the outside. But Christians and Muslims in the Middle

East are from the same culture. In fact, Christians are the original people of the region. Most Muslims here are Christians who over the years have converted. I don't care for the term minority, because it can give Christians a minority complex."

I ask Raheb, who has moved his chair away from his computer, if he feels that the Western world cares about the Palestinian Christians' situation. "I believe the West is completely indifferent," he says. "European opinion-makers use us for their own ends. We feed their hate of Muslims."

Mitri Raheb is but one of a number of people I will meet, often among the local clergy or the Western emissaries promoting interfaith dialogue, who look disappointed when asked about Christians' relationships with their Muslim neighbors. We are brothers, many of them say. The problem is Israel.

The difference between Israel and the Palestinian Territories is striking. When you cross the border into the hills of Bethlehem and find yourself among the refugee camps, the tourist traps, the peace centers, and the wealthy districts, you leave the Israeli island and enter the Arab world. Immediately I sense a different mentality, a greater friendliness and hospitality and also pride, a lifestyle both richer and much poorer. I also sense a submissive attitude. It stems partly from the very long war with the Israelis that has brought Palestinians nothing but defeat and misery, and partly because everything from love to politics in Palestinian society is more or less under strict administrative control. Civil rights are lacking in Arab societies, here included, though Palestinians are restricted far less than many others.

It always strikes me when I enter the Palestinian Territories how I can almost taste the anger behind the male self-irony, which stems from decades of futile effort. It's indistinguishable from bitterness. Every day Palestinians see the barrier that Israel began building in 2005 to prevent terrorists from crossing the border; every day they are reminded of how thoroughly they have been humiliated. In towns such as Bethlehem, the wall crowds their backyards. They are never allowed to forget what they are fighting against. In this way, Israel is a part of the reason for the mass emigration. For example, Israeli soldiers almost killed Mitri Raheb and his family.

On April 2, 2002, Israel reoccupied Bethlehem while searching for a group of terrorists behind a suicide attack in Jerusalem. A woman from the Dheisheh refugee camp, near Bethlehem, had carried out the attack a few days earlier. This was during the Second Intifada's first horrible years, which followed the optimism of the 1990s. The peace process that began with the Oslo Accords seemed to have tapped into some law of nature that would end a century of conflict. Palestinians achieved a certain degree of autonomy in their larger cities, Bethlehem included.

By the autumn of 2000, the idyll had been replaced by savage suicide attacks and an extensive, crushing Israeli attempt to stop them. Shortly before Mitri Raheb and his family experienced the consequences of Israeli antiterrorism measures, a Hamas supporter murdered twenty-eight guests at a Passover Seder in Netanya, an Israeli coastal city.

In March 2002 alone, one hundred Israeli civilians were killed. Prime Minister Ariel Sharon set into motion a reoccupation of most of the West Bank. All the powers that the Oslo Accords had given the Palestinian Authority were revoked. Arafat's office in Ramallah was surrounded. The next target was Bethlehem.

Enormous tanks rolled into the old town where Raheb and his wife and two daughters live. Their home near the Lutheran Center stood directly between the Israeli tanks and the Palestinian snipers. For thirteen hours the family lay on the floor, crawling in and out of rooms as the combatants sought out new cover from which to shoot.

A boy in one neighboring house was shot in the head, and his elderly mother bled to death in his brother's arms; it was impossible for help to reach them. A tank shot a grenade into the bedroom of their other neighbor. For several hours the media circulated the false rumor that a monk—*raheb* in Arabic—had been killed in his church. Everyone believed it was Mitri who had been killed. Calls offering condolences showered the Raheb family.

It was the worst day of his life. He was convinced that he and his family's final hour had come. Finally he walked outside his house and checked his newly-renovated center; it had been destroyed.

A few days later, he says, when twelve Israeli soldiers returned to the center, he decided to put on his clerical collar and step outside to speak with them. He peeked into his office, which fifteen soldiers had ravaged. He told them they could have behaved decently and rang the bell, that he would have invited them inside. That enraged them even further. They held him prisoner for several hours.

Only after pressure from international sources did the soldiers release him and leave the center, vandalized by three hundred soldiers over previous days. Mitri Raheb rebuilt it.

It's not difficult to understand why Palestinian Christians believe the Israelis are the greatest threat to Bethlehem. Among the many stories Raheb tells is one about how Israeli soldiers at one of Bethlehem's checkpoints prevented his father-in-law from passing through to get to an Israeli hospital in Jerusalem. He'd had a heart attack and was close to death. When they finally reached the hospital, it was too late to save the elderly man.

Experiences such as this affect people, and most Palestinians have similar stories to tell. This also might explain why Palestinian Christians are suspicious of Western observers, who they feel want to drive a wedge between themselves and Palestinian Muslims. All Palestinians, no matter their faith, share the experience of Israeli brutality. Christians such as Raheb believe that the West ignores the responsibility of Israel concerning internal Palestinian conflicts.

After reading his books, I have no doubt that the pastor is fervently contemptuous of Israel. He writes: "The Israelis hated their former persecutors but deep down were also impressed with them, wanting to become as powerful. The sense of insecurity of European Jews was transformed into a security syndrome. Security became the golden calf of the Jewish state. As Palestinian people, we are paying the price of this Israeli obsession."

This makes me believe that his anger has evolved into hatred. But Raheb considers the West to be hypocritical, appeasing Israel and offering it warm friendship. I recall watching thousands of American Christians march along King David Street in Jerusalem a few days earlier. They carried signs that declared their eternal devotion to the Jewish nation. It's true that right-wing American Christians are Israel's closest friends. These Americans seldom have much to say about their fellow Christians on the other side of the Wall between Israel and the territories.

Raheb's family has lived in Bethlehem for centuries; one of his many names comes from Emperor Constantine, who made Christianity the state religion in the Roman Empire, and whose mother, Helena, visited Palestine in 324 and established the Church of the Holy Sepulchre in Jerusalem and the Church of the Nativity in Bethlehem.

In his memoirs from 1995, Raheb recounts the strained

relationship between the Middle Eastern and Western churches. He believes that Europeans and Americans think the Church was first divided at the Reformation. But in fact the first division happened as early as the fifth and sixth centuries, when the Eastern and Western Roman Empire split. The Eastern Roman Empire was never united; it consisted of the Greek Orthodox Church (which most Palestinian Christians belong to), the Armenian, the Syrian Orthodox, the Assyrian, and the Coptic Churches, and other smaller religious communities.

That is one of the reasons why the Church in the Middle East seems so weak; there's no one who can speak up for it. When I studied in Jerusalem from 1996 to 1998, I had the impression that Christians felt like a kitten caught between two ferocious Rottweilers in the conflict between Israelis and Muslims.

The Church in Arab countries is split, scattered. The various religious communities have very little sympathy for one another; this is obvious when visiting the Church of the Holy Sepulcher or the Church of the Nativity, which are divided into sections occupied by individual religious communities.

Once I met the man whose family for several generations has kept the key to the Church of the Holy Sepulchre. He was a Muslim. The mutual animosity between the Christian communities was so entrenched that none of them trusted another Christian with such an important object. A lack of solidarity has always weakened Christianity in the Arab countries.

The differences between Western and Eastern Christianity are significant. In his book, Raheb explains that the Western Church is characterized by power. Throughout history it has allied itself with kings and princes in Europe and has created magnificent, gilded structures ornamented by the greatest of artists and architects— St. Peter's Basilica and the European cathedrals are examples.

The Eastern Church has for the past 1,400 years almost never been in a position of power in any country. After Muslim armies conquered the region in the seventh century, Christians have been the subjugated, not the subjugators as in the West. According to Raheb, the Church is powerless and therefore closer to the message found in the New Testament. The individual churches here are small and inconspicuous, and if not, then they are characterized by major liturgical confusion, like the Church of the Holy Sepulchre and the Church of the Nativity.

It's easy for me to be sympathetic toward the Church that Raheb depicts in his books. He explains that while the Western Church fought against the new scientific ideas of the Enlightenment, the Eastern Church stood for modernity in an Islamic world unable to follow along with the times. The Western Church resisted everything the Renaissance and Enlightenment brought to the world. In the Middle East, the Church stood firmly on the side of progress.

. . .

As I leave the center, I think about his assessment of Western Christians. I walk into a well-known tourist shop in Bethlehem. In the middle of the enormous room, among the copper pitchers and a large mother-of-pearl depiction of Jerusalem, I notice the classic portrait of Christ where he opens his robe to reveal a flaming heart. His hair and beard are light in color, his skin is pale; Jesus resembles a Northern European man, not the dark-haired, brown-eyed figure he surely was. Tourists visit Bethlehem not to discover the origins of Christianity, but to reaffirm the image they bring with them.

Bethlehem's famous Manger Square is a short distance away. On my way there I mull over Raheb's accusation that the only reason Europeans take an interest in Middle Eastern Christians is to feed their hatred of Muslims. I've heard that accusation before. It's true that Europeans hostile toward Islam will be pleased to read about how Muslims torment Christians in the Arab world. It's also true that Israelis will be relieved that they are not the only ones giving Christians cause to consider their future. On one of the days I'm with Raheb, someone sprays Hebrew graffiti on another Christian property, this time the Franciscan monastery on Mount Zion in Jerusalem. Israeli settlers signed the graffiti; in 2012 alone, this type of vandalism against churches and monasteries happened several times. Israelis harass Christians as well as Muslims in this region.

But such harassment is well-documented and condemned. It's a different story when Muslims are the perpetrators; for some reason it's as if an ideological fog covers these instances of provocation, a fog created in part by Christians themselves. During all the years I've reported on this situation, I've sensed clearly the suspicion surrounding this type of reporting. What is my agenda?

Choosing not to describe Muslim discrimination and hatred toward Christians, just because opinion-makers one doesn't care for will be overjoyed about what you write, is to me an unacceptable argument. It would be protecting the discriminators, not the victims.

I reach Manger Square and order dinner at a restaurant. The square, located in front of the Church of the Nativity, is calm and peaceful today; it's obvious that tourists are returning to the town, as many people have claimed. There is an understandable willingness to forget what happened not so long ago, partly because the West Bank economy in the past five years has improved. Things seem to be going better for Christians, too, even though the demographic shrinkage continues.

Ten years ago, Israeli tanks rumbled around the square after having knocked aside cars, trash cans, and small roadblocks the Palestinians had constructed. While the Raheb family dodged bullets not far away, an international political drama played out on the square. It revealed to me the miserable state of the Palestinian Christians. The Israelis had come to destroy a Palestinian militia based on the edge of Bethlehem; they had been firing on Israeli civilians and soldiers from Beit Jala, the town on the hilltop where earlier that day I had taken Communion. Back in 2002, many of the town's citizens were enraged at the militia, and several Christians said they were caught in the middle of a tribal war between Jews and Muslims.

Bethlehem, the city of Christians, became the battleground for a war that many people here felt wasn't theirs. Christians never strapped on suicide belts. Nor did they attempt to assassinate Israeli civilians. Many militant Palestinians openly speculated about which side the Christians were on. Public accusations of fifth column activity were made. And militant groups knew how to use the symbolic significance of Christianity.

Hussein Abayat was the leader of a Palestinian militia based near Bethlehem. It fought a war of attrition against the Israeli army in the first years of the intifada. According to Charles M. Sennott, a longtime Middle East correspondent for *The Boston Globe*, "the Israelis were more conscious of the negative public opinion in the Western world when neighborhoods with Christian churches were in the Israeli troops' crosshairs. This strategy, he [Abayat] believed, forced the Israelis to be more constrained in their fighting."

Hussein Abayat was killed in October 2000. The leadership of the militia was taken over by Ibrahim Abayat, Hussein's cousin, who continued to exploit Bethlehem as part of their strategy of using primitive methods to fight the high-tech Israeli army. On the morning of April 2, 2002, when Israeli tanks rolled into Bethlehem, the Abayat militia sought refuge in the Church of the Nativity and took two hundred hostages, including terrified civilians, Palestinian police officers, fighters from other militias, nuns, monks, and priests.

The hostage takers began barricading the entrance with pews. They ignored the priests, who said they would give the militia protection if they agreed to lay down their weapons. Historians believe this was the first time in the nearly seventeen hundred-year history of the church that one of the region's countless wars had in fact moved inside its walls.

Israeli soldiers and tanks surrounded the church and began a siege, with the enormous eye of the media following along as Israeli and Palestinian leaders accused each other of damaging a holy site. Israeli soldiers vandalized the area in the vicinity of the church and set up loudspeakers that broadcast loud music and animal screams to frustrate the fighters inside the church. Two cranes with guns operated by remote control were steered over the church and into the courtyard. Eight people were killed, including a handicapped bell ringer from the Armenian monastery. Twenty-two people were injured.

According to Sennott, several of the Christian civilians inside the church later related what Mohammed Madani, the Muslim governor of Bethlehem, told the hostages who had asked permission to leave the church: They were very welcome to do so, but they must understand that from then on they would be considered "collaborators." Given the malicious mood among the Palestinians in those days, it was a death sentence. The hostages' dilemma was to either die in the church as a living shield for the armed militia, or die outside the church as traitors. The choice was theirs. Since then I have thought of this as the darkest example of what Christians throughout the entire Arab world were and still are faced with.

Thirty-eight days later, on May 10, 2002, a settlement was finally reached. The Israelis retreated, thirteen Palestinian fighters were sent to various European cities, and twenty others were taken to Gaza. The first people to enter the church were met with the stink of urine, feces, sweat, and garbage. Windows had been broken, parts of the Franciscan chapel had been burned, yellow traces of phosphorus grenades marred the walls.

Mitri Raheb also wrote about the siege of the Church of the Nativity, but he appeared to be unmoved. He condemned the Israeli army but refused to criticize the fighters who sought refuge inside the church. On the contrary, he seemed sympathetic to why these fighters sought refuge in a church. Had they fled to a mosque, it would have been destroyed, Raheb quotes a Christian as saying.

The Western world also reacted in somewhat muted terms. I can't recall any significant protests in the streets or indignant declarations from leaders in the United States or Europe. It was as if a war in the cradle of Christian civilization, the symbol of something as fundamental as Year 1 in our reckoning of time, was to be expected.

In those years, many Bethlehem Christians packed up and caught the first flight out.

I pay my bill at the restaurant on Manger Square and return to my hotel in Jerusalem.

· · ·

For many years I have felt that the Western media's coverage of the Palestinians is extensive but faulty. Ten years ago, while working for my Copenhagen newspaper, I searched our archives for a generic photo of a young, modern Palestinian woman to accompany an article. There were none. Zero. When I typed in words such as "Palestinian" and "woman," the only images that turned up were elderly, veiled Muslim mothers, often crying at their dead sons' graves. I went through one thousand photos, and gradually it became clear to me that we in the West insist on viewing Palestinians this way. Tired, old, Muslim. Helpless victims, in other words. I had to give up my search for a normal, well-dressed, young, pretty, modern Palestinian woman, despite the fact that you see them everywhere in Palestinian cities like Bethlehem and Ramallah. Such a photo didn't exist in the news archive.

I realized we not only had forgotten that part of the Arab world—we had deleted it. Photographers wouldn't take photos of it because newspapers weren't interested in revealing its existence. Therefore it's not strange that many were shocked when this apparently hypothetical Palestinian woman's counterparts and sisters in the cause gathered in Tahrir Square in Cairo a few years ago to overthrow a dictator. People simply didn't know they existed.

I first became interested in Middle Eastern Christians because of such a woman. In 2003, by way of a more heavy-handed initiation than taking Communion in the Cremisan Valley near Jerusalem, I gained a sense of what it's like to be a Christian on the West Bank.

I had traveled to Bethlehem to write about donkeys. A twenty-four-year-old Christian woman, Cyrien Khano, was going to assist me. Donkeys were the fastest means of transportation from town to town during the Second Intifada's most intense fighting, when terrorist attacks took place daily and Israeli roadblocks stopped all traffic. Time seemed to race backward. These were golden days for Palestinian donkey traders.

As it happened, I came home with an entirely different article. On that January day in 2003, I found myself stranded with Cyrien's family, unable to go anywhere. The Israeli army had declared Bethlehem under military administration. I watched as everyone who ventured out on the street was frisked; tear gas and flash grenades were thrown; Israeli soldiers swarmed at door fronts. People locked themselves in their houses. The Chano family ate salmon, made small talk, watched TV, and in every way tried to pretend that nothing was happening right outside their door. It wasn't easy.

Cyrien's family was well-to-do. Their income came from manger scenes they carved out of wood and sold in Jerusalem's Old City. But the Second Intifada had driven tourists away, and it was difficult for her family to even leave Bethlehem. Her father had gone months without any income. Two of Cyrien's siblings had left the country. She longed to do the same.

Cyrien dressed as if she herself was about to enter some type of war. Her heavy eye makeup was blue and black; she wore tight blue pants, a snug, thin white sweater, a push-up bra, high-heeled calfskin boots, and a cross around her neck. The conflict had brought out in her a raging, foolhardy recklessness that her increasingly desperate parents could do nothing about. On that January day, she decided to rile up the Israeli soldiers—and dragged me along with her. We crawled out on their terrace and hid behind a tiny wall.

She succeeded in provoking the soldiers. They yelled at us, and the infrared rays from their gun sights danced on the wall behind us. Her parents opened the front door a crack and begged us to come inside. They wailed in desperation as my heart stuck in my throat. This wasn't the first time that Cyrien had scared her poor family half to death. Several months earlier, when a heavily-armed Palestinian wanted to use the family's sloping yard to fire rockets into the Israeli-controlled southern part of Jerusalem, she had thrown him out of the house. Cursed him up one side and down the other. Had he been permitted to launch his rockets, the Israelis would have retaliated by destroying the Khano family's house.

One day an Israeli tank parked outside the residence. The Israeli soldiers must have believed that something was being hidden inside, and they fired a salvo of bullets at the wall.

"I threw myself down on the floor in my bedroom," Cyrien told me. "And I thought, I'm going to be shot now. The bullets will go through the wall. I screamed until I lost my voice. My mother yelled at me from our living room to keep screaming so they could hear I was alive, but I couldn't. Then they shot our gas cylinder, it was a miracle our house didn't blow up. And I thought: Why are they shooting? Am I a peace activist? In one or two minutes I had suddenly become a suicide terrorist. I was Hamas. Then I said to myself, 'Cyrien, you must not become an animal. They want to turn you into something hideous, but you must not give them the satisfaction.'"

I have always thought of her as the most heroic woman I met during those times. Dazed, appalled, and hyper from adrenaline, I managed to leave Bethlehem that night. And I knew that although Cyrien didn't get the chance to show me the Bethlehem donkeys, her life sketched a story of a normal family's grotesque struggle to maintain their dignity, a story of the Christians' hopeless situation.

Three years later, in January 2006, Hamas won the local elections in Bethlehem. I met her again that fall, and she told me that she had cried when she saw the green Islamic flag outside her window as members of Hamas marched through the streets to celebrate their victory. She had given up and had decided to move to Dublin.

"In general, Christians have more money than Muslims," Cyrien said. "That's why we suffer more from the enormous decline we've had in the last ten years. We want to give our children a decent education, we want a decent job, and we can't live on a single slice of bread a day. And we're squeezed in between two peoples at war with each other, the Jews and the Muslims. Both are murderers," she said, furious now.

We were sitting in a restaurant, it was late afternoon, and behind us we could see an Israeli settlement, Har Homa.

"The Israelis hate us, and the Muslims treat us terribly," she continued. "The Muslims have stolen land from Christians, taken Christians' houses, harassed Christian women. The judicial system in Palestine doesn't follow the law. The Muslim police side with Muslims. That's why Christians have no protection under the law."

Few people have the courage to say what Cyrien says concerning the situation of Christians among their fellow Muslim citizens. But back in 2006, after Hamas took control of Bethlehem and several other Palestinian towns, she was on her way out. Shortly afterward, she left and spent four years in another part of the world. She was indebted to no one.

Today Cyrien Khano is back in the West Bank. This is also part of the story about the Christian Palestinians—some of them refuse to give up.

I walk along the streets of the capital, Ramallah, one morning, through the claustrophobic swarm of taxis and garbage and street merchants and men hanging around on street corners.

Cyrien has done extremely well for herself. I notice that immediately as I walk into a spacious store with bathroom fixtures, shiny stools, shower stalls, bathtubs, and tiles so clean you can see your reflection in them. It's the polar opposite of everything right outside. This store is how the Palestinian middle and upper class want to see themselves, and Cyrien, as manager, is ready to assist them.

Now thirty-three years old, a Christian woman born and raised in Bethlehem, she is wearing a dark blouse, light-colored tight pants, and high heels. She explains that much has changed in the past five years.

"During the Second Intifada a serious split occurred between Muslims and Christians. It's still no picnic, but things are much better now. I work closely with Muslims, and we have no problems. I'm regarded as a Palestinian, not a Christian."

The West Bank has become richer, the love life of people in this part of the world's otherwise restrictive atmosphere freer. For example, she tells about a Christian man she knows who married a Muslim woman, who then renounced Islam and converted to Christianity. "Earlier this was completely unthinkable, and the woman's family could have killed her for doing this. But I sense that it's become easier—especially if you're rich and influential. Then no one will touch you."

It hasn't been entirely smooth sailing for the couple. The man has received a number of death threats, even though no one has attempted to carry them out. And they can't live in the West Bank, Cyrien says. If you want to have that type of relationship, one of forbidden love, it's safest to do so in the West.

Marriage between a Muslim man and a Christian woman is more common. Islamic law permits it, and she may remain a Christian. But their children must become Muslims, Cyrien explains, because Islam is patrilineal. That's why most of the

Christian women Cyrien knows who have married a Muslim converted to Islam, she says. Ramallah is becoming more modern, however.

"Women can appear in public without so many rules about dress, and there are more mixed relationships. Women also have sex before marriage. Five years ago a man would almost certainly have abandoned a woman like that. But this is how it is in Ramallah. In the smaller towns people still live in the Stone Age."

Even though Christians continue to leave the country, the only time Cyrien feels part of a minority is on Fridays. "That's the Muslim holy day, and in some mosques there are sermons about how we should be killed, things like that." But the Christians aren't emigrating because of harassment. They leave to find work. "I think we will be okay. There will always be Christians in this country," she says.

My mood is brighter as I leave her and the chlorine-clean tiles and venture out again into Ramallah's noisy throngs that test one's patience.

• • •

There are many forms of discrimination; Cyrien had given me examples of some of them. Christians in the West Bank do not have the same civil rights as Muslims, and that goes for the entire Arab world, with the exception of Lebanon. Christians are also treated unfairly concerning faith. They are not allowed to convert Muslims, though Muslims may convert them. In my travels I have seen how distorted a society becomes when this type of hierarchy is established and maintained over centuries.

In Beit Sahour, a town close to Bethlehem, I meet with Samir J. Qumsiyeh. For many years he ran a Christian television station, Nativity TV, which he recently had to sell. The Palestinian Authority shut down the station for a period in March 2010. The official reason was that he hadn't paid his "license." According to him, the actual reason was that they didn't like the information he imparted to his viewers.

I haven't met him before, but I have read his comments in several foreign newspapers over the years. I'm aware that he doesn't share Mitri Raheb's opinions. He believes many Muslims take advantage of being a majority with respect to Christians. Over the years I have spoken with several Christian Palestinians; it is rare to meet someone as outspoken as Qumsiyeh. Most of them won't speak unless the recorder is turned off or if they remain anonymous. But he and his family have a certain status in the town, and international organizations are aware of him. This gives him a kind of protection.

He picks me up at the border, and I ride with him to his office. The walls are covered with plaques, distinguished awards, and photos of all the famous people he has met, including the two most recent popes, Yasser Arafat, King Hussein of Jordan, and leading Hamas politicians. Jesus and the Virgin Mary are also permanent fixtures on the wall. They are his employers.

Qumsiyeh plans on writing a book entitled *R.I.P.* The letters may bring to mind the Latin "Requiescat in pace" or "Rest in Peace," but the abbreviation is for a more contemporary and harsh phrase: "Racism in Practice."

"There is a hidden form of racism against Christians in this society," he says. He is wearing a gray pullover, and he has a bald spot on the back of his head. He begins cleaning his computer meticulously as he speaks. "If this hidden racism came out in the open, the West would say, 'What are you doing to the Christians?' When racism is hidden in the shadows—when it's not part of any official policy—those in power talk about how we are all brothers."

The Palestinian Authority's official stance on equality concerning Christians and what goes on unofficially in society are two different things. Qumsiyeh explains that when there is a legal disagreement between a Christian and a Muslim, the Muslim always wins. A car accident involving a Christian and a Muslim will always end with the Christian driver being found at fault by the police, he explains. "Christians are not allowed to adopt children. If an infant is left behind at a church, Christians are not allowed to adopt it. It will enter a Muslim family."

In addition, lands owned by Christians are being taken away. "Land worth millions of dollars is being taken from us. It's impossible for us to evict these criminals, and a lawsuit can run as long as fifteen years. And in the meantime they build on the land. It's incredible that Palestinian Muslims accuse Israelis of confiscating their land to build settlements on, while they do exactly the same thing."

He is not alone in these accusations. In 2007, the U.S. Department of State affirmed this in its annual report on religious freedom throughout the world: "The PA has not taken sufficient action to remedy past harassment and intimidation of Christian residents of Bethlehem by the city's Muslim majority. The PA judiciary failed to adjudicate numerous cases of seizures of Christian-owned land in the Bethlehem area by criminal gangs."

The report states directly that it seems as if Palestinian Authority officials have participated in the extortion of Christian citizens' property. "Several attacks against Christians in Bethlehem went unaddressed by the PA, but authorities investigated attacks against Muslims in the same area."

A Palestinian journalist, Khaled Abu Toameh, who writes for the Israeli newspaper *Jerusalem Post*, and is one of the harshest critics of his own authorities, has said essentially the same thing. In 2009 he reported that Muslims working for the Palestinian Authority have been seizing Christian land "either by force or through forged documents." He explained that many Christian businessmen had closed their businesses because they couldn't pay protection money to local Muslim gangs.

"As a Muslim journalist, I am always disgusted and ashamed when I hear about Christians living in the West Bank and Jerusalem, the challenges, threats and assaults that many of them have to live with," he writes. According to him, no attention has been focused on this, because the subject is "taboo."

Qumsiyeh says that the Palestinian Authority also discriminates when filling important positions in the public sector. Of the one hundred and sixty top administrative jobs, not one is held by a Christian. "We have complained about this," he says. "We want a Christian chief of police, someone who will stop the judicial discrimination."

Middle Eastern Church leaders seldom protest about the situation, he claims. "Christians are trapped between two fundamentalist groups, and our church leaders are weak. The Christian population has no respect for these leaders. They are part of the reason why Christians are leaving. Our church leadership does nothing to defend Christianity. They make Christians feel as if they are weak, but we are not weak. We must have the courage to speak up."

According to the Palestinian journalist, no one protested, for example, when the Grand Mufti of Saudi Arabia, Sheikh Abdul Aziz bin Abdullah, in March 2012 stated that it was "necessary to destroy all the churches of the region." This was a direct declaration of war with fatal consequences for Christians. "If someone had wished to destroy the Dome of the Rock mosque in Jerusalem, all the pastors would have manned the barricades, as they should," Qumsiyeh says. He himself wrote a letter of protest to the Saudi ambassador.

To give an example of the subjugation felt by Christians, Qumsiyeh tells me about the monastery in the Cremisan Valley, by the hillside where I took Communion.

The Cremisan monastery owns a great deal of land in the valley, much of which is small wooded areas. The Muslim town of Al-Wallegeh lies close to the forests, from which their citizens for years have felled hundreds of pine trees in the dead of night. They sell the wood or use it themselves for firewood.

Qumsiyeh shows me a half hour video on his computer. I watch the screen showing him as he walks around the area with the monastery guard. Tree stumps stick up everywhere; several of the trees have been recently cut down, their limbs sawed off and thrown to the side. The monastery guard tells Qumsiyeh that one day he walked over to the town to ask them to stop cutting down their trees, but he was told to get out, or else he would be killed.

"They are Christian trees," they yelled at him, meaning that it was okay to fell them.

After the interview I go to the monastery to have a look around the area. At the gate I'm told that journalists may not enter. I call the monastery's priest to ask permission, to no avail; the media is not allowed inside because journalists have characterized the monastery in a way that could be construed as being friendly to Israel. No one in the occupied territories can live with that accusation.

When I tell Qumsiyeh the next day about my failed attempt to visit the monastery, he laughs scornfully. He says that they are afraid the story will get out. "They don't wish to talk about it because they are cowards," he says. "All that matters to them is their safety, privileges, and status."

· · ·

There are many examples of Racism in Practice. When I meet Christians who, unlike Qumsiyeh, live in the towns around Bethlehem, and who are not particularly wealthy, it's obvious that they know they must act deferentially. They understand their status is below that of Muslims in the society surrounding them. Most of their Muslim neighbors don't abuse their favorable position, but some do. And in some places, especially since 2000, they have influenced the mood of their town.

A U.S. State Department report from 2012 states that the relationship between Muslims and Christians in the West Bank generally has been good. It hasn't always been that way. One October day I drive north to Nablus, a large but poor town in the middle of the northern West Bank, to see if the American assessment holds true. I want to pay a visit to the home where I spent the Greek Orthodox Christmas Eve in January 2006. I will never forget drinking a glass of port, the solemn, quiet mood, as if participating in some covert underground ceremony. The nearby Christmas tree was decorated with small, green paper ornaments, shiny blue balls, and blinking lights. It didn't take much to commit subversive activity in Nablus in 2006—imbibing port. That's how two elderly Christian men and I celebrated Christmas Eve.

Of everything I've seen, this shows best how the Islamists' ideals of purity have affected the West Bank, certainly in Nablus. The walls of the local Christian store that sold wine had earlier been sprayed with bullets, after which the owner stopped selling alcohol. My Christian hosts had therefore bought their port in Bethlehem, where it was still sold. It had to be enjoyed in secrecy, behind closed doors, in Nablus. What Christians earlier could do openly had become dangerous.

My visit in 2006 took place shortly after the death of Arafat.

The Second Intifada had ended, but kidnappings and shootings were still everyday occurrences in Nablus. In Arafat's absence, a power struggle began that has resulted in Palestinians splitting into two camps—Hamas in Gaza and Fatah in the West Bank. Christians have had to dodge bullets in this conflict, too, while the sense of being homeless in their own land has grown. Three weeks after visiting the two elderly Christians, Hamas won an overwhelming victory in the local elections in Nablus. The two gentlemen had predicted that outcome, their eyes damp with concern.

During the Second Intifada, Nablus was regarded by the Israelis as the command center of terrorism. Israeli politicians referred to the situation in Nablus and a neighboring town Jenin as the catalyst for the 2002 decision to build a security barrier to protect Israeli civilians. The worst terrorist attacks originated from there, and Nablus overflowed with weapons. Hamas and the so-called al-Aqsa Martyrs Brigade of Fatah, Arafat's party, competed to pull off the most spectacular suicide attacks, while young fighters lived by stealing cars and harassing the town's citizens. The authorities had lost all control of the town.

The story that best illustrates the town's collapse centers on someone I meet during my visit there in the fall of 2012. Hussam Abdo's photo from March 24, 2004, was seen on front pages of newspapers all over the globe. The then-sixteen-year-old boy had been caught at the Israeli Hawara checkpoint at the Nablus city limits wearing a suicide belt. Five feet tall and looking as if he might be mentally challenged, he stood in his undershorts with legs spread, appearing sad and confused as he stared off into space. The bomb around his waist had not detonated, though he had pulled its cord time and again. To me this photo symbolized an era as horrible as it was absurd.

When we meet I see a young, bullheaded man of twenty-four with greased hair, a cigarette stuck in his mouth. He constantly rolls up his sleeves to show off his muscles. He has just been released from prison after serving eight years.

A picture of Arafat hangs in the hallway of the apartment building where he and his mother live. Abdo is a member of the al-Aqsa Martyrs Brigade. His mother is also present in their living room. She is happy he isn't dead, but neither of them regret his failed suicide mission. They both claim that he now is looked up to in the neighborhood. "I would also be proud of him if he was dead," his mother says. "He did it for the Palestinian nation. In our religion, what he did was jihad." As she speaks, what strikes me as most depressing about this young man and his mother is not the grotesque nature of what they say, but how widespread their perspective has become. Terrorism by suicide is popular.

By the time of my visit, the city is doing much better. Hamas was not allowed to establish its Islamist program in the short time it was in power—Fatah's security forces quickly drove its members underground, and its military leaders were assassinated or jailed by the Israeli army. Hamas remains influential among many Nablus residents, however, and Christians are still leaving the city that is said to have had a Christian population since Jesus came by one day, fishing for souls. Currently there are only 700 of them in this city of 130,000.

After meeting this diminutive would-be suicide bomber, I drive on to see Yosuf, my host on that Christmas Eve some years back. Yosuf is an alias; he doesn't dare use his real name. He tells me that Christians are still unable to buy port in Nablus. The wine store was never reopened. It's not forbidden to sell alcohol there, but no Christian cares to try.

Yosuf is a retired driver. He doesn't want to leave; some

Christians must remain here, he says. "When supporters of Hamas learn that I'm Christian, they tell me I should convert to their religion. My answer to them is: I believe in Jesus. But many others convert, several in my family have. Mostly it's Christian girls who marry Muslim men."

• • •

Late that same evening I visit the ruins of a fourth-century Byzantine church. I sit and listen to music from the square in front of the city hall of Taybeh, the only predominantly Christian town left in the Palestinian Territories. People whose memories reach back several decades say there once were fifteen or sixteen towns in the West Bank populated almost exclusively by Christians.

Whitewashed houses and three spires from much newer churches in the small town dot the hillside behind me. Lights appear from an Israeli settlement close by, and I look out over the Jordan Valley to mountains in Jordan illuminated by the rising half-moon.

I'm at the highest elevation in the northern West Bank, about three thousand feet above sea level. Whoever built this small church understood the importance of its location. In the middle of the now open church, the vaulted ceiling of which is the starry heavens, is a stone altar resembling a pillar; someone has placed a figure of the Virgin Mary and two red candles atop it. A few tourists are kneeling in prayer.

Taybeh is not only known for its churches. Since 2005, the town has hosted the only beer festival in the Territories. It is held at the beginning of October, and a Christian Palestinian tells me it's the only place in the entire Middle East where you can see men and women on the street with a beer in hand, many of them dancing. Apart from Israel, that could be true. The town considers its lager to be "the finest beer in the Middle East," which isn't all that difficult to back up; Taybeh Beer is thought to be "the only microbrewery in the Middle East"—again, excluding Israel.

According to Maria Khoury, the wife of Taybeh's mayor, the reason for this is simple: It's tough to make a living selling beer in a place "where ninety-eight percent of the population doesn't drink alcohol." This is why they export to Germany, Belgium, Sweden, and Japan. But Khoury, who as the promoter of the festival is under a lot of pressure, gives the impression that it's not easy to keep the business afloat.

It all seemed so promising when the brewery was established in 1994. Maria Khoury and her husband returned from the United States for the sole purpose of helping the Palestinian Territories to prosper, to create jobs for its people. But the brewery is one of the few enterprises left from the optimistic 1990s. Everything else went under because of war, terrorism, and mistrust during the Second Intifada. And as mentioned, the brewery business isn't booming here.

It costs roughly $2.50 to enter the square, which is packed with people dancing to the local horn band from Ramallah, ten miles to the southwest. A tuba player and a clarinetist, as stocky and thin as their respective instruments, hop around wildly, tooting and honking on a stage bathed in lights.

For a few days, the West Bank has turned into Bavaria. Some guests are even wearing lederhosen, others bear keffiyeh, the black-and-white Palestinian national scarf; sausages, shawarma, and falafel are being served. As I walk out of the Byzantine church, past the black impressions of hands set in stone at the entrance, I'm thinking that right here and now, in this small town on this fine evening, people are determined to not give in to the gloom that has befallen many other Palestinian Christians.

Several young Palestinians swing around merrily to the tuba's honking; in a few short years they will have emigrated, as their cousins already have. A particularly downcast Jerusalemite who has traveled north to the festival tells me that Taybeh will no longer be a Christian town in ten years.

Saturday at midnight I'm on the terrace of a man who owns a local hotel, looking down on the surrounding roofs, topped with antennae and water tanks. In the distance we can see light from other houses and the moon, which has risen high in the heavens.

For months the hotel has been booked up by tourists attending the annual beer festival. I've been given permission to sleep in his small living room with large, golden sofas, icons hanging askew on the wall, a wooden cross, and a large photograph of an ancestor. Small photos of children have been stuck in the frame of a decorative plate with an etching of Leonardo da Vinci's "The Last Supper." A half-length plaster of Paris model of the Virgin Mary stands on a small round table that's covered by a damask tablecloth. Paint on her golden hair has begun to peel.

We share a beer on the terrace. His English is as bad as my Arabic. "This town. Christian," he says. Then he adds, "Out there," and points toward the land beyond the town. He bows from the waist several times, his arms stretched out above his head, modeling a Muslim prostrate in prayer.

Taybeh has a history dating back five thousand years. At that time the town was called Ephraim or Ofra, and it plays a small but spiritually significant role in the New Testament: "Jesus therefore walked no more openly amongst the Jews; but went thence unto a country near to the wilderness, into a city called Ephraim, and there continued with his disciples." (John 11:54)

This is where Jesus stayed before going to Jerusalem to be crucified. Salah ad-Din, the great Muslim general who defeated the Crusaders, gave the town its name in 1187 after the locals supplied his soldiers and their horses with water. "You are *taybeh*," he proclaimed—"You are good." Taybeh can also mean "good-tasting." The tradition of refreshment goes back many, many years.

I've been told that Maria Khoury, the mayor's wife, will be attending the service at Taybeh's Greek Orthodox Church Sunday morning. I get up early and walk up the hill; the odor of incense greets me as I walk inside.

I can't spot her anywhere in the chapel half-filled with the old and the young, so I study this beautiful, newly restored church of intense azure blue and gold, with arches supported by columns, gilded chandeliers, and paintings of saints and biblical scenes on the walls. It was built from 1929 to 1932 on the site of a seventh-century church. The church is both familiar and foreign to me, full of symbols and signs I have seen before but don't understand.

I'm struck by the same sense I had while walking through the narrow alleyways of the town the previous evening, that Taybeh is almost too pleasant, too "good" and "good-tasting." Unlike the hotel owner's house, which gives the impression of being lived in, everything here appears restored and polished. Like something found in a store display, put there for the world to see how decorative Christianity can be. Meanwhile the Christians are emigrating. What is happening here in Taybeh has been going on in the West Bank during the past fifty years. Today approximately 1,300 Christians still live in the town.

Toward the end of the service Maria Khoury enters the church. She genuflects and crosses herself, then kneels to kiss an icon on the floor. The mayor's wife also kisses a large Bible bound in silver embroidery displayed at the entrance. She walks ceremoniously over to the wall to kiss several icons. All of this is performed as a long, solitary ritual, very private.

She is wearing a black djellaba, a long loose robe patterned in gold; her long, dark hair is streaked with gray. She doesn't know I'm watching and I feel a bit ashamed, like a voyeur. She steps outside, and I join her on the small square in front of the church where we agreed to meet. The many long days of work arranging the festival have left their mark on Maria; her eyes have a harried look. She asks me to accompany her to a Catholic nursing home on the outskirts of town. The calm she displayed in church has disappeared; she drives aggressively, impatiently. Like a woman on the edge of a breakdown.

On the way she tells me that this is her swan song as the festival organizer, that her husband, Daoud Khoury, is the one who insists on holding the festival year after year to show that their town is modern and peaceful. And to provide jobs for the town's citizens. He also wants to continue living here. She is not a native; she was born in Tripoli into a Greek Orthodox family, and met her husband while studying at Harvard.

It's difficult not to sympathize with her situation, just as it's impossible to not admire people like the Khourys. Her husband has worked hard to preserve the town's Christianity. Khoury and his brother were both born and raised in Taybeh. They moved to Boston, where their grandparents had emigrated in the 1920s, but his brother, Nadim, returned in 1994 after the Oslo Accords and established the brewery. Daoud and Maria joined him in 1999.

Daoud Khoury has made known that he will go to great lengths to make sure the town and the surrounding countryside, including its 30,000 olive trees, remain in Christian hands. Each time a house or a parcel of land is sold, efforts are made to ensure that the buyer is Christian. If no one else makes an offer, he buys it himself. Maria is an unselfish woman: She raises money to help care for the elderly and to finance the education of young people. She also writes children's books. And visits the elderly, arranges stage lighting, and gives an interview to me—all at the same time.

After driving to the festival square, we manage to find two chairs, and we sit down in an empty hallway in the City Hall. I ask for her explanation as to why Christians are leaving the Palestinian Territories—and Taybeh.

"The Oslo Accords are dead," she says. "Very few of us Christians remain. There are more Christians from Taybeh in Guatemala than here. We have sixty percent unemployment in this town alone. There is no social security net, no medical insurance. People don't want to move, but there are three Israeli settlements in the vicinity, and our water is shut off four times a week everywhere except in the settlements. Pure discrimination."

Also, before 2000 it took her fifteen minutes to drive her children to school in Ramallah; now it takes an extra hour because of Israeli checkpoints. The Israeli settlers have closed the road leading directly to Ramallah to punish the Palestinians.

"They want to deny us our dignity," she says. She adds that their relationship to the sixteen neighboring Muslim towns is good. "Many of their children attend Taybeh's schools. Our schools offer a good, open, liberal education, whereas the public schools are still segregated by gender. In fact, Christians are a minority in our town's Christian schools." But the region is becoming more religious all the time, she explains. Islam has established itself, which can be seen in people's clothing. When she first came to Ramallah, only one out of ten women wore a veil. "Today it's nine out of ten," she says. "Back in the 1980s, most of the women resembled me. Now I'm a rarity, with my hair exposed. It's an enormous change."

From her chair in the hallway of City Hall, Maria Khoury tells about the worst tragedy she has ever experienced. On August 31, 2005, a thirty-two-year-old Muslim woman, Hiyam, was found dead in Deir Jarir, a town close to Taybeh. Her family claimed she had poisoned herself so as not to bring shame upon them.

Hiyam, who was single, worked as a seamstress in a Taybeh shop. The family discovered that she was pregnant. They accused the Christian shop owner, Mahadi Khourieh, of being the father—a grave offense according to Islamic law. He denied it.

On the evening of September 3, hundreds of young men from Deir Jarir marched to Taybeh, intent on burning down the homes of Khourieh and his family. The men had a list of the houses to be burned, Maria says. They set fire to fourteen homes. The families had already fled, because they knew that Deir Jarir wanted revenge. No one was hurt.

Maria speaks fast: "For six hours the mob was allowed to ravage our town. Our own house was next on the list, and they were about to set it on fire when the police finally stopped them."

The apparent poisoning of the Muslim woman went unpunished. "It was an honor killing, no one gets punished for that," Maria says. "The relationship between Christians and Muslims has been satisfactory in the past thirty years, but now we live in a land where laws are unenforced."

Another attack by young people from neighboring towns armed with clubs and guns was imminent in May 2012 as a result of a conflict between a Christian and a Muslim, but Palestinian police managed to stop them from entering Taybeh. In April 2013, Israeli settlers briefly occupied the old monastery on the hill in Taybeh and raised the Israeli flag. It takes a strong woman to endure all of this.

The attacks on Taybeh weren't the only ones in the West Bank. A similar episode took place on the Mount of Olives in East Jerusalem. The Catholic Church provides cheap apartments to many poor Christians there, and on August 20, 2012, a number of young Muslims from a nearby town stormed the area. Wielding iron bars, they threw rocks at the buildings and set fire to parked cars. This went on for ninety minutes; no Israeli police showed up, though they were called. The riots stopped only because a group of older Muslims from the neighboring town intervened. Several days later a conciliatory meeting took place in which prominent officials from the West Bank and the Palestinian Authority participated.

This was the culmination of a number of attacks painstakingly reported by *Ha'aretz*. According to the Israeli paper, this attack came about because a young Muslim insulted a Christian woman, after which the woman's husband had beaten the young man. Soon the young Muslim showed up with somewhere between a hundred and a hundred and fifty friends to wreck the town.

The newspaper cited an anonymous source: "They [were] screaming *Allahu Akhbar* and jihad. It could have been a massacre." A Christian resident said, "We don't have clans to protect us; we take the blows and move on. We want protection, which we can only get from the Israeli police. If the state won't protect us, we're doomed."

A Christian I met in East Jerusalem who wished to remain anonymous told me about the attack. "We know this isn't a place for us any longer. We live in a jungle where only the strong survive. And the Israelis are happy that Palestinians are fighting each other. It keeps them strong. In fifty years the only Christians left in the West Bank will be monks and nuns."

· · ·

A few people are trying to change the way things are going. I speak with Saed Awwad at a mechanic's garage in the center of Taybeh. The garage is being used as a small coffee shop during the beer festival. The "Fierce Warrior for Peace," which is the title of his new book, is wearing a gray cowboy hat and a T-shirt with "ARMY" printed on it.

Saed Awwad's face resembles that of the no-longer-young George Foreman, strong and thick in the way it can only be if you've lived in the United States with spareribs on the menu and a set of weights in the basement. His rhetoric bulges as much as his biceps; the subtitle of his book is "From a Captivity of Hate and Bitterness to the Freedom of Love and Forgiveness."

Awwad is an evangelist, a minority among a minority, reborn and determined to spread the joyful news to the most inaccessible Middle Eastern regions. According to many Muslims in the Arab lands, this activity is strictly forbidden; Islamic law requires the death penalty for Muslims who convert. He and his fellow evangelists are also a congregation that other Christians in the area look down on. I have never really understood why. It can't only be because they are fishing in other congregations' waters.

I struck up a conversation with him at the festival the previous evening. He was serving pitas at his cousin's miserable little booth. He asked if I was Christian, if I was interested in hearing God's word. The music at the festival was deafening, so we agreed to talk the next day. He wanted to convert me, and I wanted to get to know a missionary.

I got the impression that Awwad and the Khourys weren't

on the same wavelength—the mayor's wife gave me a strange look when I mentioned that I was going to talk to him. It's also difficult to imagine two forms of Christianity more different from each other than Maria Khoury's refined, esoteric, scholarly, tradition-minded Greek Orthodox practices and his unsophisticated American faith. The front cover of his book shows the image of a peace dove flying between an Israeli and a Palestinian flag, directly over the Dome of the Rock in Jerusalem. The symbolism couldn't be more heavy-handed.

Other Taybeh citizens seem to like Awwad. At a recently built Catholic nursing home on the outskirts of town, one of the caregivers, Nasser, tells me his incredible story. The jovial little man flew from Paris to Miami on December 22, 2001. The man who later became known as the Shoe Bomber, the jihadist Richard Reid, was on the same flight. Reid tried to blow the plane up over the Atlantic with a bomb he had placed in the sole of his shoe. The bomb didn't detonate, and he was overpowered by the other passengers.

When the plane made an emergency landing in Boston, Nasser was jailed along with Reid. A surveillance camera in Paris trained on passengers waiting to board the plane had caught the unsuspecting little man standing beside the Shoe Bomber. Because Nasser came from Taybeh and therefore not only resembled but actually was an Arab, and because it was only a few months after 9/11, Americans suspected him of being in cahoots with the terrorist.

Nasser sat shirtless and cold in a cell for a week. He imagined men in black suits and dark sunglasses showing up soon to drug him and take him to some foreign country, where he would awaken curled up in a cage, wearing an orange prison suit. Alone in the world, and on his knees, praying—begging—

to be sent home, he recalled where he came from: Taybeh, the Christian town. He had never given his religious origins much thought, but suddenly he reached out for Jesus and felt the warmth spreading throughout his body. He was born again on the floor of his cell. Shortly after, a sympathetic judge released the unlucky Palestinian, who won't be visiting the United States again anytime soon.

When he returned to Taybeh, he met bald-headed Saed Awwad, the "Fierce Warrior for Peace," who baptized Nasser as an adult. Now Nasser serves Taybeh. This born-again Christian takes care of the elderly and lives a genuinely devout life. Awwad holds a special place in Nasser's heart.

That morning, sitting at a table in the mechanic's garage, Awwad sketches out his early life. His son sits beside us, I let him play with my cell phone.

Awwad says he was wild when he was young. He fought the Israeli army during the First Intifada at the end of the 1980s and was caught and tortured. Israeli soldiers broke several bones in his body, including in his back. He still suffers from the torture.

His hatred of Israelis stems from his upbringing. As a child, the sight of Israeli soldiers frightened him to death; whenever his mother scolded him, she warned that if he didn't behave the Jews would come and take him away. He decided to fight them. "When you see an enemy, it's natural to want to eliminate him, in whatever way you can," Awwad says. One of his closest friends was killed by an Israeli soldier, and Awwad swore revenge. He wanted to kill a soldier, but he couldn't. After some time he understood that he had to make a choice: either stay in the West Bank, where he would be imprisoned or killed, or leave. "None of the Arab countries would take me. Only the United States."

First he moved to Detroit, then later to California, where he was born again. "I felt that God was telling me to let go of my hate. At first I didn't understand it. When God said, 'Forgive,' I yelled, 'What in the hell are you talking about?'" But Awwad says he discovered that forgiveness is a strength, not a weakness. Now he has nurtured a congregation that he hopes will light a fire under people in Taybeh and the Palestinian Territories.

"I don't want to change the culture. I want to change hearts." He wants me to understand that this is one of his catchphrases, and he repeats it to make sure I get it down correctly in my notes. "I don't want to change cultures. I want to change hearts. We have a great opportunity to identify with Jesus, who also was born under an occupation. Jesus said, 'Love thy enemy.' He knew what he was talking about."

Awwad refers to himself as a "tough guy." But he came to this town to help families provide their children with an education and to send students across the Atlantic. He wants his message to hit Palestinians hard. Christians to begin with, of course, but Muslims, too. He tells me that he has converted four Muslims. That is strictly forbidden here; the four converts live in the United States.

I must admit I kept an ironic distance from him in the beginning. There is something ridiculous about his pumped-up image and American appearance; had he got hold of me in Copenhagen, I would have instinctively given him the cold shoulder. But slowly, as we speak, my reservations soften. He quickly realizes that this journalist is not going to fall to his knees and praise Our Lord, and yet his American energy and optimism feel refreshing.

I have met many Christians on my travels who have given up on changing anything. This man is not one of them; he has taken on a Herculean task. He's on a mission. He is not going to permit churches to turn into museums in the Arab world.

The Church must grow, not shrink, he says, and if it doesn't do missionary work it will die.

"The Church has been on the defensive in the Middle East since the seventh century. That has to change. Jesus himself was a rebel. He confronted the powers that occupied the region. But he did it peacefully, with the power of the word, with a message of love. We wouldn't be aware of Christianity today if Jesus and his disciples had kept their mouths shut."

This sounds dangerous, and it strikes me that he is the first Christian I've met who actually believes that the Church can grow in the Middle East, who doesn't lament the fact that it is disappearing. It also strikes me that other Christians' animosity toward a man who wants Christianity to grow here shows how deeply their minority identity is embedded. Christianity must be practiced clandestinely and only by its initiates. Evangelism? That's crazy! It has been a very long time since Paul's command to spread the gospel has been practiced in this region.

Before I get my cell phone back from his son and catch the bus to Ramallah, I receive a crushing but warm handshake from Awwad. I ask him how he feels about his American born-again friends being so enamored with Israel. "It comes from not know-ing what's going on. I tell them that we are also Jews. We are descendants of the Jewish Tribe of Ephraim. So I can say with one hundred and twenty percent certainty that I have Jewish blood. That's why we're so stubborn."

· · ·

One morning in the early spring of 2013, I drive to Gaza, a region where Christians of Awwad's born-again ilk have long since taken to their heels. Christians in the West Bank are still under attack, still discriminated against, still emigrating, but their situation is improving. The reports coming out of Gaza, on the other hand, are deeply disturbing.

The nights continue to be cool, but when the sun comes up at Erez Checkpoint, the extremely well-guarded border crossing between Israel and Gaza, the temperature rises quickly. Very few people care to come here; right now, it's only me and a few UN workers. In the two years since I last visited Gaza, a short war has taken place, the Egyptian authorities have made it more difficult for Palestinians to use the extensive system of tunnels leading to the Sinai Peninsula, and Hamas has consolidated its power.

The reason Western journalists no longer swarm the narrow strip of land might be that it has become more difficult for them to enter. It requires a visa, which in turn requires permission from the government. A government that can make it very difficult for journalists to return should they write something that displeases the Hamas leadership. Also, we are—or risk being—under constant surveillance by the local so-called fixers or translators, in whose hands most journalists are placed. It's doubtful that these local fixers are nonpartisan. They often have closer ties to the Hamas leaders than they admit to. Palestinians in Gaza know this. That puts a damper on our sources. The government is listening.

This time, though, I manage to enter Gaza without a fixer tailing along. Fortunately so; it's unlikely to happen again, but this time it is necessary: Hamas doesn't want the outside world to know about the Christians' situation, and I'm told that any Palestinian in Gaza who writes about it risks immediate imprisonment.

I take a cab through the ravaged city, past donkey carts, dirty workshops, collapsed concrete buildings, faded photos of long-dead martyrs for the Islamic Palestinian cause, children playing in the median strip, women in hijabs pushing baby carriages. There are very few cars on the street, even though it's nine o'clock. I have never before seen so little traffic in this city of nearly a million. Gasoline imports through the tunnels to Gaza have almost been cut off.

It makes sense to come here. In a way, the Palestinian Authority experienced a type of Arab Spring in the years following Yasser Arafat's death. Hamas seized control of Gaza in 2007, and at that time a short civil war was fought between Hamas and Fatah, the party formerly in power. Hundreds of people were killed, supporters of Fatah were thrown out of tall buildings or had their kneecaps shot. Since that time, all protests against the Hamas government have been nipped in the bud. Demonstrators have been met by police wielding clubs and knives, dissidents have been jailed and tortured. Citizens have been forced to join Hamas to get jobs in the public sector.

Hamas is an offshoot of the Muslim Brotherhood, which briefly came to power in Egypt in the elections of 2012. "The Brotherhood's Wings," they call themselves here. Gaza can be considered a trial run for how an Islamic government in their much larger neighbor, Egypt, would have conducted itself had it been allowed to continue.

I drive from the border down to St. Porphyrius Church, said to have been established on this date in the year 407. Today, therefore, is the church's sixteen hundred-and-sixth birthday. There have been Christians in Gaza all those long years, but now their presence here is hanging by a thread. It's impossible to find out how many Christians there are left; one person says there are three thousand, another says fifteen hundred. It's estimated that there are 1.7 million people living in the Gaza Strip, an explosive growth within a very few decades. Christians therefore make up somewhere around 0.1-0.2 percent of the population. A drop in the bucket.

Before Arafat returned from exile to the Palestinian territories, there were five thousand Christians. Many say that life was easier back then, but Islamists were already beginning to destroy movie theaters and cafés. After Hamas came to power, Internet cafés were blown up, libraries leveled to the ground.

Ninety to ninety-five percent of the Christians in Gaza are Greek Orthodox. St. Porphyrius is a beautiful and lavishly decorated Greek Orthodox church, with ceiling frescoes on a background of azure blue and a large gold-tinged altar with the characteristic eye within a pyramid, a symbol of the Trinity. The odor of incense is in the air.

A procession of silk-clad parish clerks carrying candles walk up to the altar, where Archbishop Alexios blesses them. He is wearing a white, gold-embroidered miter, and like almost every priest in the Middle East he has a full beard. An icon of St. Porphyrius sits just inside the entrance to the church. In a small box lined with red velour is a bone, allegedly from the body of the church's founder.

When I ask Christians in Gaza why they are moving away, I get two different answers. Those in the upper hierarchy of the church, such as the Greek-born archbishop, say that Christians are doing fine in Gaza, that "Palestine is a nation of Muslims and Christians." They say that Christians get along well with their Muslim neighbors. They choose to emigrate; it's difficult to find work in Gaza.

A friendly elderly gentleman in a gray suit tells me that there is no persecution here. That they have everything they need. "We can practice our religion freely, and we have a good relationship with Hamas," he says. "There can be problems with some fanatics, but the government does its best to deal with the conflicts."

A minaret stands right next to the church; the man tells me

it's an old building that once belonged to Christians. "This is how it is throughout the Middle East. Minarets are placed right beside churches. That's how Christians show brotherhood."

There are many Christians who subscribe to this version. The other version requires a bit more patience to ferret out. If you hang around a while among the congregation and chat with the members, it shows up, though almost always in anonymity. According to them, Muslims in the Middle East throughout the ages have built minarets beside churches as a demonstration of power.

This more discreetly formulated interpretation is supported by events that took place after Hamas came into power. A recent example: In April 2012 the Hamas government passed a law decreeing that boys and girls must be educated separately. Many people believe this law was the impetus for several weeks of unrest and burned tires and graffiti on a Catholic school which had refused to teach boys and girls separately. The government denies this.

In 2008, a year after Hamas's coup in Gaza, twelve unidentified men bombed the Young Men's Christian Association library in Gaza, destroying eight thousand books. Danish newspapers had reprinted the illustrator Kurt Westergaard's infamous Mohammed drawing after the February 2008 arrest by Danish authorities of three Muslim men who had planned to murder him; the library bombing was an act of revenge. Hamas distanced itself from the attack. Along with eleven other drawings printed in 2005 by a Danish newspaper, *Jyllands-Posten*, Westergaard's original caricature depicting the prophet with a bomb in his turban had sparked rioting in several Muslim countries. Churches, Christians, and Christian districts in several other Arab countries also suffered during the protests at that time. An entire Christian quarter in Beirut was devastated, a fifteen-year-old boy killed a priest in Turkey: these are examples of how quickly a local event in the West unleashes hatred steeped in violence toward Christians in the Middle East.

Similarly, seven churches in the West Bank and Gaza were attacked after a 2006 speech in Regensburg by the former pope, Benedict XVI, in which he suggested that Islam was spread by the sword, not by the word. Palestinian leaders denounced the attacks. Since then, Christians in several other countries have become the victims of Islamist groups seeking revenge, both for the burning of the Koran by a fanatical American priest and for an amateurish American satirical film about the life of the prophet. Each time, Western leaders have publicly displayed indecisiveness; they don't know whether to extol the virtues of free speech or try to silence the agitators.

In April 2007, five Internet cafés, two music shops, and the Gaza City American International School were attacked by a group from the radical Salafist stream of Islam. A UN school was also assailed, presumably because it wasn't gender segregated. But worst of all was the kidnapping and subsequent murder on October 7, 2007 of Rami Ayad, the owner of the only Christian bookstore in Gaza. He was shot and stabbed several times. Earlier he had received threats, and his bookstore had been bombed twice that same year. The Hamas leadership also denounced this crime, but no one has ever been arrested, though several Christians have told me that Hamas knows the murderers' identities.

Rami Ayad was a Baptist, and his bookstore was presumably considered to be evangelical in nature by radical Islamist groups. That is one possible motive for his murder. The Baptists' mission isn't popular among the Greek Orthodox clergy, either. I speak with Archbishop Alexios in the parish hall after Mass in St. Porphyrius Church, where he tells me that the Baptists are to blame for all the problems Christians have in Gaza. They have tried to convert Muslims, he explains. That is what has caused all the trouble. Had they refrained from doing that, everyone would be living in peace. I ask the archbishop if missionary work isn't a part of Christianity.

"Jesus didn't give gifts to people to lure them into following him. He let them come to him. He insisted that people love without demanding anything in return." Today all Baptist families in Gaza have fled as a result of the bookstore owner's murder, the archbishop says. It has frightened all the Christians in Gaza.

I drive over to the much humbler, uglier, less showy Catholic church, a concrete building opening out onto a school yard. It's in need of repair. The Catholics are a small (5 percent) and poverty stricken part of the Christian population in Gaza. They claim there are only two hundred practitioners of their faith left in Gaza; others say there are even fewer. There is no love lost between the Catholics and the Greek Orthodox. Considering Christians as a whole are a dying breed, the hostility seems particularly absurd.

In front of the church, an elderly, balding man with a stubborn expression comes up to me. I'll call him Dawoud. He has just laid a bouquet on the grave of his wife, who died a few months ago. Mass is being held inside the church, but he doesn't attend.

We sit down on a red school bench leaning against a wall of the church. "There is no harmony between Christians and Muslims in the Middle East," he says. "No forgiveness. Islamists scorn us, and the young people in the mosques are taught to look down on others."

It's Sunday, the school yard is empty. A leafless tree spreads its branches far over the school yard. A few palm trees stand in front of the church, several kids are playing there. As with the Greek Orthodox Church, the yard is surrounded by a wall with an iron gate. Dawoud folds his arms and squints into the sunlight. "The Muslims don't hate us, it's more that they don't accept us. We can't find work in Gaza. It's because the government doesn't care about Christians."

He has lived his entire life in Gaza, and according to him the situation has never been worse. It all began with the revolution at the end of the 1970s in Shiite Iran, which also awakened a Sunni Islamism in the Arab countries. Nowadays, when Dawoud is home on Friday, he can hear the sermons from the mosques. Most often the hatred expressed is directed toward Jews, but once in a while Christians are the target.

The Gaza imams who appear on television go so far as to demand that both groups be murdered. Even in programs for children, Christians and Jews are referred to as "inferior" and "cowardly and despised;" suicide attacks are encouraged. The elderly man tells me that the government does nothing to stop this, and that's why the attitude of the population toward Christians is becoming more and more fierce. Especially among younger Muslims.

He has been harassed by ten-year-olds. He has also seen unveiled Christian women being called "*kuffar*"—infidel—by young children. Christian women in Gaza have confirmed this to me, that people curse them, denigrate them when they walk around town without a veil. Hamas's official policy is that wearing a veil is not mandatory, but women's daily lives are much easier if they do. A sixteen-year-old Christian girl told me that her female school principal pressed her to wear a veil in class.

If it wasn't for Dawoud's two sons, both in their twenties, he would have moved to the West Bank with the rest of his family long ago. But the Israeli government has decreed that no one between the ages of sixteen and thirty-five—the alleged age of terrorists—is allowed to pass through an Israeli border. And because the Israeli border also follows the Jordan River along the West Bank, they can't enter the West Bank by traveling to Egypt and entering at the Jordanian border, either.

One of the stories several people talk about concerns four events in June and July 2012, where Christians were "kidnapped," as they put it. The concept of kidnapping should be taken with a grain of salt; Christians may or may not have been forced to convert to Islam. Christians in the Middle East (as well as all other religions in the region, as far as that goes) have a tendency to regard fellow Christians converting to another religion as an act of insanity; it's impossible someone has converted voluntarily.

It is tempting for many Christians to convert, and has been so for centuries. Becoming a Muslim opens doors that are closed to Christians. To this microscopic congregation in Gaza it feels particularly life-threatening that young people allow themselves to be shanghaied.

The case of one man, Ramez, points to the most excruciating fear Christians have—that their children will be swayed or enslaved by Islam. I'm told that Ramez is a talented and friendly young man who was kidnapped by an Islamist group with what seems to be a respectable name: the Palestinian Scholars Association.

The group is notorious in Gaza, and its leader, Salem Salama, is a Hamas member of Parliament. One of their goals is to convert Christians, who are given cars, jobs, and an apartment when they become Muslim. I've been told a story about a nineteen-year-old who pulled the wool over the eyes of the PSA by saying he would convert. He was given a car and an apartment, both of which he sold, then he secretly fled to the West Bank with his entire family as political refugees—he had become a wanted man. But he got out of Gaza with his family and money to boot.

Ramez's case is more serious. Several days after he was kidnapped, his disconsolate mother was admitted to Shifa Hospital. The PSA allowed him to visit her, and according to several witnesses I spoke with, he arrived accompanied by several of Salama's armed guard. His mother and sister yelled at them, "You mustn't take Ramez!" Ramez screamed that he wanted to go home. Using wooden clubs, the armed men then beat up his mother, sister, a young priest, and another Christian I meet. The man I spoke to suffered a wound on his forehead.

The armed guard took Ramez away again, then released him several days later. Ramez told the press that the day before he returned home, while still a prisoner, he freely converted to Islam. He also said that he wanted to return home if his family still would have him.

I go to see Ramez's father, Hana Alamash, at his goldsmith shop in the alleyways of Gaza's famous Zaitun neighborhood. It's a shack with brown, filthy walls and a desk. He has written his son's name on a wooden plaque nailed on the front of his desk. Tongs and tweezers are scattered about. Behind him hangs a calendar with the Virgin Mary; a black cross has been drawn on the wall.

At first he doesn't want to talk about his son, but then he changes his mind. "It's not true that he has become a Muslim," he says, his voice frantic. "They brainwashed him. I am a goldsmith, I know how to sell things. That's what they did."

A young man brings in a silver ring. The goldsmith lays it on a flat stone and brings out a torch. He heats the ring up until it is white hot, then he holds it with tongs and works on it as he tells about the week the PSA held his son prisoner. He did everything he could to get his son back. He talked to the government, of which the kidnapper, Salem Salama, was a member. They could do nothing to this man, the government said. The police said the same thing; we are powerless, he is too strong.

"When Ramez returned home, I left him alone," Alamash says. "I wanted him to have peace and quiet before telling what happened. One morning he came to me and said, 'Father, I am a Christian.'"

Ramez emigrated to Sweden. It's no longer safe for him to be in Gaza. Later I am told that with the help of the government, the archbishop made a deal with the PSA, in which each side promised not to try to convert any members of the other.

Back in the courtyard of the beautiful Greek Orthodox church, I strike up a conversation with a man in his fifties I will call Simoun. He is wearing Western clothes and tennis shoes, his foot taps nervously. "If some old woman came along and wanted to take me away, I would go anywhere in the world with her. Just to get out of here." He laughs.

Simoun talks about the hate speech coming from the mosques. There are groups in Gaza who want to kill the Christians, he says. He adds that rocks are sometimes thrown over the wall into the church or the graveyard.

After Hamas came into power in 2007, something happened that almost cost him his life. A Muslim family who took care of the church was renting one of the houses next door. Simoun told how the church wanted to take back possession of the house in 2007. The courts gave them permission.

One day a group of armed men broke into the courtyard and took Simoun prisoner. They bound him and threw him into a waiting car, but he managed to escape. He then describes how the men returned five months later and beat up the archbishop. These acts were meant to avenge the eviction of the Muslim family.

"Now that Hamas is in control, we are not safe, we have no security. Anyone can attack us without consequence." The anxiety he has suffered since the two incidents has led to two heart attacks.

Another man I will call Tomas tells about an episode that took place two months ago. His brother called a carpenter to repair something in his house. Suddenly the carpenter pulled out a gun and shot his brother, his brother's wife, and their son, after which he stole their possessions. Tomas shows me photos on his phone of his brother, who is now in a coma in an Israeli hospital, a tube stuck in his mouth. His wife and son survived and recuperated.

The carpenter is in jail, and he claims he doesn't know why he did it. Tomas, however, is convinced that they were shot because they were Christians; as I've been told before, the stereotypical Christian is rich.

He also shows us photos of the threatening letters the carpenter's family has sent him. The family demands that Tomas tell the police that their son didn't shoot Tomas's brother and family. He refuses to do so. They have also offered him money to lie about the shootings. Tomas also refuses to take the money. The verdict hasn't been handed down yet, but Tomas says that if his brother dies and the carpenter isn't sentenced to death, he will kill the man himself. "I want no peace agreement with his family. Islamic law rules here, even though I'm a Christian. Therefore I will kill him."

I ask him what he expects that the revenge killing would lead to. "We believe in fate. Whatever happens, happens."

I leave the congregation and drive back to the border. I'm totally exhausted; it's as if I have been lowered into a volcano and lifted out again, bringing up with me the fear of those I have met, the fear of saying something wrong and being discovered. The subjugation, the official, understandable lies that Christians must tell to survive. The whispered stories of the lives of nameless individuals. I'm nauseous as I leave Gaza with a bad conscience and no desire whatsoever to return.

Our language can't describe the Christians' situation in Gaza. The vocabulary we use when talking about violations of human rights is not much help. No systematic persecution takes place; hate doesn't trickle down from the Hamas leadership, there's no open encouragement to victimize Christians. What is perhaps more frightening is that the anger comes from children on the street, from self-appointed Islamists who demand purity and are allowed to wreak havoc, from individual members of Parliament with shadowy connections to Gaza's security forces and authorities, from imams with flaming tongues, from the media. And the government either cannot or will not do anything about it.

We have formed our conception of hatred toward minorities from centuries of European Jewish persecutions, but that anti-Semitism was often more violent and directly sanctioned from the ruling powers. What is taking place in Gaza is different. It is milder, more hidden, more unorganized and asymmetrical, more difficult to hold a government responsible for.

While crossing the border I struggle to find the right word. Pogrom is too strong, harassment too weak; persecution is too weighty, discrimination too trivial. We must find an expression that lies in between. We are seeing something less direct, more coincidental, less controlled, leading to an intense desire among Christians to abandon the region they have lived in for centuries, since before the church built in 407 existed.

This lack of relevant concepts is even stronger in Egypt.

CHAPTER 2

Egypt

I arrive in Cairo in the autumn of 2012, just as Egypt is experiencing its worst crisis since the revolution less than two years earlier. A few days before my arrival, the Muslim Brotherhood leader then serving as the Egyptian president, Mohamed Morsi, granted himself unlimited powers, nullifying all judicial oversight of his actions. He explained that he wanted to defend the revolution and ensure that his proposed constitutional changes would be enacted. Angry demonstrators called him "Morsilini." They gathered by the tens of thousands in Tahrir Square, located in the heart of the Middle East's most populous city.

The day after my arrival in Cairo, I walk over Qasr al-Nil Bridge toward the square with a young female Christian journalist and the Western journalist and cameraman she works for as a fixer and interpreter; in other words, she translates and keeps young thugs from smashing the Westerners' equipment.

There aren't many people here; small groups of boys mill around, and tear gas from a confrontation with the police several hours earlier still stings our noses. Rocks and burned-out cars dot the streets. This section of central Cairo is in chaos. The four of us head for a side street beside the bridge leading to a grassy mound and low wall; the Western journalist and cameraman walk on ahead in search of rioting to film.

As soon as she and I reach the side street, a group of thirty or forty young teenagers force us up against a wall. For months there has been talk about these mobs of increasingly younger

Egyptians who skip school and vandalize the area around the square, intent on fighting with the police and harassing passersby. Several women have been raped on the square and in the side streets; yesterday three girls were stripped naked by three hundred of these teenagers.

Our backs are literally and figuratively against the wall; we can only try to talk our way out of this situation. The group doesn't seem to have a leader. Many of them have tied scarves around their mouths, and their eyes are red from tear gas. They look confused, filthy, their teeth are bad, they are nervous and skittish from the adrenaline rush of clashing with the police and lack of sleep. They discuss whether to smash the cameraman's equipment—he is farther down the street. Some of the boys begin fondling the woman.

She keeps her cool, smiles and convinces them that the journalists are on their side, that it would be stupid to ruin their gear. I stand there wishing for a tunnel to open and transport us to safety on the opposite side of the Nile. The boys joke a bit, make a few threats, are friendly and curious one second and aggressive the next. We sense that they could go amok at any moment.

It takes awhile, but we manage to partially separate ourselves from them and reach Tahrir Square, where an elderly doctor tries to help us shake the boys. He apologizes for their behavior. They follow us around for forty-five minutes, until finally we duck into a coffee shop.

From our table we can see the tents out in the square, where men—there are almost no women—walk around aimlessly. The tall buildings surrounding the square look empty, the balconies are filled with satellite dishes and TV cameras. The entire square seems to be a self-sustaining system of demonstrators, homeless louts, and broadcast journalists, all of them feeding off one another. And this week, when the battle concerning the constitution suddenly becomes grim, when demonstrators from the opposition and Brotherhood camps storm each other and people die, the entire food chain is once more up and running.

The journalist, who wishes to remain anonymous, tells me that although she looks like most Egyptian women, she stands out there on the square as a Christian partly because she doesn't wear a veil. For that reason, she is a potential victim. It's becoming increasingly less common to see a woman with uncovered hair, especially farther out from Cairo's center—or here, in the middle of it all.

"All my friends talk about leaving," she says. The episode with the young boys has shaken her up, even though she has been in similar situations before. As far as sexual harassment is concerned, Egypt is one of the worst places in the world, and Tahrir Square, where women were at the forefront of protests against the regime, has long been the scene of many such encounters, including some carried out by the authorities.

Soldiers conducted "virginity tests" on women during the revolution in the winter of 2011, to document how unmarried young people were sleeping with each other on the square. Hundreds of women were pawed at, groped, debased, raped, and beaten up, with no protection from men in or out of uniform.

"So don't ask why Christian Egyptians leave the country," she says. "Ask why they stay. My parents want to stay, even though they shouldn't. You have to understand how difficult it is to leave the country and city you've grown up in, and start all over in a new place, in a new country, where you can't speak the language and don't know the culture. Everything you've learned is useless, and no one respects you. Only young people can handle that type of radical change."

We leave the square, and before we part she says, "Be merciful to the Copts, Mr. Klaus."

I'm filled with conflicting emotions as I drive back over Qasr al-Nil Bridge, away from Tahrir Square and the female journalist. What she and I went through is commonplace, hardly worth noting, yet as it happened I was acutely aware that the boys could do anything they wanted to her, and I was powerless to stop them.

Egypt, like Gaza, is a type of closed society for which we lack precise terminology. The Cold War has given us an understanding of the totalitarian mentality, but Egypt can't be called totalitarian; the regime doesn't claim the same type of control over citizens as existed in former Eastern Bloc countries. The Egyptian authorities allow a vaguely controlled chaos, a freedom arising from lawlessness, street law that is given free rein, where only coincidence dictates who is punished and who is not.

I haven't really been interested in Twitter before arriving in Egypt, but I discover quickly that it's essential if you want to follow what is happening here. Hundreds of bloggers exhibit a courage and broad-mindedness that puts the ordinary opinion makers to shame. A new language has given some people a voice for the first time in their lives, and now they are shouting—screaming—at gruesome Islamists and weak sycophants. Twitter warriors can say what they want as long as they don't offend the military and religion.

Just as in Gaza, I sense in many Christians here the same anxiety that stems from the inability to point to specific persecutors who wield power. The zealots come from below, from the street, and not necessarily from Islamists. The young teenagers harassing women were against the Muslim Brotherhood. The regime has no monopoly on violence; attacks come from the most unexpected places. Christians don't even know where the authorities stand. Often they have to protect themselves from the police and the army, instead of being protected by them.

I'm also confused about my journalistic project. The stories I hear from Christians seem to blend into those of many other minorities, including the non-religious, and it seems meaningless to separate the one from the other. But Christians are emblematic of what every Egyptian minority is going through. And almost every Christian here I talk to longs to leave. Because I'm investigating why Christians are emigrating and not only if they are being persecuted, it's clear that the reasons often mirror those of countless Muslims, who also feel an urgent need to get away from a land where they are suffocating.

The revolt is reflected in Maikel Nabil Sanad, who at age twenty-seven is one of the most famous voices from the revolution of 2011—a moment that now seems ancient history. The identity of the people for whom a regime has no place says much about a country. Stigmatized people, to use a well-known Christian term.

There's no place here for Nabil. That's why I meet him in a small office on Old Square in Copenhagen on a gray, late autumn day a few weeks before leaving for Egypt; Amnesty International has invited him here.

Nabil is sharp-witted, young, comfortable with the media, and disrespectful of all authority, which is why he was the first blogger after President Mubarak's fall to land behind bars for "insulting the military." On March 8, 2011, he wrote on his blog that the military, which claimed to be protecting the demonstrators, was never on their side.

"The revolution has removed a dictator, but not a dictatorship," he said, one of the first to make this claim. He presented documents and made accusations against the military and security services for being behind a number of assaults on demon-strators, which resulted in hundreds of deaths.

On April 10, 2011, he was sentenced to three years in prison, after which he was thrown into a dark cell and tortured. He began a hunger strike, which led to an international campaign for his release. He was granted amnesty in January 2012, and today he lives in Germany, where he studies political science at Erfurt University.

Nabil is Christian, or rather, "of Christian descent." "Only three religions are recognized in Egypt, and you must have one of them written in your passport. Mine has Christian in it, even though I'm an atheist. I can't change it—or at least, only to Islam." Atheism is forbidden in Egypt; it can lead to a prison sentence. In Sudan, Saudi Arabia, Pakistan, the Maldives, Mauritania, and Iran, the sentence can be death. Only in Muslim countries do governments penalize godlessness in this way.

Nabil is a conglomeration of many of the minorities to which the Arab Spring has given equal amounts of hope and bitterness: Christian, atheist, blogger, demonstrator, antimilitarist, peace activist, open enemy of the regime. To all of that can be added that he doesn't share the hatred of Israel typical for the Middle East. He is an inversion of everything that is taking place in his country. He has Einstein-like hair, unruly and wavy, and on that autumn day he wears a burgundy-colored sweatshirt, the hood of which droops over a beige down vest. There is something of the Sunday's child about him, an awareness of who he is and what he's struggling for, as he nonchalantly sprawls out on the sofa.

Nabil is a new image of the Arab world, a new figure of opposition born from the Arab Spring. Later, as I follow him down the street to a restaurant in the middle of Copenhagen, he zips his vest up to his chin. The day is cold and gray. He is in strange surroundings in this foreign country, unwanted in his own. He doesn't seem worried about whether he'll ever be allowed to return to Egypt.

His role models are those who march to a different drummer, influential people who have weathered the storm, in particular the former German Chancellor Willy Brandt, whom he quoted as saying, "The best way to predict the future is to create it." Clearly he's a self-assured young man.

"If we were living in Oslo in 1940, watching the young dissident Willy Brandt, an exile from his country, watching him struggle against the Nazi army as it occupied Norway, not one of us would have predicted that he would one day be the leader of West Germany, play a role in German and European reconciliation and unity, and win the Nobel Peace Prize. The difference between Willy Brandt, Nelson Mandela, Aung San Suu Kyi, Martin Luther King, Jr., and us is that they believed they could make the future, that they could change things."

Delusions of grandeur or idealism? Nabil sees himself in these heroes, and he is inspired by a man who is the godfather of all liberal Egyptians, Ahmed Lutfi El-Sayed, one of the most prominent Egyptians of the first half of the twentieth century. Lutfi was the first president of Cairo University, and under his leadership Egyptian women earned a degree for the first time. He was also the director of the National Library of Egypt, and he introduced British philosopher John Stuart Mill's advocacy of free speech and women's rights to the Arab world.

Lutfi opposed Pan-Arabism, the nationalist idea of a union of Arab states promoted by Egyptian leader Gamal Abdel Nasser. He believed in Egypt as an independent country, separate from other Arab lands. This Renaissance man's glory years coincided with Egypt's era of freedom, from the mid-20s to Gamal Abdel Nasser's coup in 1952. Back then, men like Lutfi could attain influential positions. And now his young admirer walks down a rainy street in Copenhagen, unable to return home without risking imprisonment. For saying things similar to what Lutfi spoke about.

Oddly enough, I have been warned against meeting with folks like Nabil by several well-meaning people familiar with the Middle East. I have been told that the reason I'm interviewing him, the reason Westerners seek out him and his collaborators (a very small minority, at most 1 percent, they say in admonishment), is because they speak English and have the same opinions as we do.

In a country where 95 percent of the population believes that Islam plays a major role in politics, it's possible these people have a point. But sometimes the 1 percent is right, sometimes they can see clearer than the majority. Besides, I discover soon upon arriving in Cairo that this claim about Western sympathy is doubtful. The Western media doesn't wholeheartedly support Nabil and his fellow revolutionaries. Opinion is split concerning the liberal opposition in Egypt; a surprising number of Westerners blame the unrest on the Tahrir Square demonstrators, calling them undemocratic because they won't yield to majority support for a more Islamic society. The Muslim Brotherhood is often described as pragmatic and responsive. Liberal Egyptians feel betrayed by Western opinion; they accuse the West of setting different and much lower standards for Arab regimes than they ever would for their own governments. Mona Eltahawy, one of Egypt's most prominent bloggers, is among those who call the phenomenon "a racism of lower expectations."

Before meeting Nabil, I reprinted in the Danish newspaper *Weekendavisen* a column he wrote about the trials and imprisonment of Egyptians for blasphemy. He points out two cases brought against Christian Egyptians. On September 12, 2012, a court in Sohag sentenced a Christian, Bishoy El-Bihery, to six years in prison for criticizing Islam and Morsi.

In September 2011, two Coptic Christian children, Nabil Nagy Rizk, ten, and Mina Nady Farag, nine, were arrested for insulting Islam. They were caught with several scraps of paper, on which there happened to be written a few verses from the Koran. The children were later released without a trial because of their age.

Others have been prosecuted for criticizing Islam. Egyptian Christians and other non-Sunni Muslims were subjected to this long before the Muslim Brotherhood came to power. Nabil himself has been charged; while he is in Denmark, a new case is brought against him for "insulting Islam." Egyptian authorities demand that Germany extradite him to be tried in Egypt.

"What is happening in Egypt is the beginning of a new Inquisition," he says. "The world is turning a deaf ear to this." Perhaps because it won't listen to the 1 percent.

"The word Copt is used incorrectly," he says, when asked about the Copts' situation. "Copt simply means Egyptian."

The word comes from the Latin *coptus*, which stems from the Greek *aiguptios*, which is where we get Egyptian from. Coptic also refers to the Christian language, which more or less has been eradicated and replaced by Arabic. Very few people speak Coptic. In its original meaning, Copt was a term for all Egyptians, but during the past sixty years, the word has evolved to refer only to Christian Egyptians, Nabil says.

He explains that a century ago only seven countries were regarded as Arab, all of them on the Arabian Peninsula. "Along with the rise of Arab nationalism, the concept of being an Arab is being linked to the Sunni Muslim majority that also exists in North African countries," he says. "There's an attempt to foster an ethnicity that doesn't exist. The North African countries—

Egypt, Tunisia, Libya, Algeria, Morocco— they have nothing to do with Syria, Lebanon, Jordan, Iraq, Palestine, Saudi
Arabia, Yemen, and the Gulf states. Egypt is regarded as Arab
only because our dictatorship throughout the past decades has
declared it to be. In that way, Egypt is becoming less and less
Christian. Christians feel that Arabs have occupied our country."

Maikel Nabil claims that the practice of using the word
Copt to denote Christian Egyptians first began during the Cold
War, but that's not true. This has been going on for centuries.
For example, I looked the word up in the 1900 edition of a
renowned Danish encyclopedia *Salmonsens*, and already at that
time there was a clear distinction: "Egypt's original Christians
are called Copts, while the original Mohammedans are called
Arabs."

This distinction goes much further back. Before Arabs conquered Egypt in the seventh century, they called the country dar
al-Qibt, "home of the Copts." Since then, Christian Egyptians
have been considered Copts, even though ten percent of them
belong to other Christian denominations. Many Copts hold the
thinly disguised view that Egypt is their country first and foremost. They were here before the Muslims. Also, they clearly are
proud of being the oldest Christian community in the world.
The Coptic Church considers Mark the Evangelist to be its first
pope. In Coptic Egypt there exists a sense of being close to the
source of Christian civilization.

They also have a long historical awareness of being oppressed.
Christians were persecuted throughout the first centuries. The
Roman Emperor Diocletian, who ruled Egypt from 284 to 305,
was especially cruel. Copts call that period Anno Martyrum, The
Era of the Martyrs; their thirteen-month Coptic calendar, which
is still being used today, began back then. Tens of thousands
of Christians are thought to have been tortured and murdered

under the rule of Diocletian. The murdering stopped when Emperor Constantine converted to Christianity in 312.

Despite the switch to Christianity within the Roman Empire, Copts were still persecuted. The Byzantine Church broke away from the Coptic Church at the Council of Chalcedon, a city across the Bosporus from Constantinople, in 451. The purpose of the Council was to discuss monophysitism, the belief that Jesus had only a single, divine nature, that he was not both God and man. The Council rejected monophysitism, after which Coptic theology was considered heretical. The Western world shunned the Copts, while the Byzantine faith spread farther east to Russia and south into the Middle East. This split affected the history of the world.

Because the Byzantine Empire included Egypt, the Copts were suppressed. During a period in the seventh century, the Coptic patriarch went into exile. Copts therefore received Muslims with open arms when they invaded the country in 641. They were regarded as liberators.

The persecutions didn't stop, however. Copts discovered quickly that "they were shackled by a much weightier yoke than before," as *Salmonsens Encyclopedia* puts it. Bloody attacks followed, and a religious head tax, jizya, was enacted, with Muslims exempted. I have heard jizya mentioned many times during my travels by Islamic extremists, but also by Christians, who fear that the new Islamic rulers will bring back the tax. The Danish encyclopedia also states that many Arabs most likely are "true Egyptians, who throughout the years have taken up Islam to better their circumstances." This is another reason why the fear of converting to Islam is so entrenched among Christians.

The one hundred-year-old edition of *Salmonsens Encyclopedia*, written before an era of political correctness, doesn't avoid tactless and not always flattering portrayals of national character.

We are told that in contrast to Muslims, Copts are allowed to drink alcohol, and "not few of them avail themselves of this freedom more than prudence dictates."

Maikel Nabil, one of the persecuted minority of our times, of course knew the distinction between Copts and Arabs is ancient, but his point was polemic. Nationalism and Islamism have in the past sixty years changed Egypt for the worse. There are schisms everywhere in this nation. It wasn't always like this. In the first half of the twentieth century, the country had a reputation for liberalism. If you were persecuted in other countries, such as Armenians in Turkey, you came to Egypt. You were also allowed to change religions or to become atheist, he says. "I'm not saying a pure form of tolerance existed, but back then Islam was different, milder. It wasn't common to say that anyone changing religions should be killed."

Saudi Arabian oil money is flooding the country today. Radical Salafists carry the Saudi flag at demonstrations, Nabil points out. The sectarian struggle has resurfaced because a particularly stringent form of Islam has become the official version of the religion. Nabil says that many Copts are leaving the country; as in the Palestinian Territories, this has been going on for decades. "Christians sense that their lives are in danger if they stay in Egypt," he says. "Salafists are attacking churches. Everyone feels they can be victimized at some point."

Nabil sees the attacks in recent years in light of a greater, decades-long expulsion. He believes that Egyptian dictators have for the past sixty years slowly attempted to get rid of Christians—in fact, all minorities. After Nasser came to power in 1952, he initially threw out the Jews before turning to the Greeks, Italians, and Armenians, all of whom had given the open mercantile city of Alexandria a cosmopolitan character. He also deported the Nubians, who originated from the Nile region of southern Egypt and northern Sudan.

"Christians had to choose sides when the Jews were thrown out in the 1950s, and they chose the dictatorship," Nabil says. The Copts joined in with Nasser's denunciation of the Western world's so-called imperialism, and the Coptic leadership supported him when he nationalized the Suez Canal.

The 1956 war that followed, during which France, Great Britain, and Israel attacked Egypt to reopen the canal, had serious consequences: two days after the war ended, fifteen thousand Britons, ten thousand Frenchmen, and twenty-five thousand Jews were ordered to leave the country. They were forced to abandon everything they owned. It was a death blow to Alexandria. Today the city is the power base of extremist Salafi Muslims, who believe that Islam should be practiced as it was by Mohammed's early followers.

Egypt was placed under administration by Nasser. As the British historian Philip Mansel notes, Nasser transformed Egypt into a police state, with "travel and export restrictions, censorship, tapped telephones, denunciations, nighttime arrests, bulging prisons, concentration camps for Communists and Muslim Brothers."

The Coptic leadership was every bit as nationalist as Nasser, and since his rise to power they have been strongly opposed to Israel, forbidding their followers to make pilgrimages to Jerusalem. Anwar Sadat, the president who in the late 1970s signed a peace treaty with Israel, enraged them. "The Copts never thought about them being next in line," Nabil says. "What happened to the Jews is happening to the Christians, only more slowly, because there are so many of them."

The Copts have been infected by this sectarian mentality. For the past thirty years, Christians have isolated themselves, which hasn't helped their situation. They have their own schools, clubs, and beaches. They don't take part in public life. "I'm very critical of the Coptic Church," Nabil says. "That's why Copts don't like me."

I tell him that many people think it's useless to speak to people like him, people who represent the microscopic part of the population that mirrors Western opinion. "How many Social Democrats in Nazi Germany in 1944 openly expressed their opinions?" he answers. "Egypt is a closed society."

I leave him and his swooping hair and relaxed smile—not in Oslo like his hero Willy Brandt in 1940, but sitting at a restaurant on Copenhagen's Gray Brothers Square in 2012. I glance back at him as I leave; he's enjoying his meal as if he hasn't a care in the world, as if nothing can shake his conviction that Egypt will one day change course and head in his direction.

• • •

A few weeks after our meeting, while in Egypt, I think about how Nabil has his work cut out for him. Cairo is buzzing with expectations on this late autumn morning in 2012: Where will the violent demonstrations in front of the president's headquarters between supporters of the Muslim Brotherhood and enraged opponents of Morsi lead? Will they storm the building? Has the president fled? The country seems poised on the edge of catastrophe.

I'm on my way to visit Youssef Sidhom, editor in chief of the daily newspaper *Al-Watani*, and the man most people referred me to when I asked why Copts are considering exile. He is regarded as one of the most prominent and fearless Coptic intellectuals. I walk up a stairway that looks like it hasn't been swept in decades, not to mention painted.

"Copts and moderate Muslims are deeply worried," he says, when I arrive at his second floor office.

Sidhom sits at the end of a long table covered with papers. He is wearing a tie and white shirt, with his jacket draped over the back of his chair; behind him hangs a jigsaw puzzle version of the famous self-portrait of M. C. Escher, who studies himself in the reflection of a globe-shaped mirror he's holding.

Sidhom, on the other hand, is studying Egypt's Christians. Journalists at his paper have tried to find out how many are currently leaving the country. A human rights activist claimed in the autumn of 2011 that one hundred thousand people had already left, but Sidhom's paper proved that number had no basis in fact. They have called the American, British, Australian, Canadian, and French embassies; Copts are emigrating in large part to these five nations.

"All the embassies said they couldn't release that information to the press," he says. "Besides, they don't register the religion of asylum-seekers, which makes good sense." He believes that less than fifty thousand Copts have moved to the United States, which is their favored destination.

The percentage of Christians among the Egyptian population of approximately eighty-five million is also unknown. The Coptic Church's official tally is 10 percent, but that is merely an estimate, one that is definitely too high. Others say there are under five million Christians, citing censuses taken throughout the years: 8.3 percent of the population was registered as Christian in 1927, 5.9 percent in 1986, and 5.5 percent in 2000. This follows a pattern seen in all the countries that once were a part of the Ottoman Empire; whereas Christians comprised approximately ten percent of the population in 1900, a century later it was under four percent, less than thirteen million people.

Because the Egyptian population has grown significantly

since 2000, during which period many Christians have emigrated, the Copts most likely now make up a smaller percentage. That is, less than 5.5 percent. And the percentage may fall further in the near future.

"I have to admit that the Islamic movement is a wave, and the Christians are riding on top of it," the editor in chief says. "They fear the future, the total lack of law and order." I ask if Christians are being persecuted. His expression is weary. "How do you define persecution?" He sends me a patronizing look, as if speaking to a child. "No, the situation for Christians isn't the same as for blacks in South Africa. But both persecution and discrimination are a part of fundamentalist Islam, which has affected our educational system and the number of influential jobs available. It has marginalized Christians."

Also, fanaticism has led to more assaults. Christians were protected to a degree when Hosni Mubarak was in power, Sidhom explains, after a secretary serves us Turkish coffee. "Security forces treated Islamists harshly, though to protect the regime, not Christians. This protection disappeared after the revolution. Churches are attacked and plundered, and no one does anything about it. No one is arrested. That's what is new."

He also says that the president's approval is necessary before Christians can make the smallest changes to their churches, much less build a new one. This is an Ottoman law from 1856, which is still in effect. Permission can take decades. Should Christians build without permission, they risk rioting from their Muslim neighbors.

Another common criticism is that Copts are never given top posts in Egypt. There are no Coptic university presidents, deans, governors, ministers, editors in chief of state-owned newspapers, directors of state-owned businesses, employees in security or intelligence services. Christians working at the Ministry of Foreign Affairs number under 1 percent, at the Ministry of Justice—1.5 percent. In other words, Copts are excluded from the most influential Egyptian public positions. Discrimination comes from above.

I tell Sidhom that many people criticize the Copts for isolating themselves; the editor in chief agrees. "Christians outside the cities have to mingle with Muslims more, otherwise they risk being abused or assaulted. For many years I've been calling for us to reach out to Muslims."

Much of the isolation is the fault of Pope Shenouda III, who was the Coptic Church leader from 1971 until his death in the spring of 2012. For over forty years he ruled in such a conservative and autocratic manner that he has been described as a dictator. The new leader, Pope Tawadros, has already charted a new course. "He has announced that the Church will not take political stances. Individual Christians are free to express themselves politically. Now that Hosni Mubarak and Pope Shenouda are gone, there is no longer any connection between the president and the pope. We are on our own."

Since the revolution, an already ailing economy is now exponentially worse, which affects millions of Egyptians. I've seen how tourists are shunning the country; I was more or less alone while visiting one of the world's most extensive collections of antiquities, the Egyptian Museum in Cairo.

During the days I spend in Cairo, the Brotherhood and the Salafists are moving quickly to finish the new constitution and put it to a vote. "The articles having to do with civil rights are written in a way to ensure that God holds these rights," Sidhom says. "It all ends with a phrase that says that civil rights only apply as long as they don't conflict with Sharia."

And what Sharia actually is, no one knows for certain. There are endless discussions among the Islamic learned, but Sidhom is particularly concerned about the Salafists' interpretation. "They're never going to accept non-Muslims, and they will treat them as second-rate citizens. Minorities will be marginalized and stripped of their rights." Accordingly, Salafists have announced that women, including Christians, must wear hijab. They also want to ban the sale of alcohol, just as they want to prevent adultery among tourists and force men and women to swim at separate beaches.

In a country such as Egypt, which has little to offer other than its incredible cultural heritage, such proclamations are fatal. According to Sidhom, not only Christians will suffer if Sharia is implemented—everyone will. "If it happens, no civilized country will accept the type of punishment Sharia metes out. Thieves will have their hands cut off, unfaithful women will be stoned."

I ask if there is a difference between how the Muslim Brotherhood and the Salafists interpret Sharia. "The Salafists are more fundamentalist, and therefore they're also more honest," he says. "You can believe what they say. The Brotherhood is widely mistrusted. They want to camouflage their politics until they have gained full control of the country. Ask a high official of the Brotherhood what they wish to do, and you'll get a reassuring answer. But we in Egypt have learned to never trust them. They say this, that, and the other, but they never stop dragging our country toward an Islamic state."

Analysts are groping in the dark to explain what the Muslim Brotherhood really wants. It's a mysterious movement, but its leading members have made statements that support Sidhom's predictions.

The enormously popular television cleric, Sheikh Yusuf

al-Qaradawi, whose weekly show on the Qatar-based Al-Jazeera network is seen by sixty million people, said in January 2012 that "Sharia should be implemented gradually. This is Sharia law and the law of nature." For many years he has been regarded as a spiritual leader of the movement and the most important Sunni Muslim voice in the Middle East. "People do not understand the Sharia properly," said the Al-Jazeera cleric, who was once thrown out of Egypt because of his ties to the Brotherhood. "We have to teach people the laws of the Sharia and explain them, before anything else. I think that in the first five years, there should be no chopping off of hands."

But al-Qaradawi is an ambivalent figure; he has openly declared that he supports democracy and liberalism, and he speaks in conciliatory tones about Christians. At the same time, he has declared that alcohol is the first thing that must be forbidden, that it's not something Islamic law can compromise on, even if a majority should prove to be against its prohibition.

Al-Qaradawi is often described as moderate and democratic in Western media, despite a statement during the Gaza war in 2009 in which he commended Hitler for putting the Jews in their place. In addition, he has praised Palestinian suicide attacks. He believes that homosexuality should be punished by death, and he has defended "mild" abuse of wives by husbands. It's difficult to see anything moderate and democratic about that.

On the other hand, he has spoken out against attacks on Copts: "Islam does not condone the killing of the innocent civilians of any nation or nationality except for a prescribed penalty." On other occasions, he and other leading figures in the Muslim Brotherhood have stated clearly that the movement regards Copts to be a part of Egypt.

These conciliatory statements do not ease Sidhom's mind. But he also explains that I shouldn't expect the Copts I meet to dare speak out forcefully about their situation. "If we speak out too loudly, we risk being assaulted. We could be considered traitors."

Before I leave, I ask him who could explain to me why Egypt is caught in the grip of Islamization. He promptly gives me the number of a teacher, Kamal Mougheeth, a "one-man army against the Islamism that has strongly influenced the educational system and ruined an entire generation."

The change in Egypt over the last several decades is obvious when I step into the time capsule that is Café Riche. It was established in 1908, back when Cairo was called "Paris of the Nile," when Egypt's capital was linked with smoky salons, Oriental mystique, and a touch of decadence.

The café is close to Tahrir Square, on Talaat Harb Street. If you had been a frequent visitor over the past hundred years, you would have spotted the twentieth century's entire cast of famous Egyptians expounding on the world's troubles.

Kamal Mougheeth, now a retired teacher, rises from a chair and greets me as if we were old friends. He has set aside his newspaper and laid his reading glasses on top of it. Something immediately becomes clear to me: This man, like others who were present back then, regards the eighteen days on Tahrir Square in the winter of 2011 as the dream of moderate Egyptians. Eighteen days of utopia.

"It lifted my spirits to see that Muslims were protecting Christians, just as Christians were protecting Muslims," he says. "No one asked anyone else about their faith. The Tahrir revolutionaries wanted me to become the minister of education. I felt very honored."

Mougheeth is a well-groomed man about sixty years of age; he wears a gray suit and black shoes polished to a sheen, and he keeps his cell phone and a glass of Stella beer at hand on the red-checkered tablecloth. An Egyptian flag is pinned to his lapel. Café Riche is more a museum than a café, even though the three bullet holes in the dark wooden wall bear witness to how this café also has been affected by the recent revolution. "Since 1952 our country has been steered in a single direction," he says.

The educational system's collapse quickened when Anwar Sadat came to power in 1970. Nasser's successor allowed the Islamists to spread their ideas. For the first time in Egypt's history, a moralistic movement appeared whose followers attacked girls without veils and Christians who demanded the right to practice their religion. "The reason why the state accepted these extreme ideas was that it had no educational project of its own," he explains. "There was a mutual understanding between Sadat and the Islamists: as long as they stayed out of politics, they could do what they wanted."

Which they did. In the 1970s they burned down nightclubs and assaulted weddings that had dancing and music. That it was the Islamists who in 1981 killed Anwar Sadat is an irony of history. But Sadat's successor, Mubarak, continued this understanding between the two camps: don't mess with me, and your hands are free.

It's no coincidence that Islamization spread to the educational system. The Muslim Brotherhood had long been encouraging teachers to adopt Islamic principles in the schools. But more important, both Hassan al-Banna, the Brotherhood's founder, and Sayyid Qutb, the chief ideologue of the movement, were both teachers. They knew that students could be profoundly influenced by Islam through education.

In addition, help arrived from the outside. "Many teachers now working in Egypt taught in Saudi Arabia and the Gulf states in the 1970s," he says. "They brought the Wahhabi ideology back with them." When the teachers returned, many of them worked their way up through the hierarchy, and by the 1990s they occupied all the influential positions in the educational system. "Starting when they returned from Saudi Arabia, we began to see books based on the Wahhabi mentality. And for the first time women were being urged to wear veils. Suddenly everything being taught was based on Islam. If you are looking for an explanation of why so many Egyptians believe our constitution should be based on Sharia, there it is. It's their school days." Because over twenty percent of the population is believed to be between fifteen and twenty-four years of age, the influence of education can't be underestimated.

Café Riche is almost empty, tourists have abandoned Cairo, and the Nubian waiters mill restlessly around us. "When I was young, Islam took up little space in our textbooks," Mougheeth says. "Now half of all textbooks are based on Islamic thought." He emphasizes that it's not that Christians are denigrated in history books; it's more that they are not even mentioned.

"It sounds absurd, but Muslims more or less know nothing about Christians, even though they make up a large part of the population and are in fact the original Egyptians. Egypt was Christian for six or seven centuries. The sad thing is that for many years the history books skipped from Cleopatra to the Muslim conquest of Egypt. The Christian era was gone. Disappeared. An enormous hole."

Mougheeth says he fought for the inclusion of at least a few pages about Christians in the history book most used in schools, and after twenty years of protests he finally succeeded. Today the story of Egypt's Christians takes up 7 of the 250 pages in the book. "Not enough, in my opinion, but at least it's something. But the seven pages aren't part of the official curriculum, students aren't tested on them. That's why very few feel obligated to study the subject."

He wants me to understand that Islamic tunnel vision in Egypt has strengthened sectarianism. "We haven't taught children about coexistence and understanding of others. The entire conversation about society today is based on a sectarian mentality—'I'm right, you're wrong.' We are small islands in a great ocean." Despite this, Mougheeth is an optimist. "I'm convinced that political Islam in Egypt is a small cloud in summer. Islamism will fail."

I ask if he is Christian. "That's a personal question," he replies bluntly. His reading glasses have slipped halfway down his nose, and the authoritative look he gives me over the top of them makes me feel ashamed for asking such a question. Then he smiles. "I know all about Islam. I've studied at Al-Azhar." Only Muslims are permitted to study at the Cairo university, which is considered the most prestigious in the Sunni Muslim world.

. . .

Later that day I hail a taxi and ride out to Maadi, an affluent, leafy suburb of Cairo, to speak to a fifty-seven-year-old Dutch sociologist, Dr. Cornelis Hulsman. He considers it his duty to minimize the conflict and point the Western press—anti-Islam, or at least factually confused, in his eyes—in the right direction. He calls it "media surveillance." He has lived in Egypt with his Egyptian wife since 1994. He is well known here as an advocate of intercultural dialogue, an idea which has been spreading for many years.

Hulsman has arranged a lecture by an Islamist this afternoon for his circle of volunteers and other guests in his Center for Arab-West Understanding. I'm here to take a closer look at this "small cloud in summer," as Mougheeth optimistically calls Islamism, to observe these people who have come into power via the recent social upheavals.

There is plenty of time to mull things over in the perpetually logjammed Cairo traffic, so while drivers are honking and yelling and threatening, I sink into my seat and think about my visit the previous evening with Dr. Hulsman in his Maadi home.

During our long conversation, I had the sense that the more critical my questions about the Christians' situation were, the more peaceful their lives were, according to him. It was a type of literary skeet shooting: I tossed up the clay pigeons, he knocked them down. As the evening wore on, I was given the impression that Christians were the ones being intransigent. He said that Copts often close themselves off in a "mental ghetto," that it was much more difficult to enter into a dialogue with them than with the Islamists.

Now at the lecture this afternoon, the sociologist is again eager to ward off every attempt to portray Christians in Egypt as being threatened. It takes place in a small room on the fourth floor of a rundown building. Most of the audience comprises young Europeans studying with Hulsman. He stands at the front and begins by describing how the media often exaggerates: "It's so easy to say that Muslims are attacking Christians." Three men in Muslim skullcaps, or *kufis*, full beards, and Arab dress—the main speaker and two members of his entourage—sit in the front row.

"But one must observe what's happening from different perspectives, from the social and educational aspects. One must also look at what is being done about it." He takes a deep breath. "Yes, churches are being burned down. But if one studies the situation, often it's about a Christian man having a relationship with a Muslim woman. In that way it's not just a sectarian attack on a church. Not to justify the burning down of churches. Of course not."

He continues by saying that we must understand the importance of the nuances involved. When this type of event is described in Western media, without the whole story coming out, it creates fear. "Islamophobes use these types of images and claim that Islam is a threat to Western liberties." In his view, that's the real problem: Islamophobes. He mentions that American foundations have donated $42 million to spread misinformation about Islam. "Don't let Islamophobes gain control of the general public," Hulsman says. "Show them that it's all very complicated."

On an overhead projector he presents a photo of Christians and Muslims demonstrating together in Alexandria against church burnings. "This is the type of thing you never see in Western media," he says. "Lots of new churches have been built in Egypt. You never hear about that, either. So no, you can't claim that Christians are being persecuted. No. Definitely not."

He introduces the speaker, Dr. Mohamed Salah, as a member of the al-Nour party, the political arm of the Salafists. He says that dialogue means always listening to others. "In this way we see that people are not always who we think they are. Welcome to these people from the al-Nour party, who are excellent people with excellent principles."

Hulsman wears glasses and is clad in a dark suit with a dark striped tie. He has gray hair and a gray beard; he's probably a few decades older than the speaker he has just introduced, who now rises. For a short moment they stand together before Dr. Hulsman sits down.

Dr. Muhammad Salah's appearance is surprising. He shatters our prejudices of Salafists; in his midthirties, he wears khaki-colored clothes, a jacket, a V-neck sweater, and an open white shirt. He looks like a British archaeologist from the 1920s, hunting Pharaonic treasures in the sand. The two men, Dr. Salah and Dr. Hulsman, are not so dissimilar in appearance. The only thing that stands out about Dr. Salah is his full red beard—his mustache has been shaved—and his white, finely crocheted kufi.

Any last vestige of prejudice about Salafists falls to the ground when he begins to speak. He's funny and sympathetic, and he entertains us in fluent English; all the Europeans in this room would be happy to be able to speak as eloquently. Dr. Salah has his own television show, on which he answers religious questions. The show airs on a station called Huda TV. He says that it's seen by ten million Muslims all over the globe. He begins by stating that he is neither a Salafist nor a member of the Brotherhood, but he sympathizes with Islamists. His reason for being here today is to bring a message about "communication."

"All problems are created by a lack of communication," he says. "We cannot say that all Americans are like Timothy McVeigh." Dr. Salah's message is that idiotic prejudices are destructive, such as when he once heard while in the United States that all Egyptians eat with their feet. "They believe we are living in the Stone Age." He laughs, and we all laugh with him.

Then comes a more serious accusation. Like Hulsman, he believes that "we are seeing a lot of Islamophobia. For the most part it is based on lies." He sees it as his duty to rebuild the churches that young Muslims have burned down, so they will understand that they acted wrongly.

"I want to avoid bloodshed. Blood only leads to more blood. Every time I read that Muslims are forcing Christians out of the Middle East, I have to say that it is not what Islam is all about. We are totally against these acts of individuals, and Muslims must not be judged by them." He says that Christians often approach him because they want to convert to Islam. He rejects many of them. They don't really want to become a Muslim, but they have fallen in love with a Muslim, he says. Their declaration of faith isn't genuine. Therefore he refuses them.

And though it may be difficult for Christians in Egypt to build churches, he says, it's practically impossible for Muslims in the United States to build a new mosque. "So I say to all the minorities here in Egypt who want the same degree of freedom as in the West, to those who demand a quota for women or a certain percentage of Christians in Parliament, to them I say, okay, let's play by the rules."

He poses a question to his audience: How shall we define democracy? When no one answers, for whatever reason he turns to me and asks, "What is democracy?" I answer that democracy is more than elections. It's a whole package of things, including minority rights, freedom of speech, and the rule of law.

"How typical it is that you begin with minority rights," he says, and then addresses the entire room. "I would happily accept the American constitution here in our country. It says nothing about any groups having special rights. The majority rules." He asks us to imagine that we are driving around outside in a car with two drivers, each with their own steering wheel. Can that work? "Shouldn't we be allowed to be governed by Sharia, if that's what the majority in this country wants?" The answer is self-evident.

The audience applauds, and Dr. Salah takes a break, during which he finds a place to pray before taking questions.

After we return to our seats and Dr. Salah once again is standing in front of us, an elderly gentleman in the first row introduces himself as Professor Abdallah Schleifer, from Albuquerque, New

Mexico. He says that he has built a mosque there, and he invited all the city's dignitaries to the opening ceremony. "Never speak badly of Christians and Jews," he says, and adds that, if that tack is taken, Americans would welcome Muslim mosques.

"Because I'm Muslim, I don't need to be so polite to you," says Professor Schleifer, who now lives in Egypt and for decades has worked as a journalist. He gets directly to the point. "Where do you stand on the issue of a Muslim wanting to convert to Christianity?"

Dr. Salah's demeanor turns serious. "I have nothing to hide. I have been educated at Al-Azhar," Sunni Islam's leading theological university. "If you study Sharia law, there is agreement that Muslims may not abandon their faith. The Koran says that those who do shall be executed. When you accept the Muslim faith, it is irrevocable."

He explains that this is why he doesn't convert people to Islam just because they ask him to. "One must have some experience in what it means to be a Muslim, and to know the consequences. But for many decades the judgment of those who renounce Islam has been done away with. They are not executed. This is why it's not about whether one becomes an atheist or begins to worship the devil. It's only serious when the fallen pose a threat. And they only do that when they announce publicly that they don't believe in Islam, when they defame the religion. That is why they are not sentenced to death if they convert and say nothing about it. It only happens if they go public with it. That is to say, persecution is not about the conversion, but the betrayal of Islam by declaring it to the media."

He urges us to understand that it's the same with criminals. They are also stopped. They are also a threat to society. "When you attack Islam in Egypt, you attack ninety to ninety-five percent of the population. But—," Dr. Salah holds a short dramatic pause—"according to Islam, it is up to the state, not the individual, to execute the sentence."

He asks the elderly professor in the first row how the American military treats a soldier when he deserts and joins the enemy. "Does the army have the right to sentence him harshly?"

"Yes," Professor Schleifer says.

"The same goes for someone who renounces Islam," Dr. Salah continues. "If a Muslim threatens a Muslim state, it is permissible to sentence this person harshly."

The elderly professor asks how this can be in agreement with what the Koran says about forbidding "coercion in the religion." "There is no contradiction here," Dr. Salah says. "There is an early stage before one converts, and a later stage after being converted. At this later stage, one should be aware of the situation one is in."

Professor Schleifer looks at the learned man suspiciously. "I feel bad when I hear someone say this. I was born a Jew. I embraced Christianity. Then I became a Muslim. I was not punished. I would be if I converted back. It's called equity."

Hulsman speaks up now, perhaps to ease the tension in the room. He tells about interviewing a famous Egyptian imam for Dutch television. He asked the imam what he would do if his son, who sat beside him during the interview, converted to Christianity. I would kill him, the imam answered. Hulsman now appeals carefully to Dr. Salah. "You scare people when you speak this way."

A young Dutch woman sitting beside me asks the Islamist about the fairness of imprisoning all the bloggers who are accused of "attacking the religion." He answers by talking about the so-called "naked blogger," Aliaa Elmahdy, who in 2011 put up a nude photograph of herself on her Facebook page to confront what she believes is widespread sexual chicanery and persecution of women in Egypt. She became known all over the world. She received a storm of death threats and now is seeking asylum in Sweden.

"Does she want to have sex outside marriage?" Salah asks. "That's her business. But she attacks the entire nation with that photograph. If a Muslim blogger speaks badly of God, it will create chaos in society. People might go amok, it could lead to assaults, deaths. We must prevent that. The concept of freedom has been grossly misinterpreted. Certain websites have been blocked in American schools for the sake of children. We must also protect our country."

When the lecture is over, I walk up to Dr. Salah to greet him, and I ask for his phone number. A while later I call him to wrangle an invitation to his television studio so I can watch him live on Huda TV. I want to see if Hulsman is right when he says that once we get to know people like Dr. Salah, we will have a better impression of them and be less prejudiced against them. The television cleric's talk about executing those who leave Islam has made me unsure if that really is the case.

There is another reason why I want to go there: I have the feeling that Dr. Salah's way of thinking is representative of Islamists throughout the Middle East who have come to power, which will have consequences for everyone, including Christians. A new elite of learned, media-savvy, articulate, and highly intelligent Islamists have appeared on the scene.

What are they capable of?

Dr. Salah's base is in the enormous Media Production City on the outskirts of Cairo. I take a cab there, but no one is allowed inside the area without a permit. I ask the taxi driver to call Dr. Salah for help in getting me in. One of his assistants picks me up in a car. The assistant, a young man, has the same long beard with no mustache as Dr. Salah. The seat belt alarm blinks red as we drive in silence toward an enormous hall. He doesn't fasten his seat belt, but finally he turns to me. "The sound irritates you for your own good. It's good for you." The thought comes to me that his boss must feel the same way about the Islamism he presents night after night to his viewers from all over the world: it irritates you for your own good.

I walk into the hall and up to the third floor, where I am led into his office. There is less than a half hour before his show, *Islam Unveiled*, and so he doesn't really have time to talk to me. Everyone there is polite; several have the same long, mustache-free beard. A man with a very large prostration mark on his forehead, a *zebiba* (literally meaning a "raisin" and considered a mark of piety), walks in and shows the television host something on an iPad.

I understand that Huda TV, which broadcasts in English, has financial problems and is seeking funding, though from whom, no one will tell me.

This evening Salah is sitting at his desk in front of a computer. There are several books behind him. His desk is a mess, littered with dirty coffee cups and empty plastic bottles. Notes and papers are scattered about. He wears something that resembles a doctor's white coat, whiter than white, with a white silk kufi cap on his head.

He asks me what I'm writing about. Christians moving out of the Arab world, I say. "There is nothing in the American constitution about political minority rights," he replies, with a hint of aggression. "Muslims cannot demand special rights in the USA, even though they number eight million. In Egypt Christians are protected, but as citizens, not as Christians."

And yet Christians in Egypt have been allowed to administer their own civil law, he continues. "For example, divorce is forbidden in the Coptic Church. It is not forbidden in Islam, but we permit them to keep this rule." When he puts it this way, it sounds as if Islam in Egypt is more liberal than Christianity. And as if the Western world is every bit as unsentimental toward its own minorities as the Arab world.

A Koranic verse in calligraphy hangs behind him. It says that God swears by the pen, he tells me. "When they are resurrected in heaven, all writers will be asked to give an account of what they have written. If it is evil—for example, if a writer has described how to make a bomb—the writer will be condemned."

We walk down to the studio. I am seated at a glass table to the side of his studio desk, and I watch as he sits down. The set is in pastel colors, mint green, beige, and a golden red like a flame on the wall behind him. Everything is bathed in light; the introduction to the show could be mistaken for one from American TV, something like the lead-in to a sports program. If Islamists have a problem with the West, it has nothing to do with technology or appearance. The studio's style is Western, and the program is in English, spoken perfectly.

When the camera comes on, Dr. Salah is no longer smiling as he did during the lecture. This is a solemn event. *Islam Unveiled* is a program where Muslims from all over the world call in with questions about their religion. The first viewer wants to know how to perform the obligatory pilgrimage, the hajj, to Mecca. Salah constantly uses examples from the prophet's life to explain what he is talking about, and often he cites the Koran in Arabic. The prophet's life and deeds are to be emulated.

The television cleric's demeanor is mild and fatherly. He speaks slowly and makes an effort to explain things. If you are looking for someone in whose hands to place your life and thoughts, this man in white garb is a good candidate.

An Egyptian woman calls in to hear if it is permitted to listen to Islamic songs accompanied by music. "They aren't Islamic songs if there is music in them," he says, implying that music is forbidden in Islam. "But Islamic songs are permitted. Songs are just talk. Talk can contain permissible and forbidden verses. If the verses are good, fine, listen to them. If the song tells about something evil, it is forbidden. It is not permitted to read or discuss a novel about love affairs."

He ends the conversation with several verses from the Koran, then says there will be a short pause. A jingle sung by a gloomy male choir is played, an assistant hands Salah a glass of water, and short ads for other programs appear on the screen.

Back on camera, he takes a question from a Pakistani, who judging from the question is calling from a non-Muslim country. "I can afford to take another wife, but my culture frowns on such things. Should I obey my religion or my country?"

Salah answers that Allah has not written that a man must have more than one wife, only that it is permitted to have as many as four wives. "One can, however, be in a situation where one has to have several wives. Do it! I don't care what your culture says. It is halal."

The program ends, several men sing about "passing the decisive test," and the lights in the studio go off.

When I return to the hotel that evening, I sit in front of the computer to watch Dr. Salah's programs on YouTube. There is no end to the subjects addressed. Is it allowed for men to urinate while standing? Only if they make sure that no drops of urine touch the clothing. May Muslims force Islam on non-Muslims in Muslim countries? They may not, but they must fight non-Muslims if they revolt in Muslim countries.

One program is about the *niqab*, the veil that covers everything but a female's eyes. A viewer asks if she must wear one, and Salah answers that there are two interpretations in Islam. One states that it is voluntary, the other that it is mandatory. Salah recommends the latter.

A woman calls in to another of his shows and asks if her friend, who is in her late thirties, may marry a Christian. According to him, she may most assuredly not. It is worse than adultery. If she does so, she will be among the infidels.

In one program, it is confirmed that Shiite Muslims are to be regarded as infidels. They are not a part of the Muslim community. Dr. Salah calls them a sect.

In a broadcast from June 2009, he talks about why Arab armies in the past decades have lost wars to Israel; they fought in the name of nationalism, he says, and they drank and danced. Allah wanted to teach them a lesson. They should have fought in the name of Islam, and as a result everything went wrong.

It's clear from watching his shows that he believes Muslims in the West have lost their Muslim identity. But Salah is most implacable when it comes to Zionists and Israel. He talks about them in a program on the Palestinians in Gaza. "I'm addressing the Jews. I'm addressing the Zionists. I'm addressing George Bush. I'm addressing the West. What do you expect of us? Do you think that we're afraid of death? No, I swear by Allah. It is either victory or an eternal life in heaven."

He demands that Western countries throw Zionists out and close their embassies. It is forbidden to do business with them, help them, sell or buy from them. They may not even be given water. "These people live to harm the international community. These people are much worse than any disease we have ever known. We have to confront their evil by strength, by unity … The day shall come, and it will be very soon, we will have the rightly guided leadership ... We just wish, and we hope and pray, to be in the army that will liberate Jerusalem."

I look for others who have shows on Huda TV. They are named on Huda's website, they're called "Huda Stars." Are they as implacable as Dr. Salah?

I notice that one of the "stars" is a famous Indian cleric, Zakir Naik, who has spoken ambiguously, almost sympathetically, about Osama bin Laden. He believes that Jews control the United States and are the worst enemy of Muslims. He also subscribes to the theory that America is responsible for 9/11. Naik is barred from entering Great Britain and Canada. He appeared as a guest on Dr. Salah's show.

Haitham al-Haddad, another known cleric, has been a guest host on Salah's show. The London-based Palestinian imam has justified suicide attacks and the circumcision of women, and in 2001 stated that Jews are the Muslims' real enemy, that they are "the descendants of apes and pigs." Al-Haddad later claimed that he had been "mistranslated."

This claim is not unusual. Morsi said the same thing before he became president. In 2010 he urged Egyptians to raise their children to hate Israel and Zionists. Several months later he talked about "... these bloodsuckers, who attack the Palestinians, these warmongers, the descendants of apes and pigs." He has since stated that his comments "were taken out of context," and that he has nothing against the Jewish faith.

Among Salah's other fellow commentators is an American convert, Yusuf Estes, who believes that homosexuals should be put to death. Devils, he calls them. In July 2010, Dr. Salah and Dr. Estes were in Hong Kong to spread their message to the Chinese.

There are other guests on Huda TV, clerics who have been

quoted as saying similar things. It's clear that they all, including Dr. Salah, belong to an impressive group of English-speaking, extremely popular, and well-traveled TV imams who know each other, appear together in public, travel together, and are to be found on a great number of satellite channels, websites, conferences, and seminars.

On Huda TV's website, the unusually fiery British-born convert, Abdur Raheem Green, is presented as a "star." He enjoys speaking in Hyde Park's famous Speaker's Corner, and he makes no attempt to dampen his astounding hate of Jews. In mid-May 2013, he visited Denmark to speak in Nørrebro, a district in Copenhagen. He has a similar contempt for other religions. He has stated—though not on Huda TV—that one should never make close friends with Jews, Christians, and other "non-believers." Green is also a proponent for reintroducing the special religious head tax, jizya, for Jews and Christians. "The purpose of the jizya is to make the Jew and the Christian know they are inferior and subjugated to Islam, okay?" he has said. "In the Muslim state, although the Jew and Christian are free to practice their religion, this is allowed, but they are not permitted to display their cross and even in the time of Umar, (the seventh century CE caliph who ruled a vast swatch of land stretching from Syria and Egypt all the way to what is now modern-day Armenia and the Caucasus, and who was renowned for his fairness and tolerant attitude toward minorities) they were not allowed to reconstruct or construct new churches. All of this is to create an atmosphere where it is encouraging the people to come to *iman* and Islam, not to remain upon *kufr* and misguidance." As concepts in Islam, iman is faith, and kufr is infidelity.

These clerics' statements are what Copts and other Christians in the Middle East are scared of hearing; the sources of similar testimonials range from the most radical Islamists to Egypt's secular Muslim elite. As Magdi Abdelhadi, a former Arab affairs analyst for the BBC, wrote in 2012, Egyptian sectarian animosity is more widespread than commonly believed. "Those who think it is confined to rural Egypt and the poor communities should abandon that illusion. I was shocked to hear abominable opinions of Copts among Egypt's affluent and supposedly well-educated Muslims. 'They want to take over the country,' 'They should know their place,' etc. A Muslim architect once told me: 'Guns are the only language they understand.' And then there were those who spoke of 'monasteries being turned into fortresses and weapons depots.'"

Abdelhadi believes that the Egyptian authorities remain passive when speakers at public events or on television shows denigrate Christianity and call it a primitive religion. "The logical conclusion is that they seem to condone what amounts to incitement to hatred of Copts ... Egypt has a chronic sectarian problem, and the main obstacle to addressing it is official and popular denial that it has one."

But to be fair, groups other than Christians are treated more harshly by the Huda Islamists. Apart from the injustice of Muslims not being permitted to convert to Christianity, the Huda Stars rage even more fiercely against homosexuals, Muslim women who marry non-Muslims, apostates, those openly critical of Islam, Shiite Muslims, and Jews, especially Israelis.

And against Muslims who do not share their opinions. Dr. Salah expresses his hopes in one of his programs: "Oh Allah, destroy the hypocrites from amongst us. The hypocrites from the Muslims."

When I hear this, I think about the driver who has taken me around for days and is convinced that I am Jewish. This is why he has done his utmost to show me the very best side of the city. With the Koran lodged under the front windshield to protect us from bad luck, he has driven me past churches, mosques, and the only synagogue still in use, talking about peace and understanding between all peoples. He is also the one who drove me out to Media Production City, the one who called Dr. Salah to help me get through the gate, who waited for me behind the fence and guards while I watched the show.

After the show, Dr. Salah accompanied me to my waiting driver. The television cleric was extremely friendly, inviting me to lunch the next time I come to Cairo, and asked me to keep in touch. He also shook my driver's hand and left us with a friendly smile.

Dr. Salah drove away in his big car, and my driver said that every Egyptian could see from the cleric's appearance that he is a Salafist. My driver is a cheerful man, but now he sounded worried. "I called him to come get you. Now he has my number."

• • •

Finally I shut down my computer and go to bed, but I can't fall asleep. After all my journeys, of all the people I've met, Hulsman, the Dutch sociologist who arranged the meeting with Dr. Salah, is the one I can't get out of my head. I don't understand why he wants to play down the danger Christians and others are in. When introducing the television cleric to the audience of young Europeans, Hulsman clearly denied that Christians were being persecuted, and he called the Salafists "excellent people with excellent principles." Excellent principles—really?

Jakob Erle, the director of the Danish Egyptian Dialogue Institute, which is financially supported by the Danish state, has also stated that neither the Christian minority nor the West should fear the Islamization of Egypt, and he has called the Muslim Brotherhood "an extremely moderate organization."

These opinions aren't shared by many of the Egyptians I speak to. They don't believe that Christians shouldn't be worried. I ask myself if entities like the Dialogue Institute are trivializing the problems. Who are they protecting? The minorities or the majority?

For whatever reason, such downplaying of danger is prevalent in the Middle East institutes of some Western universities. One of the reasons I began my investigation was my frustration over a book, *A History of Christian-Muslim Relations*, by Professor Hugh Goddard, director of the Prince Alwaleed bin Talal Centre for the Study of Islam in the Contemporary World at Edinburgh University, an institute named after the immensely wealthy Saudi business magnate and philanthropist. The book was translated into Danish by the prestigious Carsten Niebuhr Library with a new afterword concerning the ten years leading up to the date of publication. Those years were horrible for Christians, especially in Iraq, but the book remains more or less silent about what Christians have been subjected to recently, not to mention throughout history. It seems more concerned with criticizing how Islam is spoken about in the West.

Like Hulsman's and Erle's institutes, Goddard's center is committed to "advancing tolerance, mutual understanding and cross-cultural dialogue between Islam and the West." It's difficult to be against this statement, and had it come from my Egyptian driver, it would make sense. But Goddard is connected to a university, and I sense that behind the slogan greater efforts are being made to dim rather than spread enlightenment.

When I finished Goddard's book, I thought about how a researcher would have been treated had she or he written cloyingly of the relationship between Christians and Muslims in the former Yugoslavia without even mentioning the expulsion of Kosovo's Albanians. The researcher would have been ridiculed and shamed. Nothing of the kind, however, happened to Professor Goddard. He continues in his post as director of a center at a renowned university, his books are being translated and published by my country's most distinguished publishing house. How can this be?

One evening a few days later I visit St. Mark's Coptic Orthodox Cathedral, the headquarters of the Coptic Church, in the Abbassia neighborhood of Cairo. The enormous arched building was consecrated in 1968.

I have arranged to meet Samuel Tadros at the broad stairway leading up to the church. Tadros is connected with the Hudson Institute in Washington, D.C., a leading think tank involved in the study of violations of religious freedom. He has written ominously on the Copts' situation in Egypt for *The Wall Street Journal.*

I'm early, the traffic was remarkably light, so while I'm sitting on the steps I consider why it's mainly the Western right that concerns itself with the Christians' situation in the Middle East. When I search for books and websites, I often find myself in places that are alarmingly far out on the nationalistic, theological, and Islamophobic fringes. The Hudson Institute is not in that territory, though it is considered to be right-wing.

Interest in the subject is far from mainstream. It strikes me as peculiar that so very few books about the Christians' hardships exist. The extraordinary treatment given Professor Goddard and his book is symptomatic of the disgraceful coverage of the subject. True, the press does mention the Christians' situation regularly, but for years I have searched the Middle East's quite extensive airport bookstores for books about it, just as I always plow through the Middle East sections of metropolitan bookstores in the West. My search bears very little fruit. The books that exist are often written by Christians in the West who take a theological view of the tragedy, instead of focusing on the human rights aspect. And rarely if ever do authors bother to travel to the Middle East and report on what Christians themselves have to say.

It's not because of a lack of interest in the Middle East. Larger bookstores offer numerous volumes about Islamist groups, and there are detailed works about the Taliban in Afghanistan, Hezbollah in Lebanon, and Hamas in Gaza, in which capable Middle East correspondents expose the inner structures of the Islamist movements. There are excellent books about Middle Eastern history, and Christianity is naturally included. There are stirring, courageous works about the countless wars in this part of the world. And there are insightful books about Israel and Judaism and the dismal situation of the Palestinians. These books sell extremely well. But books exclusively dedicated to the historical and contemporary troubles of Christians are few and far between.

The few who do show an interest in the plight of Christians are on the religious right, and it's difficult to fault them for that. It is much more difficult to understand why the outrages taking place aren't a perfect target for the secular left wing to focus on. I see a blind spot, an inner conflict of principles and prejudice.

Several years ago, I read an opinion piece by Ole Wæver, a professor of international politics at Copenhagen University, that I have come to agree with. He believes that the persecuted Christians in the Middle East are "unfortunate victims of an unholy alliance" made by the large human rights organizations, which have paid little attention to the Christians. The Danish newspaper *Kristeligt Dagblad* ("The Christian Daily") wrote in 2008 that "the religion section of the Danish branch of Amnesty International has disbanded itself as a consequence of a strategy change within the organization. They will no longer prioritize religious persecution." It should be said, however, that Amnesty International has in the past few years issued several good reports that were of significant help in my research.

But an old problem lingers; it's noteworthy, for example, that the director of the Human Rights Watch, Kenneth Roth, in the winter of 2013 (before the removal of the Muslim Brotherhood from power) encouraged Western governments to show respect for the new democratically elected Islamist governments. "Embracing political Islam need not mean rejecting human rights," Roth wrote, without even considering that the statement might be an oxymoron. This famous human rights organization thus believes it has a pragmatic political role to play in the Middle East, beyond simply reporting violations. It wants to educate Western politicians, to influence them into showing moderation toward clearly dubious political and religious parties. How did it get to this point?

Professor Wæver puts his finger on the problem. He believes that human rights organizations and the left wing not only are "afraid of further inciting Islamophobia in the West, but also Western countries engaged in wars in Iraq and Afghanistan are not interested in being regarded as Christian, because Islamists are attempting to conjure up the vision of religious wars in which the Christian West is engaged in a crusade against Muslims."

These two reservations explain the silence in the West. "But," Wæver continues, "it should not be all that difficult to focus attention on the problems without seeming to be defending special Christian considerations. After all, it's about civil rights and protection of minorities."

Samuel Tadros from the Hudson Institute finally shows up, and I rise from the stairs and follow him behind the Copts' principal church. He leads me to a shrine in which the remains of the church's first pope, Mark the Evangelist, are to be found. They were brought from the Vatican to Cairo in 1968 as a gift from the Catholic Church to the Coptic Church. We remove our shoes before walking on the soft carpet.

The body of the recently deceased Pope Shenouda III, the 117th Pope after Mark, was brought into this church seated on the papal chair for a final photograph. The Coptic neighborhoods of the city display numerous copies of the photo in which he wears a golden red episcopal vestment, his eyes closed, his ashen face topped by a large round crown of gold, his hand holding a scepter. The photo hangs on large posters outside the church, facing the street. Dealing with the dead here is less laden with taboo than in many places in the world.

The coffin containing the earthly remains of Mark is in the middle of the room, a tall, square shrine with a Bordeaux-colored cloth over it, tapestries of the evangelist and the lions that symbolize him hanging from its side. Modern iconic images draped on the wall depict Mark's martyrdom in Alexandria, presumably in 68 A.D., where he was beaten and stoned by Roman soldiers and dragged through the streets with a rope tied to his feet until he was dead. Light pierces through the crowd of people, culminating in a halo around his head.

A painting on the shrine depicts all the leaders of the world's religious communities delivering the deceased Mark to the Copts. It is a victory parade, a historical monument to commemorate the homecoming of the Copts' first bishop. To Egypt. The home of the original Christians.

Tadros tells me that a journey in the opposite direction is taking place nowadays. As we leave the crypt to find a place to sit, he explains that he no longer lives in Egypt.

Earlier that day he handed in his manuscript for a book about the Copts, and while we look for a coffeehouse he talks about when large numbers of Copts began emigrating—as in the Palestinian territories, it's been going on for decades.

We find a small coffeehouse on a corner. Coffee is practically free, the tables wobble on the uneven tiles. The façade is covered with woven reeds, and a tree stump is covered with a rug. An old, tired air conditioner, black with dust, has been dumped against a wall. A Coca-Cola refrigerator stands empty and unplugged in a corner. It's late in the evening. Tadros orders a hookah and a Turkish coffee, which is served with a glass of water. I have the same, minus the hookah.

After the war with Israel in 1973, Tadros says, Sadat became much more accommodating toward Islamism, and his rhetoric often turned against the Christians. The president released many of the Islamists that Nasser had imprisoned. "That's when the serious threat against Copts started, especially in southern Egypt. Four churches were bombed in 1980." Other attacks took place as well. The worst massacre happened on June 17, 1981 in Cairo, when eighty-one people were murdered.

No one knows how many Copts have recently moved away, but everyone is talking about it. "Ninety percent of all my Coptic friends on Facebook write me to hear how they can get out. Not all of them leave the country, but all of them are considering it." More than half of his closest family live in other countries, he says. An aunt in Great Britain, an uncle in the United States, an uncle in Ireland, his sister in Germany, a cousin in Oman, a cousin in Saudi Arabia, a cousin in Canada, etc. "My parents have no one left to take care of them."

For his book, Samuel Tadros tallied the number of Coptic churches outside Egypt in an attempt to estimate how many Copts are living abroad. "In 1970 there were seven Coptic churches in Germany and only two in the USA," he says. His research showed that in 2012 there were two hundred and two Coptic churches in the United States, forty-seven in Australia, fifty-one in Canada, and twenty-nine in Great Britain; many Coptic churches are also located in Germany, France, Austria, Hungary, Sweden, and Italy—and one in Denmark. In addition, there are Coptic churches in Bolivia, Mexico, Thailand, Singapore, Japan, Fiji, New Zealand, China, Malaysia, South Korea, Taiwan, Pakistan, and the Gulf states, and between sixty and seventy churches exist in Africa. "From the number of Coptic churches, I believe that in the United States alone there are half a million Copts," he says.

Tadros is a member of the Coptic Church in Fairfax, Virginia. "About three thousand Copts belong to the church. Since the revolution in 2011, in our congregation alone we have seen between fifteen and twenty families arriving every month. Our congregation has grown by a thousand, a thirty-three percent growth in two years, and that's in Fairfax alone."

In other words, a wave of emigration is taking place. It is being caused partly by the postrevolution attacks. Whereas those at the top of the governmental hierarchy in Egypt want to protect the Copts, often giving them at least some economic compensation for the attacks, there is no control of what goes on in the streets. This includes soldiers and police. And though it is extremely rare to hear Egyptian leaders endorse violence against Christians, they're in no hurry to punish the perpetrators.

In a report on the sectarian violence in Egypt, Amnesty International reports that in the past three decades fifteen major terrorist attacks and acts of violence have taken place, but in 2011 alone there were at least six attacks on churches or battles between Muslims and Copts.

Hassiba Hadj Sahraoui, Amnesty's Middle East and North

Africa deputy director, said in March 2013 that "Coptic Christians across Egypt face discrimination in law and practice and have been victims of regular sectarian attacks while authorities systematically look the other way." Countless attacks have continued after the military coup; Human Rights Watch has condemned them. Christians have been assaulted and accused of acting in collusion with the military leadership that overthrew Morsi.

One of the worst series of assaults started with an otherwise commonplace marriage episode six months before the revolution in 2011. There is something symptomatic about the events that set it all in motion. It also reveals how essential female loyalty to faith is for both sides. Women's virtue is the sectarian conflict's major battleground. In this area the Copts are no better than the Muslims. I found few people with much to say on the matter.

On July 18, 2010, a twenty-four-year-old woman, Kamilia Shehata, disappeared from her home, ostensibly after an argument. She was the wife of the priest in Deir Mawas, a town approximately two hundred fifty miles south of Cairo. Five days later she was returned to her husband and children. By the police.

Why did she leave home? This is not some modern version of Ibsen's *A Doll's House*, though enough material exists for a genuinely tragic drama. The episode led to large demonstrations and possibly was the cause of two horrific terrorist attacks, one of them in a city in another country hundreds of miles away, and other assaults and burnings of churches.

Each side has its own version. The Copts claim that Shehata was kidnapped by Muslims and converted against her will. The police brought her back to her family because of the fear of Coptic riots across the entire country.

The Muslim version: The woman wanted to convert and therefore sought refuge with the local sheikh. She had been moved to do so by Islam and its precepts. There is, however, a video recording in which she tells her story and denies that she ever had anything to do with Islam.

A third version also exists. *The Economist*, which in September 2010 published a detailed account of the case, reports neighbors saying she was unhappy in her marriage and wanted out of it. Because the Coptic Church doesn't permit divorce, while Islam does, conversions have in the past led to very serious incidents. If she became a Muslim, she could get a divorce. According to this version, she professed faith in Islam. Perhaps more from necessity than conviction.

This latter detail has been of little importance. To the many thousands of Islamists, the question wasn't whether or not a sheikh had kidnapped a Christian, but if a priest was holding a Muslim convert captive. Christian kidnaps Muslim woman! That accusation reeks of violence.

The director of the Egyptian Initiative for Personal Rights, Hossam Bahgat, criticized church leaders as well as state security officers, who "may think they have contained the seeds of a sectarian conflagration by turning over an adult citizen to her family as if she were a piece of furniture." Twenty-four-year-olds are old enough to make their own decisions, such as about changing religions. Or getting a divorce. The police violated her rights, according to the Egyptian human rights organization.

As so often is the case, Copts suffered most from what followed. Al Qaeda groups caught wind of what had happened and got involved. From Iraq, where these extremely violent groups have spread death and destruction, it was proclaimed that all Christians in the Middle East would be legitimate targets if the Coptic

Church didn't release the woman. In Egypt in 2010, twenty percent of all Muslims supported Al Qaeda, which meant that the threat to Copts was genuine.

The story about Wafa Constantine, another runaway wife, resurfaced. On November 27, 2004, this forty-seven-year-old woman left her husband who, like Shehata's husband, was a Coptic priest. Allegedly, she converted to divorce him; she was also brought back to the priest and, according to Muslims, locked up. The case had not been forgotten six years later. On October 31, 2010, armed terrorists took more than one hundred churchgoers hostage in a Syriac church—in Baghdad. They yelled, "All of you are infidels. We are here to avenge the burning of the Koran and the jailing of Muslim women in Egypt." Shortly after, fifty-eight people were dead.

Two months later, on New Year's Day 2011 in Alexandria, the worst terrorist attack against Christians in Egypt in a decade took place. A suicide bomber walked among the more than one thousand Copts leaving St. Mark and Pope Peter's Coptic Orthodox Church in the Sidi Bishr neighborhood after a service celebrating the new year. The man set off his bomb and killed himself and twenty-three other people, including the Muslim bookstore owner across from the church. Ninety-seven people were injured.

No one has been arrested or charged, no group has taken responsibility for the attack. But there is a lead in the case. A press release on an Islamist website a few weeks earlier had urged Muslims to detonate "explosives at churches during celebrations." And the church bombed in Alexandria was mentioned. Whether Al Qaeda was behind the action is unknown, but militant Islamists, especially in Iraq, had for months been talking about the two women and demanding revenge.

Other attacks followed. On May 7, 2011, two churches in

the Imbaba area of Cairo were stormed by what locals described as Salafist groups, who believed that the Coptic woman was being held in one of them. They ravaged and burned down one of the churches. Video clips show the attackers lifting their swords and pistols and crying out, "Allahu Akbar." Several buildings and businesses owned by Copts were also vandalized. Later the police fired directly into the crowd. Fifteen people were killed, including both Copts and Muslims. Many more were wounded. The army paid for rebuilding the church. Forty-eight Copts and Muslims were put on trial.

Samuel Tadros and several others have told me that attacks on Christians have changed after the revolution in 2011. The Egyptian security apparatus more or less broke down, and any sense of protection Christians had felt disappeared. A state of lawlessness developed, and now the Christians I meet seem worried and vulnerable. The police and the army have even turned on Christians in isolated instances, one of which took place as early as February 23, 2011, when the Monastery of St. Bishoy in the Wadi Natrun Valley built a wall around its entrance. The monastery wanted to protect itself against the thousands of prisoners who had escaped from nearby prisons during the revolution. The army demanded that the wall be removed immediately, and they attacked the monastery, using antitank weaponry. It was the first time since the revolution that the army opened fire on civilians—but it wasn't to be the last. Four employees and one monk were wounded; one of them had to have a kidney removed.

A little over a week later, on March 4, 2011, a church in Sol, a village near the town of Atfih, about twenty miles south of Cairo, was burned to the ground. A rumor had spread of an affair between a Christian businessman in the town and a Muslim farmer's daughter. The girl's cousins went to her father and demanded that he hand her over to them. They were armed, and they intended to kill her.

He blocked their way and refused to give up his daughter. During the ensuing gunfight, he and one of the cousins were killed. Young Muslim men then attacked the village church, Shahidayn, while the police stood by and watched. It took the Muslims twenty-three hours to destroy it. The army later paid for rebuilding the church.

This instance of rioting was also filmed, and it's obvious who the guilty parties are, but no one was arrested. According to Human Rights Watch, two of the church's lawyers handed a list of one hundred suspects to the government prosecutor. "This is not a case where the public prosecutor has no information," one of the lawyers said. "He just refuses to make a decision." Similar apathy toward Christians has been in evidence in the wake of the bloody coup in the summer of 2013.

The list of attacks against Copts since the revolution is long. An example from 2011: The destruction of the church in al-Marinab, Edfu, Aswan Province, on September 30. This episode is worth detailing because of its extensive consequences. Priests had been given permission to rebuild their church, which was in danger of collapsing, but they were accused of building it twelve feet higher than permitted. They were given fifteen days to correct the matter.

When the deadline passed without the church being lowered, a local Muslim imam incited the town's Muslims to destroy the church. A mob of three thousand gathered and left the church in ruins. The homes of three Copts were also burned down.

The governor of Aswan, Major General Mustafa El-Sayed, later claimed that "Copts made a mistake and, therefore, they should be punished." He added that the Copts' mistake was promptly corrected at the hands of Muslims, and that should be end of story. Seldom has such a highly placed politician, a governor at that, expressed contempt so clearly. Copts across the country were in an uproar.

All this resulted in extensive protests on October 9, 2011, in front of the Maspiro TV headquarters in Cairo. Fifty thousand demonstrators, including a large number of Muslims, demanded that the governor be fired and the people responsible for destroying the church be brought to justice. They also demanded that the church be rebuilt, that Christians no longer be required to seek permission from the president to restore or build new churches, and that religious discrimination be banned.

The demonstration proceeded peacefully to begin with, but everything went horribly wrong. Twenty-eight people—twenty-six Christians, one Muslim, and one soldier—were killed, either shot or run over. More than three hundred suffered injuries, some of them critical.

Video clips show armored military vehicles driving directly into the crowd. One particularly gruesome clip shows two men with their backs turned being run over and killed by an onrushing armored vehicle. One of the men didn't see what hit him; the other glanced back just as he was being hit. They were no more than a bump for the armored vehicle, which weighed several tons.

In another video clip, taken immediately after the demonstrators were suppressed, a soldier is heard yelling from a bus at a crowd of delighted onlookers, telling them that he had shot a demonstrator in the chest. One of them congratulates him and says, "You are a man, by God."

The whole world witnessed an attack by individual soldiers of the country's security forces, with jubilant Islamists alongside them, aided by Egyptian state television, which besides mistakenly claiming that three soldiers had been killed, encouraged Egyptians to help the soldiers fight the Christian thugs. Other news channels announced that the U.S. Secretary of State, Hillary Clinton, planned to send American troops in support of the Copts. Islamic television stations reported that a Koran had been burned on the square. None of this was true, but a number of Islamist gangs formed and fought the demonstrators. They also attempted to attack the large Coptic hospital in Cairo, where the injured and dead were being brought.

This episode was perhaps the greatest shock of all to the Copts. The military had assaulted them directly, stirred up by bloodthirsty, lying media. Despite enormous protests, the government directed the army to investigate itself, but only after first arresting thirty-one civilians, including two bloggers, Bahaa Saber and the famous Alaa Abd El-Fattah, who were accused of inciting demonstrators to attack the police.

Three soldiers were court-martialed, accused of killing fourteen people by running over them in armored vehicles. They were found guilty of involuntary manslaughter; two of them received two-year sentences, the other three years. Anyone who watches the video clips can easily see there was nothing "involuntary" about the killings. The Maspiro tragedy was the culmination of a year, Year One of the revolution, in which six churches were attacked and Christians were killed or injured all across the country.

Samuel Tadros quickly recounts the many attacks, and in my eagerness to write it all down I spill a glass of water on my notebook. Words and sentences flow together into one black, meandering inkblot. We call for the waiter to wipe up the pool of water, as another brings coal to replenish Tadros' hookah.

He says that a disturbing pattern has formed since the revolution in 2011. Rumors of such things as a purported relationship between a Christian man and a Muslim woman lead to a large group of Muslims, often several hundred, attacking the man's house or burning down a church. Assaults also occur from rumors of a Christian insulting the prophet. The suspected blasphemist is attacked if he hasn't already been arrested and jailed. Most disturbing is how several times since the revolution an entire Christian population in a village or district of a large city has been evacuated because of a conflict between one Muslim and one Christian.

Usually it happens this way: A large crowd of Muslims attack a church, a business, or a home; the police arrive too late; the authorities don't know what to do, so they urge the other Christians to leave town; the local priest and the local sheikh meet with other town dignitaries. "They kiss each other, and everyone talks about how brotherly they are," Tadros says sarcastically.

And no one gets punished, except for the family of the Christian who has been accused of having a relationship with the Muslim woman or in some way has angered his Muslim neighbors. "We call it 'reconciliation,'" says the young Hudson Institute researcher.

Dispute resolution meetings to smooth the waters have in some places only worsened the situation, such as the events that took place in Sharbat, close to Alexandria. The Egyptian Initiative for Personal Rights has documented what happened.

A Christian, Sami Girgis, woke up on January 27, 2012 to find an irascible crowd of Muslim men, led by the local sheikh, in front of his house. They demanded that he and his family abandon everything they own and leave town immediately. They claimed that a video had been circulating that showed a sexual relationship between his son, Murad Sami Girgis, and a Muslim woman from town.

Whether or not the accusation is true is still unknown, and it should be irrelevant. While the situation grew increasingly tense, influential members of the town's leading Christian and Muslim families met to solve the conflict. They agreed that the Girgis family had to leave.

Perhaps the mob's demands increased as the dignitaries tried to hammer out an agreement that would meet everyone's approval. In any case, their proposal didn't satisfy the mob, which after growing all day numbered approximately three thousand. They yelled out slogans, threw rocks, and threatened with sticks, guns, and Molotov cocktails. The Girgis family barricaded themselves on the second floor. Three ground floor shops belonging to family members were plundered and set ablaze. Some of the crowd went looking for other local Christian homes whose owners either were entrenched behind locked doors or had already fled. Some Christians fired out on the crowd without hitting anyone. Several houses and shops were attacked with rocks and, as with the Girgis family's shops, plundered and burned.

For several hours the police didn't react. The angry mob kept them at bay when they finally did arrive, and they waited until things settled down the next day. Then the town's decent Muslim citizens took the law into their own hands and stopped the attacks by forming a barrier around the houses of Christians. They also prevented the home of the accused son, Murad Sami Girgis, from being burned down.

Though peace returned to the town for a while, the demand for revenge wasn't satisfied. A dispute resolution meeting was held between Alexandria's governor, several Muslim Brotherhood members of Parliament, Salafists, and other notable Muslims and Christians in town. Once more it was agreed that the family had to leave. In the meantime, the police had jailed the family's son. He was locked up for fifteen days.

This compromise also proved to be unsatisfactory. Hundreds of young Muslims took to the streets again, demanding that all the young Christians in town be thrown out. They threw rocks at several houses and set fire to one of them.

Another meeting took place, this time with the police leadership attending in addition to Islamist members of Parliament, the heads of seven of the town's Muslim families, and several Christians. They wanted to put a stop to the unrest, and this time the majority of those at the meeting were more sympathetic to the demands of the crowd. A proposal was formed: Eight Christian families must leave town without being allowed to take anything with them, and their houses and all their belongings were to be sold within three months. The Christians at the meeting didn't at all care for this, especially because it punished families who had nothing to do with the episode. Why should they be thrown out?

Their protests were futile. With the blessing of the members of Parliament and the security forces—the police who were unable to protect the town's Christian citizens in the first place—the proposal to run the eight Christian families out of town was passed.

And that's what happened. A Salafist leader was appointed to sell their property, and the families were warned that no one could guarantee their safety should they return. As the Egyptian Initiative for Personal Rights puts it, the police—the long arm of the law—acted unlawfully. The verdict of the human rights institute is scathing:

"Shame on executive and legislative officials for providing legal cover for crimes in an ostensible 'reconciliation' that punishes the victims and acquits the offenders. As long as the Egyptian judiciary and the elected People's Assembly do not intervene to relieve this injustice and restore the rule of law, they are complicit in these crimes."

It doesn't even take a rumor of an interfaith love affair for confrontations and expulsions to take place. A commonplace event can be enough for a Christian neighborhood to suddenly become prey. This is another source of anxiety for Christians—the unknown, unforeseen threat. They can become victims of an everyday conflict to which they haven't the slightest connection.

The Egyptian Initiative for Personal Rights once again gathered information about an episode on July 25, 2012, in the town of Dahshur, Giza. A Christian laundry employee, Sameh Nesseem, must have left an iron on the shirt of a Muslim, Ahmed Ramadan, and forgotten about it. In any case, it burned a hole in the shirt. When Ramadan got his shirt back, he flew into a rage.

The next day he rounded up twenty friends and went to the laundry, intending to beat up whoever burned the shirt. Nesseem locked himself in his apartment, made a Molotov cocktail, and threw it down from the roof.

A twenty-five-year-old Muslim, Moaz Muhammed, happened to be passing by on the street below; the bottle hit him and exploded in flames. He died later at the hospital. Shortly after, two thousand people stood outside the laundry, demanding revenge. Other residents in the building were attacked and vandalized; someone set fire to the building. An attempt was made to destroy a church two hundred yards away, but local Muslims managed to stop that.

The police were called. They arrived quickly, but did nothing. Again, a number of citizens showed courage the authorities lacked. Sameh Nesseem's cousin was injured, and Nesseem and his father were jailed for fifteen days, accused of murder. The police looked for five Muslims, but—need it be said?—no one was arrested.

According to *Al-Ahram*, the widely circulated Egyptian newspaper that investigated the case a week or so later, the town's Christians felt threatened, and the police ordered them to leave because no one could guarantee their safety. They did so before Moaz Muhammed was buried.

In their absence, several of their homes were plundered and destroyed. The thirty-six Christian families were later allowed to return, and the state gave ten thousand Egyptian pounds ($1,700) to those whose homes or businesses had been destroyed, plundered, or burned down. Ten thousand Egyptian pounds is a drop in the bucket if everything you own has been ravaged or stolen.

"Islamists feel they are growing stronger," Tadros says. "They are making the visions of the Muslim Brotherhood come true on a local level. Even though the leadership never demands that women wear veils, that is what is happening on the street. No authorities close stores serving alcohol, yet they are being closed. The Brotherhood never says an unkind word about Christians. And yet they are attacked. I am less afraid of one Morsi that I am of ten thousand small Morsis spread out all over Egypt."

It is now midnight at the café and new coals have been placed on the hookah's aluminum foil. Samuel Tadros's blue shirt is untucked, his face is covered with stubble. He sits with his brown jacket on his lap. It's warm, and noise from the street forces him to lean over the table to be heard.

"The Copts pay collectively," he says. "When one Copt does something regarded as illegal, all Copts are considered to be guilty. And you see the police doing nothing. No one is arrested."

I ask why.

"An entire population is guilty. Who do you point a finger at?"

He asks me to think about *Mississippi Burning*, Alan Parker's 1988 film featuring Gene Hackman and Willem Defoe as two investigators, each with their own method of solving the murder of a young black activist and his two white colleagues in the Ku Klux Klan-infested South of the 1960s.

"The police are part of the system in Egyptian villages, just like in the film's southern towns. They protect the assailants." Tadros sees the same things happening to the Copts that happened to the Jews here, only at a slower pace. But there is one significant difference. "Egyptian Jews could flee to Israel. There is no 'Israel' for Copts."

He says that currently Copts in Egypt have only four options. "You can stay and fight for change. You can bow your head and accept your status as a second-class citizen. You can retreat and live your life inside the church and congregation. Or you can emigrate."

The final option isn't so easy. The West doesn't want to take in several million Copts. Only those who speak English and have a good education and money can emigrate. That leaves the poor, the old, and the uneducated.

I ask him if what has been happening over the past several years can be called "persecution."

"There are no 'rivers of Christian blood' flowing," he says. "It's not so much persecution as suffocation. Part of the proud Islamic self-perception is that Christians are 'tolerated.' Christians are allowed to practice their faith, but their status in society is being downgraded. That's why it's not a type of Christian Holocaust we're witnessing. The goal of the Egyptian authorities is not to kill all Christians, even though we can point out local pogroms."

According to Tadros, the reason the West is not in an uproar about what is happening is that many Westerners regard Christians in the Middle East as being a part of the West's own culture, as a strong majority religion, a group in power. That's why the stories of violence against Christians, of how they are being driven out, conflict with the West's self-image. As he puts it, "Christians are not persecuted. We are the persecutors."

I ask him how he feels about the many international organizations striving to create a dialogue between the West and Islam.

"It's one of the modern world's great myths. If only Palestinians and Israelis could sit down and talk, all their problems would be solved. Bullshit. I don't think much of these organizations. Dialogue is not a solution to actual conflicts."

He tells the story of Sarah Ishaq Abdelmalek, a fourteen-year-old Coptic girl. On September 30, 2012, she and her cousin were on their way to school in the town of El Dabaa, west of Alexandria. Amnesty International-Egyptian Action has investigated what happened after Sarah disappeared in a bookstore. Her father went to the police. He received a telephone call from a man who said that he would never see his daughter again. She had converted to Islam and had married a Muslim man.

"According to Salafists, girls are old enough for marriage at puberty," Tadros says. "Even though Egyptian law says she wasn't old enough to convert or to marry, the Salafists' law says she was." The authorities assured the father that something would be done. Nothing happened. Sure, the family learned that the girl's husband was a twenty-seven-year-old shopkeeper by the name of Mahmoud Abu Zied Abdel Gawwad. A month after the kidnapping, a group called the Salafist Front issued a statement warning human rights organizations not to return the fourteen-year-old girl to her parents, stating that the girl was free to convert to

Islam and marry because she had reached puberty.

On November 3, 2012, the government prosecutor in her district demanded that the missing girl's husband be arrested, not least because the police knew who was holding her as well as where she was. Nothing happened. Sarah Ishaq Abdelmalek has not been returned to her family, even though everyone knows where she is. "This story proves that law and order has collapsed. Even when the authorities know what they should do, they don't know how to do it," Tadros says.

This is not the only kidnapping of a young Christian girl; some claim there are hundreds taken every year, but there's no way of corroborating the numbers. The kidnapping of Christian girls is a touchy subject. It's not always possible to know which of them are actually kidnapped and which ones fall in love with a Muslim man and, against the will of their parents, voluntarily convert to Islam.

Cases such as these and countless others are driving Christian Egyptians out of the country. As for Tadros, he left in 2007 to study in the United States, and he has returned only to gather material for his book. "Because of my opinions, I don't think I have a great future in Egypt," he says.

Despite my protests, he goes inside the coffeehouse to pay the bill. When he comes back, he suggests I interview Charles Malik's son when I get to Beirut. Charles Malik was a Lebanese diplomat and philosopher who helped draft the UN's Universal Declaration of Human Rights, and according to Tadros his son is one of the most perceptive writers on the situation of Christians in the Middle East. I thank Tadros and promise to follow up on his suggestion. I watch him disappear down the street in the warm Cairo evening, his light brown jacket under his arm, on his way to somewhere far from Egypt.

I stroll through the city and back to my hotel in the wee hours of the morning, thinking about the many people driven from their homes simply because they are Christians. Clearly they are often the object of a rage that police can contain only by herding the Christians out of a city or village until it blows over. The ones who must give ground are the victims. I also think about the Muslim civilians who revolt against the crimes of other Muslims. They do what the authorities can't as yet bring themselves to do.

· · ·

On the outskirts of Cairo, on the slopes leading to Mokattam Mountain, lies one of the city's strangest districts: Manshiyat Naser, or Garbage City, as it is called. The name fits perfectly. To understand why all the Christian Egyptians I meet talk about leaving the country, Garbage City is the place to visit.

I drive up the narrow, dark dirt roads, up past four-story brick and concrete houses, their doors practically in the street. They look as if they had been built in a matter of days. A stench hangs heavily over the town. I pass mounds of large clear plastic bags filled with plastic bottles, glass, cloth, copper, and cardboard; legs of lamb dangle from hooks in the doorways of slaughterhouses, banners with the image of the deceased Pope Shenouda III are stretched out fifteen feet above the street, donkey carts and trucks squeeze by, goats munch on fruit peels. Lemons, cucumbers, and bananas sit in piles. Bakeries sell *korban*—the Coptic holy bread. Old ladies sit in small, unfurnished concrete rooms, sorting the day's garbage.

Finally I turn and drive through a tunnel; light returns at the top of the slope, and all of Cairo spreads out below. Farthest up is a church carved out of the cliff, with room for several thousand worshipers, the Garbage City cathedral. This is where exorcisms and other miracles take place. I have seldom seen anything so magnificent, so kitschy and spectacular. A figure of Jesus has been carved from the stone wall, with biblical verses in Arabic as well as English for the many tourists who visit.

This is Christianity in its rawest form: fierce, wild, grim, bloody, passionate, primitive, and uninhibited. I can't help thinking about one of modern art's most controversial works, by the American art photographer Andres Serrano, *Piss Christ*. His 1987 photo of Jesus on the cross plunged in a vat of urine sparked fiery debate about U.S. taxpayer support for artworks deemed obscene. The only path up to the church winds past heaps of garbage. You literally have to start at the bottom to reach the top.

Samaan Ibrahim is the Garbage City priest. He receives me in what once was a grotto in a depression of the cliff. Now it's his office. He sits at one end of a long table; many citizens have lined up at the other end to listen to him. Their eyes beam with veneration for this man. Coptic priests are treated with a reverence otherwise bestowed only upon those recognized as saints. But this is also his church in more ways than one.

"I have been here for forty years," he says. "But God gave the church to us." The priest says God ordered him to come here, that he was sought out by a man who collected his garbage every day. This was in the 1970s, before Ibrahim became a priest, back when he was thirty and unstable.

The residents of this town, *Zabbaleen*, as they are called, have been Cairo's garbage collectors for many decades. Thirty thousand of them live in Garbage City, thirty thousand more live in other parts of the city. Ninety percent are Christians. Every morning the young Zabbaleen pick up the city's garbage for a modest fee and haul it all up here, where the older citizens sort it and sell it as recycled goods or melt it into such things as car tires. I am told that 8,500 tons of garbage are collected every morning, along with 4,000 tons of organic material. Eighty percent of the city's garbage is recycled—an enormous percentage compared to other cities in the world. The organic waste used to be fed to the town's pigs, which the citizens either ate or sold to international hotels.

"I didn't listen to the garbage collector," Ibrahim continues. "After all, I couldn't preach, so I ran from my fate. I saw there was no running water, no electricity, no roads. This was no place for humans. The smell was horrible, much worse than it is today."

Forty years ago this town was regarded as a neglected, ramshackle, demoralized slum. But for two years the old garbage collector kept telling Ibrahim that he had to start a church, that he had to teach them about Jesus. "Finally I asked them to find me a place where I could pray. I needed to know what God wanted me to do with my life and this town."

He pauses when a Japanese tourist wants to take his picture and kiss his hand. He allows the former but strictly forbids the latter. He smiles at the man from behind his long gray beard. He is wearing a knitted black cap; an enormous cross fastened to a solid chain hangs from his neck.

After the tourist takes his picture, Ibrahim explains that the garbage collector found a large cave under a cliff where the priest prayed every Sunday for three weeks. It was the very place we are in now. The priest prayed and prayed, but for three weeks nothing happened, until a short-lived whirlwind blew across town, whipping garbage and paper up in the air. A page from a book landed at the priest's feet. Two verses from the Bible caught his eye, Apostles 18: 9-10:

"Then spake the Lord to Paul in the night by a vision, Be not afraid, but speak, and hold not thy peace: For I am with thee, and no man shall set on thee to hurt thee: for I have much people in this city." The framed page with these verses hangs in the back of the room, brown with age, tattered and dirty.

A sign of God; all doubt was swept away. He became not only the town's priest, but a kind of mayor who was instrumental in the building of their houses. People who have lived here for thirty or forty years say that it's a different town today.

I can also see that Christianity is growing stronger and more radical, just as the Islamism that was given free rein in the 1970s. There are parallels. Ibrahim is doing for Garbage City what the Muslim Brotherhood has done for countless villages and the poor all over the country, namely giving them what the state cannot or will not. Obviously religion is part of the package. The priest explains he is the head of one of the largest congregations in the world. "Thousands of people come here. We exorcise demons. We have brought four people back from the dead. We have caused the blind to see."

As he tells me this, I am thinking that he wouldn't have cared for the comparison to *Piss Christ*. It's also unfair, because there is nothing "ignoble" about the town, which is orderly—the plastic bags are stacked in piles, for instance. In a town of garbage you have to be unusually tidy to not quickly become part of the surroundings. But in the rest of Cairo, the Zabbaleen, or garbage people, have been regarded as the dregs of the city, as swine living among swine.

"We are the ones who clean up," the priest says in answer to that accusation. "The others are the garbage people. We simply pick up after them. That's why they should take care of us, but they have never done so. Years ago they just pushed this group of people out on this mountain, hoping it would devour them. But God gave the people life."

The Egyptian state has never helped them. A typical example is from June 2009, when swine influenza was labeled a pandemic by the World Health Organization. At that time, panic had already spread throughout the world. Countries have various methods to deal with such things. In April 2009, Egypt chose to slaughter all pigs in the country, 300,000 of them, even though the virus is carried by humans and no pigs in the country had been found to be infected. The UN called the decision a gigantic mistake.

Photos spread throughout the world showing pigs being beaten with iron pipes and hammers, loaded onto trucks, and driven out to the desert to be buried more or less alive in the sand. They were then covered with lime and chemicals. The state compensated the owners, paying them one hundred dollars per pig. The authorities maintained that the pigs were killed because they constituted a health risk. The priest sees it differently. "The pigs were murdered because they are *haram*, forbidden. I wish they had killed them in a decent manner."

He can take heart from a type of higher justice, however, that came with the revolution in the winter of 2011, two years after the pig massacre. "Just think, the people who killed the pigs, the president and his men, are today in prison."

The citizens of Cairo also experienced a type of justice— lower, not higher. To protest the slaughter of their animals, the garbage collectors refused to carry off the organic waste. The streets quickly began to stink, just as Garbage City always has. They killed the pigs, now the mess was theirs to clean up.

The priest is not happy now about the revolution. Its aftermath arrived at Mokattam Mountain on March 8, 2011. I drive down through Garbage City to a large building at the town's entrance, which looks out onto an enormous dump. The family living here was among those who suffered during the violence that day. Skinny dogs run around, poking their snouts in the black sooty ground. Gigantic green, white, and gray plastic sacks are piled up in front of the long stairway. The view is barren and foggy.

It's difficult to imagine a greater contrast when I enter the home of Shehat al-Mekades. I'm blown away by the magnificence that greets me: the pistachio-green rug on the wall with dark green leaves and the imprint of children's hands; the pillar in the center of the room, turquoise with splashes of gray paint applied with light strokes, as if they were pigeon feathers; two cages with canaries, a stuffed fox cub, a sculpture of an eagle, and a whinnying horse painted in gold; cacti in pots; two enormous pictures glued onto the wall, one of them a bridge with a waterfall and green hills, the other a pond with storks in the garden of a large Arab house. Two large standing ashtrays have been placed in the middle of the room. Smoking is permitted, and a hookah stands ready. There are also many pictures of Jesus, the Virgin Mary, and Pope Shenouda. The pope is wearing his round black hat, a melancholy expression on his face.

The man living here is prosperous, an animal lover, a friend of birds, a bon vivant, an aesthete. I have never seen anything like this. *National Geographic* should stop by. The house is also new. "Muslims from the neighboring district burned my old house down," he says. He could afford to rebuild it. "My father was a big man in town. He went on a pilgrimage to Jerusalem." His fortune was inherited. Just like his piety.

Mekades explains what happened on that early spring day in 2011. Four days earlier, on March 4, 2011, the church in the village of Sol was burned and leveled by hundreds of Muslims. I had spoken with Samuel Tadros about it a few days ago. Young people living in Garbage City make up one of Egypt's largest groups of Christians, and they demonstrated against the authorities' obvious indifference toward the many attacks Christians were being subjected to.

The young Christians walked down to the main road below the city and blocked it. Some of them carrying large crosses climbed onto cars. The road was heavily trafficked, and word spread fast about the Christian troublemakers. According to Mekades, several thousand young Muslims gathered on the other side of the road two hours later. The army also arrived with tanks.

A rumor started circulating: The Christians had kidnapped two girls and ripped off their clothes. It wasn't true, but it incited aggressive Muslims from the neighboring districts. Video clips show the young Christians on a bridge above the main road, along with a few tanks; a crowd comes running from the opposite side of the bridge toward the Christians; shots are heard, and the Christians flee back to Garbage City.

Mekades says they were attacked with bottles, acid, and heavy ammunition. The video clips document that the army made absolutely no effort to stop this small civil war on the outskirts of Cairo. "They just watched the murdering," he says.

When the shooting was over, the Muslim assaulters stormed the area and burned down six factories and eight buildings. The photos taken afterward show what looks like a war zone. The Mekades family's house was the first one to be burned down. "There were too many of them," he says. "We couldn't defend ourselves. We had to leave our houses and seek shelter farther up the mountain." Ten people were killed, nine Christians and one Muslim. A few of the dead are visible on one of the clips; a boy not more than fifteen was shot in the heart from the side. Fifty people were injured. The clips also show the temporary, overcrowded field hospitals.

Mekades states that the riots lasted until that night, when Pope Shenouda finally convinced the minister of defense to step in. Ten hours went by. "The army claimed that it wanted to stop the riots, but after a young Christian knocked an officer down, the soldiers did nothing to help us."

According to Human Rights Watch, Christians captured eleven Muslim men setting fire to a store. They handed the prisoners over to the army and presented the names of the men to the government prosecutor, demanding that they be brought to justice. When Human Rights Watch published its report two months later, no action had been taken. A year and a half later, Mekades says that still nothing has happened.

I've heard elsewhere that Garbage City is full of weapons, but this mustachioed, tunic-clad man won't confirm that.

"They were the ones with machine guns. If we had had weapons, we would have used them. Listen—we get up early in the morning to pick up garbage. We are not criminals. We are not Hamas. We are not Mafia. We are in a business that society regards as the lowest of the low. The only weapons we had were glass bottles sorted out from the garbage. We have tons of glass bottles, we threw them at the attackers."

Mekades is a small, thin man in his early forties with a calm expression. He speaks without batting an eye. For a short moment he is visible on one of the video clips, standing on the steps of his burned-down house. He looks unaffected, like a man who knows that houses can be rebuilt, that life goes on. Perhaps his relaxed demeanor comes from being the oldest in his family—he has eight sisters. He became a father at the age of fourteen, and today he has ten children. He is already a grandfather. There is a rich exuberance everywhere you look. One of his sons walks by; he could just as well be Mekades' little brother.

We walk out behind his house. He raises chickens, goats, and pigeons to provide food for his family. The pigeons live in a tall, pistachio-colored, cone-shaped tower dotted with holes and perches. He finds a large can filled with food that he throws out to the birds, who have surrounded him with wings flapping. For the first time I see him smile.

They fly back up into their tower. "We are a minority in this country, and we are growing smaller in number. We are becoming a new Iran."

I've heard that complaint before, and I'll hear it again in Lebanon, my next stop. But I've never before heard the pigeon man's idea of how to solve the problem. "If only the pope allowed us to marry more than one woman. Then we could be as many as them."

CHAPTER 3

Lebanon

Charles Malik's story can be taken as a sign that liberal ideas not only thrived in the Arab world; they originated there. In that sense, this Lebanese giant in the field of human rights proves that the deplorable state of affairs in the Middle East today is no natural one. Things can change for the better.

Or he can be seen as an example of how badly things have turned out. To me, Malik's fate shows a bit of both sides. He both contradicts and affirms the twenty-year-old idea of the clash of civilizations proposed by political scientist Samuel P. Huntington, which has shaped how we understand the post Cold War world. In terms of the West and Islam, that is.

I see Charles Malik as embodying the narrative about the Christian struggle for equality in the Muslim world. He also exposes the rise and fall of Lebanon in the nearly one hundred years the small Mediterranean country has existed as a somewhat independent state. This narrative can only be seen in one way, however: it is not a happy story.

Malik was born into a Greek Orthodox family in 1906 in the northern mountain town of Bterram. When he was fourteen, Lebanon was granted a measure of autonomy, though France retained control of the area. The country was called Greater Lebanon, and it included areas populated chiefly by Sunni Muslims and Druze.

In reality, France handed the country over to the Maronites, Lebanon's largest Christian group, just as the British promised the land to the south, Palestine, to a small but growing Jewish minority. Today it's clear that the Jews have done much better for themselves than the Maronites to the north, although the Christian Lebanese made up the majority of the population to begin with, unlike the Israelis in Palestine. According to a census in 1932—which, it must be said, is suspected of having been manipulated—fifty-four percent of the population was Christian.

The special treatment by the French skewed the country from the start, even though the second largest group, the Sunnis, also gained a share of power. The Christians were given the presidency and the top leadership of the military, while the office of prime minister would be held by a Sunni. The ratio of Christians to Muslims in Parliament was set at six to five. But the Sunnis were clearly at a disadvantage. And just as the non-Jewish groups in Israel turned against the Jews, the non-Christian groups in Lebanon turned against the Maronites.

This sectarian division meant that demography became the X factor in the country. As the years went by and Christians emigrated and bore fewer children than the Muslims, the size of the religious groups changed. The constitutionally guaranteed dominance of Christians became more and more scandalous. It could only go wrong.

In 1926, Lebanon became a republic, but already in the 1930s it was clear that the Sunni leaders wanted to unite with other Levantine Arabs. Many Sunnis didn't regard Lebanon as a nation. There was only one Arab nation, which stretched from Iraq to Oman.

One of the men who proudly called themselves Lebanese was Charles Malik. He had a vision he often elaborated on in interviews or when lecturing, a vision of Lebanon as a meeting place between East and West. The Lebanese had access to the most holy of both parts of the world, which was why Christians and Muslims there understood each other's cultures so deeply, he claimed.

Malik was a man of the world; he spoke Arabic, French, English, and German fluently. At first he studied mathematics and physics before taking an interest in the philosophy of science. He entered Harvard University, and in 1935 he won a scholarship to study with the German existentialist Martin Heidegger at Freiburg University. His years in Nazi Germany turned him against totalitarian states, Nazism as well as Communism, the latter of which fascinated many intellectuals of his generation.

After World War Two, he was summoned by the United Nations to work with a Chinese, a Frenchman, a Canadian, and an American on a declaration of human rights, which became the most important document of the twentieth century. Charles Malik played a decisive role; he demanded that Article 18, one of the declaration's most central, be included.

It's important to have a look at Article 18, because it is at the heart of what this book is about. It highlights the rights that Christians *don't* possess in most of the Middle East, rights that in many places they haven't possessed for centuries:

"Everyone has the right to freedom of thought, conscience and religion; this right includes freedom to change his religion or belief, and freedom, either alone or in community with others and in public or private, to manifest his religion or belief in teaching, practice, worship and observance."

Charles Malik's Article 18 threatened established dogmas: a direct challenge to the Koranic interdiction of renouncing the prophet's faith and the Muslim world's resistance to Christian evangelism. It was a blow against the discrimination in the Middle East against Christians, Jews, and other minorities since

Muslim armies conquered the region in the seventh century. Malik wanted that article included because throughout history Lebanon had been a haven for Christians persecuted after having converted from Islam.

The proposal caused a stir in Muslim countries. Egypt's UN delegation squirmed but ended up voting for it. They promised that they "intended to apply and execute it in all honesty." Pakistan's foreign minister was more receptive. He said that the right to religious freedom and the right to change faiths had the full support of his country. It was a matter of Islam's honor.

Adherents to the clash of civilizations argument must be puzzled that an Arab demanded the inclusion of this article and that large Muslim countries voted for it. And based on my travels in the region, I think it would be a good idea to remind the Muslim countries about what they agreed to. Saudi Arabia was the only one to refuse to ratify the resolution in 1948; it abstained from voting. But in the end, all thirty articles of the Human Rights Declaration were passed.

At a memorable ceremony on December 9, 1948, Malik presented the new declaration to the international press corps. For the first time in history, he stated, the world had gathered to form a "synthesis" of all existing traditional rights, from Asia to Latin America. It was a triumph for humanity, a distillation of all human experience.

This imposing Lebanese man was in his forties at that time, and later he would become the leader of the United Nations Commission on Human Rights. In 1956, he returned to Lebanon to become foreign minister in the government of liberal Christian President Camille Chamoun.

Could he create at home what he preached abroad? The UN diplomat believed that his country was a meeting place for East and West, but within Lebanon itself East and West were moving rapidly apart. Malik's image of a beautiful interfaith mosaic is still shared by many here, though not in the rest of the world, where it sounds much less convincing after the sectarian civil war which began in 1975 and lasted fifteen years, resulting in 150,000 casualties. The term "Lebanonization" was coined after that war—by Israeli politician and Nobel Peace Prize winner Shimon Peres, no less—and it has absolutely nothing to do with "cultural coexistence."

In a way, the civil war ended with all the country's sectarian groups fighting against the Christian Lebanese. The aging Charles Malik remained in Lebanon during that time. He lived in the mountains overlooking Beirut while mortars flew over his head and destroyed the capital's Christian quarter. He condemned the many Christians who in those days sought out more peaceful places in the world to live. He predicted that Christian culture in the Middle East would fail without a shift in the direction of events.

Charles Malik died in 1987, eighty-one years of age. Foreign correspondents wrote that "none of Lebanon's Muslim or pro-Syrian politicians or militia leaders mourned his death." There is something heartbreaking about these words, that the man who in December 1948 believed the world's wisdom was embedded in the Human Rights Declaration went to his grave as a hated man, in a country at war.

When the civil war ended in 1989, Christians felt they had been defeated, even mortally wounded. For many of them, the concept of living peacefully with Muslims was buried deep in the Lebanese mountains. In the West, the Maronite Phalangist militia's 1982 massacre of Palestinian refugees in Sabra and Shatila remains the most intense image of the horrors. Perhaps it's the only image still remembered today.

While many in the West believe that they had been deceived by a Christian group with murderous and fascist ideals, the Maronites contend that the West had abandoned them. They also feel that enemies from both within and without are slowly taking over their country. Even now, twenty years after the civil war, their disappointment is omnipresent. Never in my life have I heard such strong criticism of Islam as that voiced by the Christians of this country.

Charles Malik's son, Habib Malik, is the man that my acquaintance in Cairo, Samuel Tadros, recommended I seek out. He greets me on a cold, rainy day at a Starbucks in a fashionable mall on Beirut's outskirts. Like his father, Habib Malik is a well-read, opinionated man educated in philosophy (one of his books is about Kierkegaard, the Danish philosopher). He is also a giant of a man, with hair retreating from both sides of his high forehead. He lacks his father's beaked nose and bushy eyebrows, however. He also doesn't share his father's optimism regarding his country. A generation has passed since his father's death, and the mood is entirely different.

We sit down in large upholstered chairs. The tiled floor gleams. We could be anywhere in the world, in Tallinn or Singapore or Salt Lake City, and the mall would have looked like this. But the story he tells is uniquely Christian and Lebanese. Here in a Starbucks between lingerie boutiques and toy stores I am introduced to the schizophrenic Maronite feeling of mission and despair. He has documented this melancholy in a small, dystopic book from 2010, in which he explains that although this part of the globe is often referred to as the cradle of three monotheistic religions, only two can be said to be thriving in their respective geographic areas: the Muslim and the Jewish. Although Christianity has spread over the entire world, here where it all began, it is dying.

Habib Malik divides Middle Eastern Christians into two categories: the free 10 percent, who in reality can be found only in Lebanon and on Cyprus, and the suppressed 90 percent, who live in the other Muslim countries. The ninety percent feel much more a part of Islamic culture than a Christian community in the Muslim world. Malik calls them *dhimmis*, which refers to the subordinate legal and social status that non-Muslims, such as Jews and Christians, have had while living under Muslim rule. The dhimmis were allowed to practice their religion and administer their own religious laws, but because of loyalty concerns they were not allowed to join the army and, therefore, were forced to pay jizya. The dhimmi Christians and Jews have also historically been forced to wear specially-colored clothing; they weren't allowed to practice their religions in open public areas; they were forced to ride sidesaddle on their donkeys or mules and keep to the side streets and alleys. Funerals were to be conducted in silence.

"Strictly forbidden as public manifestations of kufr (infidelity) were the ringing of church bells, the display of crosses and other religious symbols, or loud singing during church services. Moreover, dhimmi Christians were not allowed to sell alcohol or carry any weapons and they were exempt from military service. They enjoyed no political rights whatsoever," Malik writes.

The dhimmi rules are no longer part of modern legislation in Arab countries, but echoes of the mentality persist in the prohibition of evangelism in Algeria, where such action by a priest can result in five years in prison, and conversion in Yemen and Saudi Arabia, which in principle can result in the death penalty.

Habib Malik tells me that actual violence against Christians began when the ideals of the Enlightenment reached the Middle East from the West in the 1800s. These ideals, which later were spelled out in the UN Human Declaration of Rights, conflicted with the dhimmi concept and gave non-Muslims almost equal status as citizens. The special privileges of Muslims, their superiority in relation to Christians and Jews, disappeared.

Muslims reacted by committing pogroms against Christians and Jews in the 1800s; tens of thousands were murdered in Lebanon and Syria. Malik sees the massacres as an attempt to maintain the privileged status of Muslims. Because the influence of the Enlightenment came from Christian countries in the West, today Christians in the Middle East are seen as fifth columns and traitors.

But shouldn't it have been in the interest of Christians in Arab countries to establish equal rights? Wouldn't it have made sense for them to support Charles Malik's liberals? Here is where the words of Malik's son become seriously radioactive. He believes that the centuries of subjugation and fear have resulted in a type of Christian Stockholm syndrome, in which Arab Christians are allied with the men whose feet are planted firmly on their necks.

Some background here is necessary. Two dominant, despotic ideologies have plagued the Arab world since World War Two. The first is the idea of Arab unity, pan-Arabism, which is secular, socialist, and nationalist. The second, Islamism, is religious. The past several years have witnessed a shift in the tectonic plates of the Arab world. Gone are Hosni Mubarak in Egypt, Saddam Hussein in Iraq, Muammar Gaddafi in Libya, and Yasser Arafat in Palestine, all nationalist Arab leaders. Bashar al-Assad of Syria, a peer of the aforementioned men, is clinging to power by the tips of his fingers. Islamism is on the rise everywhere in the Middle East, in some places through the use of violence.

Pan-Arabism's goal was to unite all Arabs into a single entity. Language, traditions, and history, all of which were shared by Muslim and non-Muslim alike, were emphasized, while the religious aspect was given a more modest role. Christians and Muslims could agree on pan-Arabism; this explains why the pioneers of this ideology were Christians—dhimmi Christians, as Habib Malik scornfully calls them.

In Egypt, Nasser had his own version of pan-Arabism, which was destructive to Egyptian business life and resulted in the expulsion of tens of thousands of people. A different form, Baathism, cropped up in Syria and Iraq; it's one of the last totalitarian ideologies in existence. Michel Aflaq, a Syrian Christian philosopher, formulated the obscure thoughts that crystallized into Baathism; to him it was a matter of erasing "Western civilization's invasion of the Arab mind."

"To do so he imported thinking from Western civilization," Malik says. Aflaq was inspired by the 1930s German ideals of racial purity, and by nationalism, socialism, and cult worship—ideals shared by other modern Arab intellectuals. "They identified and adopted all the worst ideas from Europe with amazing accuracy, then identified and rejected all the best ideas, such as political liberalism and human rights, every bit as accurately," Malik adds.

Baathism ruled in Iraq for thirty-five years, the final twenty-three years under Saddam. Syria has embraced the ideology for half a century, with the Assad family, father and son, leading the way for over four decades. The consequences for these police states have been catastrophic.

Here in Starbucks, another Western import, we have forgotten to order anything to eat or drink. We sit in their cozy chairs and talk, making ourselves at home.

The gruesome paradox is this: In Lebanon, where the Maronites want to maintain a state with far more freedom than their Arab neighbors, pan-Arabism has brought the country to its knees. The split between free and unfree Christians still divides the Lebanese Christians' ranks. There are traces of accusations of treason in the big Lebanese man's words that throughout my travels I gradually have begun to understand.

The struggle against an independent Lebanon has been waged by Arab military dictatorships—mostly Syrian—over the past fifty years, based on an ideology formed by Christians. Thus the treason simmering in Habib Malik's words. For decades the free Maronites have had to fight off pan-Arabs, who want to do away with the borders of this small country and be absorbed into a great Arab utopia—the Syrian version, to start off with.

Which brings us back to the Universal Declaration of Human Rights and Charles Malik. The one thing pan-Arabs and Islamists could agree on when they weren't fighting each other was that these rights were Western. In the West, pan-Arabs and Islamists faced a common enemy.

Many Western intellectuals agree that human rights are "Western," which makes this story all the more tragic. This cultural relativism flourishes among European and American academics; one needs only to consider the concept of "Orientalism" formed by the Palestinian-born man of letters, Edward Said, which has dominated Western studies of the Middle East for decades. It accuses Western observers throughout history of an imperialist and racist view of the Muslim world. It's also seen in Huntington's influential ideas about civilizations: Westerners have one type of rights, Easterners another. Pan-Arabism and Islamism are completely in agreement with this.

These efforts to divide East and West collapse when confronted with men like Habib and his father. If human rights are Western, where does this put the Lebanese? Does a Christian in the Middle East have less need of avoiding discrimination? Was the UN on the wrong track in 1948? Should the author of Article 18 have understood that this right is foreign to the Middle East?

As Habib Malik walks away on this cold winter day in Beirut and disappears down the escalator, I recall the lament his father wrote in his diary one day in 1946: "The loneliness, the unutterable loneliness of Lebanon."

• • •

I have enlisted the help of Raymond Merhej, formerly a liberal political activist in Lebanon who knows people in power here. He shares Habib Malik's view of the Maronites as the last free Christians in the Middle East, and one early afternoon I tag along with him as he pays his respects at a Maronite church in Beirut.

An elderly lady, Wadia'a, died that morning after a long illness, and now her family and friends sit in a row on Louis XVI chairs upholstered in red velour. The floor of the long hall is covered with Persian rugs.

Raymond didn't know her well, but it's customary to show grieving families respect in this manner. And besides, our presence will be noticed, Raymond says. It's good for business. The burial will take place tomorrow, more condolence visits will be arranged the next day, and finally the old Maronite will be at rest, her family comforted.

Raymond has dark curly hair. He flashes a perfect set of teeth; he is a dentist, with a small clinic on the outskirts of Beirut. He would like to work less and earn more. His plan is to lure Danes from expensive dentists in their own country, offering a cheap vacation in Beirut that features luxury hotels, nightlife, and licensed dental work.

Medical tourism, it's called. India is luring Americans away from their too-expensive hospitals with an affordable vacation and medical treatment. Raymond offers his clients a "Hollywood smile"—cosmetic surgery on their teeth. The only thing that could keep well-to-do Westerners away is Lebanon's poor reputation, he says. You have to admire his optimism when he claims that this reputation can be improved.

A Syrian archbishop greets us in the doorway. He has temporarily left his shattered homeland for Lebanon. Raymond kisses his hand. Inside the hall, most people are dressed in black, the women with bowed heads and moist eyes, the men well-groomed and well-fed, with thinning hair. Some carry silver-tipped canes. We walk down the row of soft hands to be shaken, past Raymond's uncle (the wealthy and influential monsignor of Beirut) and the woman's son and husband, both priests. They are the youngest in a long line of family priests, men wise enough to marry and have children before being ordained—Maronite priests are forbidden to marry.

We sit at the end of the row and wait silently until it's appropriate to leave. A waiter serves us Turkish coffee. I think about what a human rights activist from the American University of Beirut, Wa'il Kheir, said to me yesterday evening about the Maronite church. It sends out an annual newsletter, listing the births and deaths within the community. The newsletter shows that only elder Maronites have stodgy names such as Wadia'a, the name of the deceased. The young are called Maria or Nathalie.

"That way their names won't prevent them from becoming a part of the lands and continents their parents expect them to grow up in, like the USA, Canada, South America, Australia," Wa'il Kheir said. "Lebanese Christians feel like they're living in airport departure halls."

Lebanon might be the Arab world's freest nation, but it is also the one with the most emigration, Muslims as well as Christians. All the wars are bleeding the nation dry of its citizens. Three large cities—New York, Montreal, and Paris—have taken in many Lebanese; in Brazil alone there are many more people of Lebanese descent, in particular Christians, than in Lebanon. There are between seven and ten million Lebanese or Lebanese descendants living in South American countries; they have been emigrating there since the latter part of the 1800s. It's estimated that sixteen to twenty million people of Lebanese descent live outside Lebanon. Seventy percent of these people are thought to be Christian. During the Lebanese civil war, it's estimated that forty percent of the population—both Muslims and Christians, in equal numbers—left the country.

The population of Lebanon today is thought to be 4.5 million. When Lebanon achieved full independence in 1943, the majority of the population was Christian, while today it's believed they make up slightly over a third. According to a report from the Lebanese Information Center in 2013, it does seem as if the stream of exiting Christians has finally stopped. The percentage of Christians in the population may even increase in the future.

After sitting in silence for fifteen minutes, nodding sorrowfully at the people arriving and shaking their hands, we discreetly take our leave.

A sentence is stuck in my head. A few days earlier, I met with Raymond at my hotel on Hamra, the city's principal street in the modern Muslim district near the American University. Several times he cited Pope John-Paul II's words from 1997: "Lebanon is more than a country—it is a message." So many times that I finally suspected he really meant it.

"I feel closer to Muslim Lebanese than I do to Christians from other Arab lands," he said. "It's because of the freedom we have cultivated, and we want it to stay that way. If we have less freedom, we would rather emigrate. We value being able to practice our religion without discrimination."

It is true that democracy does exist here, albeit a wounded democracy. The country has an open economy, and Beirut is justifiably famous all over the world for its wild nightlife. Lebanon also has a somewhat free press, even though many writers and journalists have lost their lives by criticizing Syria's presence in the country. Their big neighbor to the northeast has always been touchy about people who long for true Lebanese independence.

But Lebanon as a "message"? Even though the civil war ended with members of Parliament divided equally between Christians and Muslims, the law continues to be based on injustice. Christians still have more power in the sectarian Parliament than their numbers dictate. I am also thinking about the sectarian division of law, which no one knows how to change even though everyone can see that it's wrong. As a prominent Lebanese judge who wishes to remain anonymous has told me, Lebanon is "an apartheid state without a single race in control of others."

There isn't one set of civil laws that covers everyone—eighteen civil codes exist for the eighteen legal religious groups in the country, each of them responsible for administrating their laws. A multicultural and multijudicial nightmare. It is impossible for two people of different faiths to marry, therefore such marriages take place outside the country, usually on Cyprus. A Christian cannot inherit from a Muslim and vice versa.

According to the judge, Muslim groups are preventing the introduction of national civil law, because it would conflict with Sharia. He calls it a sickness that is corroding the entire Middle East. "Nations are based on a principal of equality and laws that apply to everyone. You can't base a country on segregated laws," he says.

What is the message in that?

When I talk to Raymond and other Christians in Lebanon, I sense they are walking a thin line between pride and arrogance. And yet they have a point. I would put it in more modest terms: Lebanon is the least unfree country in the Arab world.

• • •

Perhaps the message is that the alternative is worse. Christian Lebanese don't need to look far to see what their situation could be. In a country where all religious groups live by their own laws, in the end the law of the jungle prevails and dictates which groups have the upper hand. People here are painfully aware of this.

One Saturday, Raymond, his girlfriend, and I drive north to a small town that can be seen as a warning to Christians of what they can expect wherever in Lebanon they become a minority. Raymond wears a checkered suit, black coat, scarf, and sunglasses. He listens to classical music on the radio in his squeaky clean black car as he blows cigarette smoke out the window.

We are headed toward Tripoli, Lebanon's second largest city, the Sunni Muslim bastion against the north. Our destination is the small town of El Mina, meaning the harbor. El Mina is on a small peninsula along the coast, connected to Tripoli by bridge. The town is sided on the north, south, and west by the azure blue Mediterranean. On our way into the harbor town we pass by a wall where someone has written in English, "Suicidal Misanthropy." Well-chosen words that encapsulate the mood among the Christians in this fishing village. The air is fresh, only a few clouds dot the sky.

El Mina's history stretches five thousand years into the past. Christians settled here in the decades following the crucifixion of Jesus, and disciples used the harbor to sail to Turkey and Greece to spread the message. The town has always had a beautiful coastline; it's a tourist destination that boasts an open, welcoming atmosphere, a place where Christians and Muslims have lived together in relative peace and tolerance, because the shipping trade unified its citizens. Christians could seek shelter here, and Armenians and Greek Orthodox in particular have taken advantage of that.

Relative, I say. Turks massacred Armenians here around the time of World War One, back when the area was still a part of the Ottoman Empire. Turkish soldiers requested all Armenians to gather on the outskirts of town, where they would be given food. Instead they were murdered and thrown into a pit. Between one and one-and-a-half million Armenians and Assyrian Christians are believed to have been killed in those years by the so-called Young Turks, the secular nationalists who seized power when the Ottoman Empire fell.

One of the El Mina citizens I meet tells me that when he was young he watched the mass grave being opened (a house was to be built on that site near the coast). He picked up several bones from the hundreds of skeletons and took them home. He still has the bones. He takes us past that dilapidated house, now abandoned, its shutters closed, with a smashed-up, unpainted rowboat alongside the gable wall, looking like some half-devoured carcass.

Lebanon is a country where Christians, Druze, and Shiite and Sunni Muslims live together in the same areas and cities. This is why it doesn't make total sense to divide the country along sectarian lines. But whereas Shiite Muslims dominate southern Lebanon, especially through the paramilitary Islamist group Hezbollah, Sunni Muslims dominate the north in cities such as Tripoli.

Emigration from Tripoli began before the civil war. I am told that the Christians in the city were merchants, and it was easier for them than other Lebanese to make connections and settle in the United States, Canada, and South America. But the emigration surged during the war, not least of all because of Muslim radicalization in the beginning of the 1980s.

For three years starting in 1982, a Sunni Muslim militant group, Tawhid, spread terror in the town. They established a self-proclaimed Islamic emirate there. In the middle of a round-about, the group placed a green memorial with "Allah" written in gold, along with the message that Tripoli was a Muslim city. It is still standing; apparently nobody has come up with a reason to rip the chauvinistic declaration down, thirty-three years after its erection. Perhaps because the message has been heard. Large pictures hang on the wall of a house on the square, depicting a few Islamist martyrs who probably were blown to bits.

In the 1980s, Tawhid closed restaurants, bars, tennis courts, and golf courses in Tripoli. They loudly preached that Christians should leave. The serving of alcohol was banned. In the past the city had built cabarets and the country's first casino, but Tripoli's Christians gradually felt less and less welcome. Modern life seemed to be on the retreat. Many people headed west over the Mediterranean to seek a new life.

The Syrian army defeated Tawhid in 1985, but Islamism continues to be strong in Tripoli, and poverty is entrenched. Salafists have seized control of parts of the city thanks to financial aid from Saudi Arabia, which wants to counterbalance the support the Shiite Hezbollah to the south receive from Iran. Long ago, the harbors of Tripoli and Alexandria were the two most important in the Mediterranean. But today Tripoli is one of Lebanon's poorest, most overpopulated cities, with sky-high unemployment among youth and 57 percent of its citizens living below the poverty line.

We drive through the city and into the Zahria district, down Churches Street. There is also an Archbishops Street and a Nuns Street, names that tell of a bygone era. Cables and ropes are stretched above the street, some with the Islamists' green and black flags flying from them. Kids hang out, cars and scooters slow all traffic—including us—to a snail's pace. Beautiful, newly restored churches still exist on Churches Street, but very few Christians are left to attend them.

The eruption of a small, proxy version of the Syrian civil war is a constant threat in the city. Alawites, the sect of Syrian leader Bashar al-Assad, live in a district farther up the mountain. Because the Syrian uprising is a fight between Sunnis and Alawites, the same groups shoot at each other regularly in Tripoli. Together with the Lebanese Communist Party, the Alawites helped the Syrian army crush the Tawhid movement in 1985; six hundred Sunni Muslims were killed, which is why Sunnis in Tripoli hate Syria and the Alawites so intensely.

Many Tripoli Sunnis are suspected of having joined the fight against the Syrian regime. Armed Shiite members of Hezbollah, which dominates southern Lebanon, have also gone to Syria to help Assad. People in Lebanon are horrified at the thought of what battle-hardened, agitated Islamists will do if and when they return. Another proxy war, this time in Lebanon, can be glimpsed on the horizon.

And what of El Mina, out on the peninsula? What about that little free town?

One hundred years ago, approximately 40 percent of this fishing village's population was Christian. Today I am told it has fallen to around 8 percent, though the official number is 15. And within the last two years, the exodus has picked up.

We walk to a Maronite church with a school inside its court-yard. A marble statue of the Virgin Mary stands behind bars. We are permitted to enter the courtyard, and we strike up a conversation with the church priest, Chouhry. He invites us into the parish hall's main room, which is filled with sofas. I notice a single gloomy drawing of a black-clad Virgin Mary, a halo glowing behind her head.

The priest sits down. He is a stocky man with short hair and rimless glasses. Only a few weddings and infant baptisms take place in his church now, he says. Twenty-five percent of the students in his school are Christians, the rest are Muslims, both Sunnis and Alawites. "This is good," he says, "for there is much illiteracy in the city. We raise the educational level. Muslim parents send their children here because they know that it's a good school, and they trust our way of teaching."

The school was built in 1963. Today it's a private school, though poor parents are allowed to pay just under five hundred dollars a year, which isn't even a tenth of the normal fee. The state pays the rest. Almost twice as many students apply as the school has room for, which is why the priest has recently bought an old, long-defunct movie theater to establish another one. There will be room for more students and work for more teachers. He intends to build yet another school, but he lacks the funding.

"I've applied for funds in the EU and with individual European governments. We make no profit from the schools. We can provide jobs for over one hundred teachers and give over one thousand children an education. Our goal is to save the city from extremism, save it from ending up having only one color, one religion. But Europeans no longer believe in the Church as an institution. Europeans only give money to NGOs, because they are secular. We are not an NGO. We are Christians. Europeans don't like that."

According to the priest, the European disdain means there will be no support for a church that would help education in the area. "I'm not a fundamentalist," he says. "But we have to realize that although the Church has made mistakes, it has done much for societies all over the world. We believe in peace and forgiveness and fellowship."

After talking to the priest, we meet a guide who takes us around El Mina. Palms grace the avenues. A tall sculpture made up of bicycles and dusty computers stacked into the form of a spiral stands by the ocean, as if a monster had swallowed the modern world's most important creations and vomited them onto the seafront.

We walk down to the brown-tinged water. This stretch of beach should be every tourist's dream—escaping the northern climates, watching the sun go down over the Mediterranean, eating grilled fish and drinking cold white wine behind the glass windows of the fish restaurant, and then heading south to get their teeth fixed by Raymond.

Today we are more or less the only ones here admiring the last rays of the orange sun. The bridge leading out to a small island is blocked by a large blue iron barrier. Barbed wire tops the barrier to prevent anyone from crawling over. According to our guide, it's to stop young, unmarried lovers from finding a spot shielded from the area's omnipresent eyes.

Our guide, a short man with a goatee, broad smile, and a cap with the bill pointing backward, was born in El Mina. He left the country for twenty years and returned home five years ago to an entirely different town. Muslims and Christians used to protect each other in the old days, he says, but many new people have moved into town, poor people who can't read and who have changed the local mood and demographics.

He leads us up to a small side street in El Mina where all the bars are located. The actual name of the tiny, narrow street is Yaacoub Labban, but everyone calls it Minot Street, a nickname that comes from combining Mina and Beirut's Monot Street, one of the capital's most celebrated nightlife strips.

We walk past Cava Bar, Mike's, and Gosha, whose motto is "Simply the Best." The bars would have already begun to fill up on a Saturday afternoon like this a few years back, but today they are practically deserted. Mike's has closed down. Cars are parked against their façades. The Hollywood Bar by the arcade also looks run-down. Five years ago there were twenty pubs along this short stretch.

Today the owners complain that there are no police patrols to protect their customers from being harassed, and recently El Mina's town council, in which Christians are a minority, decided to change Minot Street from a pedestrian thoroughfare to an actual street. Now cars drive down it and park, and the bars have had to stop serving outdoors. Plants are not even allowed outside.

We meet the owner of a bar, Simoun. I explain that I am here in El Mina to find out why Christians are leaving town. "Do you want to know why?" he says. He is fifty years old or so, with beard stubble, salt-and-pepper hair, and a strong chin. And he is enraged. "I'll tell you why. The town council is a bunch of fanatics, they lack only beards. They want to run Christians out of town. They are not interested in tourism. And they won't do anything about the people who break my windows and destroy my chairs." Simoun says that despite the ban he placed a few small trees in large pots in front of his bar. He was fined five hundred thousand Lebanese pounds, roughly three hundred dollars.

Rusty New Year's decorations hang from a telephone pole nearby. On a wall, someone has painted a window with blue curtains and poppies on the sill, another wall has a stairway that disappears into the gray concrete. Farther down the street, past the row of bars where it curves, is painted a hammer and sickle. And farther down, another hammer and sickle.

Later we say goodbye to the guide, and Raymond, his girl-friend, and I enter one of the beachfront fish restaurants and sit down. Something striking has happened to my companions' mood. The drive from Beirut to El Mina had been fun, the mood had been light, but now they are silent, pale, grumpy; the air is heavy with intimations I can't decipher.

Our food is served, no one really says anything. They eat very little. I'm still in the dark, but small hints of an explanation begin to seep out, perhaps triggered by my mentioning the Soviet logo on the walls. Also something our guide had said— he had used the word "progressive" to describe the people who fought Tawhid in the 1980s, Communists in cahoots with the Syrians. They are still around today, the Communists, as we can see from the arcade walls. Was it one word or was it perhaps a sentence our guide spoke that caused the tense mood in this empty restaurant?

Much later that evening, after driving the coastal road back to Beirut, while sitting with Raymond at a bar, I finally pry out of him the common knowledge in Lebanon that Communists have been or could be Syrian agents. The lives of Lebanese have been poisoned by Syrian agents for decades. That's all he will say.

Whether or not our guide is a Communist, not to mention a Syrian agent, we will never know. He is presumably totally innocent, but now I perceive something else: the nerve-rack-ing mistrust that has crept into relationships among Lebanese, where everyone has been at war with everyone else. Including Christians against Christians.

Later I decide to go for a walk in West Beirut. I allow myself to believe I can sense the oppression in the countries I visit; it was certainly present in El Mina and Tripoli. I've experienced it many times in Arab countries, a tension in the air, rage, outrage, taboo. It's there in the faces, it crackles in the rooms.

In West and East Beirut, though, the air is free of all this invisible clutter. The city is pleasant, attractive. I've seen photos of how it looked twenty-five years ago, and now it's difficult to believe it's the same city. Some places are doing better now in this country.

Yet I suspect that the freedom Maronites talk about is simply another word for Christian dominance. Lebanon's so-called "message" is the Christians. That's what Raymond is actually saying. Isolating a special Christian right to freedom, which leads to the idea that Christians have some sort of birthright to power, seems contemptuous to me. But then I didn't learn my ideals of freedom in church. The concept of special Christian ideals of freedom is also contradicted by this country's Christians themselves, who have resisted Lebanese independence and supported the Syrian police state's leaders, and by the Muslim politicians and opinion makers in Lebanon who share a longing for freedom; many Muslims have lost their lives in the struggle against Syria.

But I also can observe for myself. It's hardly a coincidence that a certain degree of freedom has been established in Lebanon that doesn't exist in all other Arab countries. There's no getting around that Christianity and civil rights are linked in Lebanon. Not even for someone like me, who was taught from childhood that Christianity in Europe fought against the ideals of the Enlightenment.

The district where I'm staying, West Beirut, is Muslim, but there's nothing obvious about that in the quarter I walk around.

Perhaps Islam's absence on the streets creates a more relaxed atmosphere. No visible evidence exists of an adamant Islamic set of morals; many, though not all, women are unveiled, and some restaurants serve alcohol. The bars behind my hotel are open until the early hours of the morning. Young students are everywhere, animated and drunk, like young people can be all over the free world. There is something reassuring about cities where people can drink long past midnight.

As I travel around, it strikes me how closely linked alcohol and tolerance are in this part of the world. I'm not at all sure how pleased I am about this insight, but it's a fact: bars, taverns, liquor stores, and alcohol are a sign of freedom in a Middle Eastern country.

Obviously it's not the only sign. Because of Lebanon's grotesque situation, it's easy to depict the country as a nation torn apart. What will happen, though, if Christians lose their disproportionately large political influence in the country? If emigration lessens their numbers? Will Muslim governments treat the Christian minorities decently? Will they treat their own minorities decently? Will they protect civil rights and permit Muslims to convert to other religions? Will Beirut continue to be Beirut? Will the bars still be open, as they were in El Mina until recently?

• • •

It's difficult not to be surprised that Lebanon still exists, that it hasn't been annexed or crushed by larger nations with immensely superior military capability. The Lebanese Christians have likewise been under pressure for decades, both internally and externally. One evening Raymond takes me to one of the men whose family has been through it all. Dory Chamoun is the current leader of the party his father established in 1959, the National

Liberal Party, which Raymond also belongs to. Clearly Lebanon's special status exists because, unlike all other countries in
the Middle East, it has been dominated by Christians.

The Chamoun family's history encapsulates the Maronite
spirit—or, if you will, cultural self-assertion. It reflects why
the accelerating decline of Christians in Lebanon is every bit
as much a result of the Christian clans' self-destructive lust for
power as the wars against Palestinians, Israelis, Druze and Syrians, pan-Arabists, and Islamists. The reaction of Raymond and
his girlfriend to our guide's behavior in El Mina was an after-
shock of the earthquake that has struck the relations between
Christians within the last forty years. And between Lebanese Lebanese—meaning Lebanese nationalists—and Arab
Lebanese.

But most of all the Chamoun family's political downfall
shows why Charles Malik's vision of Lebanon as the Middle
East's only free nation has been so costly, given that Christian
rivalry and Syrian brutality have undermined the country. The
family's fortunes also show why this vision is still alive. Despite
everything.

Still, the Chamoun family is the nearest thing to a political
dynasty the Maronites have, a type of Lebanese Kennedy clan,
glamorous and filled with heroism, marred by spectacular mistakes with tragic consequences. Dory Chamoun, the oldest son
of former president Camille Chamoun, is eighty-two. He greets
us with a whispery voice. His nose is shaped like a dagger, his
smile is mild and ironic. He gives the impression of being a man
of the world, yet in a way this politician has lost the battle. It
wasn't the National Liberal Party which formed Lebanon, which
in this country of families and clans is the same thing as saying
it wasn't the Chamoun family. Two civil wars and two assassinations have amputated it.

Dory's father was president from 1952 to 1958. Charles Malik, the father of human rights, returned home in 1956 to become foreign minister in the Chamoun government. Muslims and Christians were to be united by the National Liberal Party, and the world would then admire this tiny country that brought together two cultures who for ages have fought each other. Only a year went by, however, before the first signs of the national earthquake appeared.

A civil war broke out in 1958. It was helped along by Egypt's Nasser, who was in line to become the leader of an Egyptian-Syrian union. In fact, his ambition was to become the leader of the entire Arab world, and the Lebanese president stood in his way. Camille Chamoun was forced to ask the United States for help. For the first time in almost a century and a half, America intervened militarily in the Middle East. American soldiers had to pass by water-skiers and bikini-clad Lebanese sunbathers on Beirut's fashionable coast. The intervention ended the conflict— and Camille Chamoun's presidency. The short-lived civil war was a foretaste of what followed.

Camille Chamoun's successor in the family was Dory's younger brother Dany, a natural talent who combined a life of leisure with patriotism.

Dany was a flamboyant figure, well-dressed, articulate, and charming. His first wife, Patti Chamoun, had been an Australian model and actor. They were married in 1958. She created quite a stir by parading through the streets of Beirut in her Alfa Romeo, dressed in Capri pants, a Grace Kelly coiffure, and sunglasses. Patti Chamoun helped give Beirut the reputation of being the Paris of the Middle East in Lebanon's Golden Age from 1960 to 1975. Dissident writers from the entire Arab world came to Beirut to publish their books or pamphlets. In 1970, half of all the magazines in the Arab world, from Morocco to Oman, were published there; Lebanese newspapers were read in the entire region.

Patti Chamoun's nose for business opportunities led her to attempt to export her style to the rest of the Arab world, where she ran its first modeling agency and a television production company, but it all fell apart at the beginning of the civil war in 1975. Later she was kidnapped, and her house was bombed five times. By 1982 she'd had enough. She divorced Dany.

Initially the Christians concentrated on the war against the Palestinians. Israel had created a flood of Palestinian refugees from the wars of 1948 and 1967; two hundred thousand of them settled in Lebanon, though they have never been granted citizenship. Led by Yasser Arafat, these Palestinians attacked Israel and terrorized Lebanon with roadblocks, extortion, robberies, and assassinations. By 1975 there were four hundred thousand Palestinians in the country, fifteen percent of the population. Arafat's headquarters were in Beirut, and his militia was judged to be stronger than the Lebanese army. Chamoun and many others believed that the Palestinians were planning a coup. They had to protect their country.

That Dany Chamoun became the leader of a militia is a symptom of the basic faults of Lebanon's governmental system. The Lebanese army was weak, which led to the creation of private militias, also by the National Liberal Party; because the state couldn't protect the various sects, they had to do the job themselves. Not all of them showed restraint in implementing the power over life and death they suddenly had acquired.

Camille Chamoun founded the Tigers, a militia whose name came from his middle name, Nimr, which means tiger in Arabic. Dany was its leader. The Chamoun family thereby played as much a part as anyone else in the bloodbath that followed. The British historian Philip Mansel writes that Dany Chamoun was considered to be "the last person in the world you would have thought could become a fighter."

Spain's General Francisco Franco inspired the Phalangists, a far more radical Christian militia led by the other great Maronite clan, the Gemayels. They were rivals to the Chamouns, and they fought just as much for control of harbors through which weapons and other goods were being smuggled as they did in the name of ideologies and principles.

Journalist Thomas Friedman, author of *From Beirut to Jerusalem*, one of the finest books written about the Lebanese Civil War, characterized the Christian clans as a "corrupt, wealthy, venal collection of Mafia-like dons, who favored gold chains, strong cologne, and Mercedeses with armor plating." Mafia-like also was the method by which family conflicts were handled. Friedman described the slaughter of Dany Chamoun's Tigers by the Phalangists on July 7, 1980, in East Beirut's Safra Beach Club. Along with innocent bystanders, the Tigers were mowed down by machine guns and executed by bullets to the head. Others were thrown out of the windows of the Safra Hotel. Eighty-two Tigers were killed.

The massacre of these sunbathing soldiers was the beginning of the fall of this otherwise influential family and the shattering of the dream of a free Lebanon based on national, Christian, and civil principles. "Tigers," Dany Chamoun said afterward, became "just little pussycats." He escaped with his life, but his militia ceased to exist.

The next attempt against the family came ten years later, when Syria in 1990 finally stopped the war. Dany Chamoun, his new half-German wife, and two of their small children were murdered. The identity of the killers has never come to light. The Syrians had captured the Christian quarter of Beirut the previous week, and presumably they knew who was going in and out of the Chamouns' apartment complex. The family was killed in their apartment; only an eleven-month-old daughter survived when the babysitter hid her in the laundry room.

One of the family's Christian enemies was charged with the murders and convicted, but older brother Dory claimed that the man was innocent, that Syrian agents killed his brother's family. Like his father before him—and his older brother after him—Dany was a life-long opponent of Syrian involvement in Lebanese politics.

Power in the Middle East is handed down from father to son in influential clans, and that goes for both Christians and Muslims. Though he had never been interested in politics, it was up to Dory—who else?—to take up the reins of the family party after his little brother's murder.

Dory Chamoun, the head of his family, the clan chief, the political leader, explains to us on this quiet evening that his country's nearest neighbors, Syria and Israel, have been disastrous for Lebanon. Syria's intelligence agency expanded into Lebanon, in particular after 1990. Politicians and journalists were affected; they spoke out about how Lebanon was better off without Syrian's assistance. Dozens were murdered.

The worst episode took place in the heart of Beirut in 2005, when the anti-Syrian, Sunni Muslim former prime minister, Rafik Hariri, and twenty-one others were killed by a gigantic car bomb in the middle of Beirut in 2005. After these spectacular murders and subsequent massive international pressure, Syria officially withdrew its forces from Lebanon, though it covertly kept its agents and henchmen in place.

Dory Chamoun has always refused to be intimidated by Syria. A portrait of his father, the president, hangs above his desk. They resemble each other, but the son looks less stodgy, authoritarian, and formal. His more relaxed demeanor may be the result of him never having borne the heavy responsibility of leading his country, as his father had.

He has refused to hold office in the Lebanese government, because he believes his country to be under Syrian occupation. He also hasn't allowed his party to participate in elections he felt were rigged. This is why the party is dwindling rapidly in number, just as the family's influence, previously so strong, has been minimized. He has characterized various Lebanese presidents and military leaders as being Syrian yes-men and has referred to government officials as "rotten." He kowtows to no one.

Including me. I try to ferret out his opinion as to why Christians are leaving the region, but he prefers to talk about why Western journalists finally are beginning to cover Middle Eastern Christians. Their newly-arrived-at interest stems from the fact that Muslim immigrants in Europe are behaving as they always have in the Middle East. "It's making Europeans nervous," he says. There is a hint of schadenfreude in his voice.

"What will happen to your old continent, you're asking yourselves now. I am not calling for a religious war. But you should understand that many Muslims imagine that their faith compels them to Islamize the country they live in. This has also happened in Lebanon." But Lebanon's current problem isn't so much Muslims as the direction of its demographics. Too many Christians leaving, too few children being born to those who remain.

"If you Europeans really are the Christians you claim to be, you should help us. The diaspora must return. Good jobs and circumstances must be established for them. Europeans can help by investing in Lebanon."

His expression shows that he is not counting on such help in the immediate future. "A senile old man," is how he described the West as far back as thirty-five years ago.

"For decades the USA has looked on us as a small toy," he says. "If it hadn't been for some stubborn Maronites, there would be no Lebanon today. We Christians were in this country long before Islam. We have fought and fought. We were second-class citizens in the Ottoman Empire. But we held on to our country. We didn't buckle under. We paid a great price, but even when you're up against a superior force, you don't have to lower your trousers."

He calmly looks me in the eye and assures me that the Maronites will survive. Even if they have to do it alone. They will also survive the Baath regime's henchmen in Syria, who took the lives of his brother and so many others. The Maronites have survived against all superior foes. "They can't oppress us. No one has been able to. Not even the Ottoman Empire. We are mountain people, we are tough. We talk with goats. We talk with sheep."

After meeting with Chamoun, we drive through Beirut in Raymond's car. He tells me he also knows what it's like to confront the Baath regime to the northeast. When he was young, he was the leader of a student movement that demanded Syria leave the country. Several times the Lebanese intelligence service picked him up, threw him in jail, and beat him. The intelligent service takes its instructions from Damascus.

Raymond may be one of the mountain people, but he is visibly nervous when he takes me one evening to meet a man with a claim to the title "Your Excellency." This man was the deputy spokesperson for the Lebanese Parliament after Syria took control of the country in 1990, to the extent that Hafiz al-Assad, Bashir's father and predecessor in power, could elect and overthrow governments. While the Chamoun family's fortunes fell, His Excellency's star was on the rise.

Dory Chamoun would claim that Elie Ferzli is one of the "Syrian yes-men." Habib Malik would have referred to him as a "dhimmi Christian." Both men would in all probability believe that hell holds a special place for those who betray the free Lebanese cause.

We meet Ferzli in a concrete room containing only an empty bulletin board, a telephone, a bare desk, and a few chairs. There is something spooky about this room; it's as if a man in a black suit and sunglasses is about to come in and tie our hands behind our backs, shine lamps directly in our eyes, and yell at us.

I can't bring myself to call him Your Excellency. I notice that Raymond can't, either. Ferzli doesn't let that affect him. He says that he has just returned from the Bekaa Valley along the Syrian border for this interview. He attended the funeral of four Lebanese soldiers killed several days ago. They had attempted to arrest members of a militant rebel group hiding out in Lebanon, though they were fighting the Assad regime. Two of the rebels were also killed. The civil war in Syria constantly spills over the border.

Elie Ferzli's past can be seen in his face—not in his left eye, though it is blind and half closed, but rather from the scar on his right cheek, the reminder of a bombing in 1985. The bomb was meant for his friend Elie Hobeika; the two of them were in church when it went off. Hobeika was uninjured.

Elie Hobeika, His Excellency's old friend, frightens those familiar with the conflict. He is an important bogeyman: If Christians in this country can justify their disproportionate power only by pointing to worse alternatives, the pan-Arabs or the Islamists, he is standing at the end of that slippery slope, justifying mass murder. His crimes are a stain that neither Maronites nor Israelis have been able to wipe away. Hobeika is the seamy side of the Maronites, representing an extreme cultural arrogance, and his story has to be included to understand the reputation of Maronites outside the country, just as he is a prime example of the duplicity and treachery within their ranks.

Even at a young age, Hobeika became known as an extraordinarily violent Phalangist warlord. He is thought to be behind the murder of eighty-one Palestinians in the town of Yarin in July 1977; between twenty and thirty civilians were lined up against the school wall and shot. He was only twenty-one at the time. Hobeika worked both for the Israelis and the CIA, and he made sure that political enemies were liquidated.

He also was a bodyguard for Bashir Gemayel, who was elected Lebanese president in August 1982. Three weeks later, Gemayel was killed in a bombing attributed to the Syrians. It was meant to avenge the massacre committed by Hobeika-led Phalangists in September 1982, where between seven hundred and two thousand unarmed Palestinian refugees in two camps, Sabra and Shatila, were slaughtered while the Israeli soldiers guarding the camps turned a blind eye.

By the time of the 1985 church bombing, Hobeika had formed an alliance with Syria. With the enemy. Just as His Excellency had. Due to an unerring sense of which way the wind was blowing, Hobeika switched sides and just as fiercely served the interests of the Assad regime. Hobeika quickly established himself in luxurious surroundings in Damascus. He spoke about "Arab identity" and Syria's important role in Lebanon's history.

For several years in the 1990s, Hobeika held ministerial posts in the Lebanese government despite his bloody past; at one time he was even the minister overseeing thousands of internal refugees. Many people saw this as a special Lebanese form of black humor—the man responsible for displacing hordes of people had been appointed to serve their cause. Something had to give. In 2002, someone managed to kill Hobeika with a car bomb in Beirut. No one knows who was responsible, but many had reason to eliminate this shameless and gruesome renegade.

Elie Ferzli, Hobeika's Syrian-friendly ally, is an unusually talkative man, but at first he talks about everything except what I ask him about. And besides, it's difficult for me to listen to him; I can't help staring at his eye and cheek. His black hair parted on the side, his dark blue suit crackling with static electricity, his ingratiating hospitality, and his endless arm gestures make him look like a film gangster who eventually suffers a swift and bloody death.

When he does finally respond to my questions about his dubious connection to Syria, he seizes on Western apathy toward what is happening inside Lebanon's big neighbor. "Look at the Christians' situation in Syria now." He speaks calmly and self-assuredly, as if all his opponents perhaps should have known better.

"It's unbearable. The Christians in Aleppo, Homs, and Damascus are in flight. If the Muslim Brotherhood comes to power in Syria, you can be sure that the Christian presence in Syria is over."

A man enters the room carrying blood-orange juice. I ask Ferzli how he could support the Syrian police state. "The West simply doesn't understand. You don't fight Muslim fundamentalists by slapping them on the cheek. Now the West must take the consequences. Look at Libya. Look at Turkey. Look at Iraq. Look at Egypt. Look at Mali. What is it you wanted? Listen, this is the Middle East. You want democracy. After you installed 'democracy' in Iraq, Christians had to flee the country in horrific numbers. The same will happen in Syria as a consequence of the so-called 'Free Syrian Army' supported by the West."

I ask him what he has to say to all the Maronites who believe that Syria, which he supports, has ruined Lebanon. "When

Syria was in Lebanon, we had a certain degree of stability. If you look at the Christians, they were leaving in droves before Syria stepped in. That stopped while Syria was here. When the Syrians left in 2005, the instability returned."

I say that the instability was caused by Syrian agents and countless liquidations of critics of Assad. "Syria gets accused every time there is an assassination attempt. But up to now no court has confirmed these accusations."

He glances at his watch; still profusely polite, he says that he unfortunately has run out of time. Raymond stands up, walks over to Ferzli, and whispers in his ear that he, Raymond, was tortured ten years ago in prison by the Syrian-controlled Lebanese intelligence service. Ferzli's friends.

For the first time, the former spokesperson for the Lebanese Parliament looks startled. The side of his face with a blind eye hangs a bit, as it sometimes does with people who have had a stroke. But now the other side of his face hangs also. He doesn't answer Raymond; instead he walks somewhat confusedly toward me, as if he wants to escape this nasty accusation whispered in his ear. He holds both hands out and says, "Welcome, welcome, thank you, thank you."

But Raymond is not going to waste this opportunity to plague his tormentors' lackey just a bit; he asks me to take a picture of the two of them. Ferzli complies without a word. The two of them stand together, two Christian Lebanese shoulder to shoulder, the National Liberal and the Pan-Arab, each on their own side of the decades' front line, one with a wonderful set of teeth, the other with eyes darting in every direction.

• • •

It's Friday, and Raymond, animated in the wake of his modest but satisfying revenge over His Excellency and his Syrian world, takes me to hear L'Orchestre Philharmonique du Liban in the Église St. Joseph des Pères Jésuites. We listen to a performance of Mendelssohn's Symphony No. 4; the large cathedral is bursting at the seams with Beirut citizens young and old who listen attentively. An appreciation of classical culture may be declining on the old continent, but not in Lebanon.

This city has more to offer than magnificent symphonies. Afterward we go to the Hole in the Wall, Raymond's favorite bar. His girlfriend from the trip to El Mina is with us, and she has brought along a friend who after three or four shots of tequila begins to lean into the unmarried and not completely unreceptive Raymond. A fantastic female guitarist has the packed bar in an uproar.

Raymond is something of a prankster; he knows the bartender, and later that evening Raymond convinces him that it's my birthday. The bartender eagerly rings the bar bell; immediately the guitarist stops, and while the crowd cheers I'm called behind the bar to be honored as the birthday boy by this well-oiled gathering. I generously accept this undeserved tribute while wondering if I'm expected to buy a round for what looks like half the population of Beirut. Behind me somewhere I sense Raymond's sly smile. I take a page from Elie Ferzli's book: I buy a little time and defuse the situation by urging everyone to cheer for the guitarist instead, while I sneak away.

She sees right through me. In acknowledgment she plays "The Gambler," Kenny Rogers's old hit.

> You got to know when to hold 'em,
> Know when to fold 'em,
> Know when to walk away,
> Know when to run.

. . .

Maybe it's the hangover settling in this morning that brings to mind the accusations I've heard during my travels, namely that I've picked out a single group and made it the object of a special investigation. Why does the Christian exodus from Arab countries interest me? Am I not building sectarian barriers? Why am I not interested in Shiites, who are suffering in Sunni Muslim countries? Interestingly, research by the Washington, D.C.-based PEW Research Center indicates Muslims are persecuted to a greater degree in the Middle East than Christians—but by other Muslims, obviously. So why don't I turn my attention to the Alawites in Syria, who have more to fear than Christians if the regime falls? Is it because Christians remind us of ourselves? Is it a type of cultural chauvinism? Look at Lebanon—haven't Christians been brutal in the sectarian fight for survival? Is our sympathy shielding them?

I don't believe that the blood they have on their hands is a reason to not write about the Christians. Just as it's no excuse that groups in other countries are suffering more. Infinitely more people are dying in the civil war in Congo, but that doesn't grab our attention in the same way. It's too bad, but public focus has nothing to do with the amount of suffering. We have historical, cultural, and religious reasons to be interested in this group. And the degree of attention given to Christian Arabs isn't all that great, either. It has always amazed this unbaptized observer that there is so little focus on them.

When I'm around Christians in Arab countries, I begin to doubt our own alleged Christianity. Gradually I have come to the conclusion that Christians in the Arab world are very, very different from, say, Northern European Protestants, American Evangelicals, or Mexican Catholics. I told Raymond about an issue currently being discussed in Denmark: a congregation in Jutland had placed an ad for a minister who was a "believer." He nearly died laughing. The priest in El Mina applying for funding to build new schools in his long-suffering town was surely onto something when he accused European governments of supporting only secular NGOs.

The Christians I meet strike me as familiar and yet completely foreign. What do I have in common with armed Maronites fighting for their rights? What is my connection to Greek Orthodox Palestinians with their incense and icons and strong sense of family? What do I have in common with Copts who believe in miracles and exorcism? The more I speak with Arab Christians, the more I realize there is a distance, that we in the West don't share the same historical experience.

One evening I meet with Professor Wa'il Kheir in front of the American University of Beirut to understand the nature of this distance. Kheir, the former director of the Foundation for Human and Humanitarian Rights, is a lawyer who teaches human rights at the university. He has written several books on diverse subjects.

It's drizzling, he's standing in the gateway with his folded umbrella in hand. We greet each other and walk in silence near the university to find a place to sit. He uses his umbrella as a cane. We find a café filled with students. He takes off his wet overcoat and sits down.

Kheir says I must understand that the Middle East and the West went their separate ways in the Middle Ages. Since then, the European world has been influenced by a number of landmark events in history. The first was the Renaissance, during which the ancient world was rediscovered.

"You discovered that the Greeks and Romans made magnificent achievements in science, art, and philosophy. You discovered there is a world outside of Christianity, a parallel path that isn't Christian."

The second was Protestantism. "Along with Martin Luther, you went back to the sources, the religious sources. The Church as an institution had lost its sacred meaning. A direct connection between man and God arose, outside of the Church. Catholicism still dictates that our souls can only be saved through receiving Communion. The Church remains a vital link between man and God. Protestants have done away with that link."

Next came the Catholic Reformation. The Church was reformed, and the Jesuits established several modern educational institutions. Kheir takes a pause from his point-by-point argument about why the chasm between the West and the Middle East has become so vast. "Up until now, none of this has affected my part of the world, the Middle East," he says.

The fourth break with the past came with the Enlightenment. "For the first time in history comes the idea that our humanity is innate, not something from outside us. This is a revolution. Until then, it was believed that the source of our humanity came from class, clan, city, or God."

The fifth and final landmark event was the Industrial Revolution of the nineteenth century. It created the concept of "society," or rather, an awareness that groups in society also should have rights. "It became difficult for politicians to ignore social groups. They demanded to be heard. This has changed you."

This has changed you, he says. He isn't a member of the club. He comes from the Middle East. "None of these five epochal developments took place in this part of the world," he says. "We are stubborn, just as Europe was before the thirteenth century. On the surface it may seem that we aren't so far from the Western world. But deep inside us exists a culture unaffected by these five steps."

Kheir asks rhetorically how Christians have managed in this medieval society. "A Christian in the Middle East is given his humanity from an external source—his religion. It's the same for Muslims. This affects the way Muslim countries are governed. If you are a Muslim, you have 'rights.' If you are not a Muslim, you are 'protected.' But you have no rights."

In this lies a fundamentally different view of the individual. In the West, you are first and foremost a human, he explains. Humanity is innate. Therefore Westerners can better understand that human rights are universal. They are rights that all humans have through their humanity. They are not rights derived from religion, as in the Middle East.

Of course it's not that simple. The Middle East changed as influence from the West spread at the beginning of the twentieth century. The circumstances for Christians improved. Arab countries were given constitutions, relatively independent judicial systems, a certain freedom of the press.

"But after the war, in connection with the creation of Israel in 1948, our freedoms began to shrink again. The leadership of this part of the world was overtaken by military regimes."

These regimes had no popular support among the people. They lacked legitimacy, he says. The only way they could gain legitimacy was through actions such as supporting Palestinian nationalism and an awakening Islamism. "The military regimes were oppressive, but they had an Islamist slant. This is also why Christians began leaving the region."

Wa'il Kheir is wearing a blue cotton cardigan and a gold and blue tie, his shirt is pale yellow. His large wristwatch has a gold band. I'm guessing that he is about sixty years old. A mustache helps define his face, his forehead extends up onto the crown of his head, his eyelids hang low. He is a refined gentleman.

In Europe, a man who considers himself a human rights activist would rarely dress so conservatively, and even more rarely would he be so adamantly Christian and critical of Islam. As he sketches out the differences in the history of ideas between the East and West, I begin wondering if opinions like those of Kheir are rejected or ignored by many journalists and human rights activists in Europe. He believes so.

My friend Raymond often complains that the West seems to take sides with either the Palestinians or the Israelis—but never with them, the Lebanese Christians. Why is Palestinian or Israeli nationalism worth fighting for while Lebanese nationalism is not, he asks. And when Kheir is asked to explain why so few books are written about Christian Arabs, even though they are leaving the cradle of Christianity, he says, "The Western world is no longer very Christian or interested in Christians. The West is secular and, to a degree, hostile to the Church."

Christian Arab immigrants therefore often become demoralized after settling in the West. They develop an identity crisis, they feel rootless. They long for their homes, they bond with others from their homelands to search for what they have lost. "For over two hundred years Europeans have been cutting religion out of their lives," he says. "But the Arab Christians remain in the West, even though they are disappointed. It's because they are treated like humans."

Kheir isn't giving this short lesson in the progress of the Occident to bolster Western self-satisfaction. He believes that the absence of religion in the West is a loss. "You are finally beginning to understand that religion is part of human nature. In the past you believed that humans can be molded by education. But if that's true, why did the Soviet Union collapse? Why did the Russian Church prove to be much more important than Communism?"

Contempt for religion has been so destructive that it has affected how we—Europeans—think about the Middle East. "If religious arguments are brought into an issue, they are swept aside," he says. "This is why it is difficult for you to think of Christians in the Middle East as Christians. You're not allowed to concern yourselves with a religious group, especially if it's Christian. But other kinds of arguments are completely okay. You have nothing against national or ethnic arguments. You can concern yourselves with groups like Syrians, Palestinians, Kurds, Israelis and so forth."

Christians in the Middle East are not included.

We say our goodbyes and walk outside; the rain in Beirut is even heavier now. As he strolls off, he uses his umbrella as a cane again. I walk down Sidani Street, past a hyperrealistic painting on the gable of a building; it depicts a bald person with full lips and an intense, friendly expression. It's impossible to tell whether it's a man or a woman, black or white.

I am drawn in by Kheir's strange accusation against Europeans; he exposes a blind spot concerning Christians in the Arab countries. They make up no ethnic group, no independent nationality. They resemble Muslims in appearance, live among them, eat mostly the same food, wear mostly the same clothes, speak the same language. The only difference is religious: the church, the liturgy, the New Testament. And all of this is detested by "post-Christian" Europe, as Kheir calls it.

When you think about how unpopular and repugnant nationalism has been for decades because of World War Two's monstrous European annihilation, his words expose a hypocrisy in the northern hemisphere's modern mentality: nationalism is harmful in Europe but not in the Middle East.

Kheir also describes the double standard in Europe concerning the religious critique running parallel to the struggle for human rights. The critique was limited to Christianity, not religions as such; Islam was never focused on by the European human rights movement in the same harsh, damning way. To me this seems a deficiency bordering on contempt: the critique of religion is reserved for the Christian world, while Muslims must be protected against this type of thing.

This patronizing attitude also explains a feeling I have had for many years, that important human rights organizations such as Amnesty International and Human Rights Watch until recently have neglected the victims of Islamism and Arab nationalism. This includes the Muslims and Christians and countless other minorities who have suffered under these two Middle Eastern absolutist ideologies. It's as if human rights violations are mainly committed by the Western world. Only Westerners are capable of being butchers. When the regimes of Arab countries committed gruesome acts against their own populations, it must have been because of earlier Western colonialism or some form of modern Western exploitation. Responsibility was taken from them, which changed them into something less than individual people.

"We hate ourselves much more than we love others," according to the French philosopher and writer Pascal Bruckner. This built-in cultural arrogance in Western self-hatred is not our finest quality. I'm soaked to the skin when I finally reach my hotel.

• • •

One Sunday morning Raymond drives me up to his childhood home in the mountains. He wants to have a look at his apartment, take me to lunch at his uncle's enormous house, and go to church with this post-Christian European. He also wants to show me where the tragedy of his childhood took place. We drive through Beirut and immediately up into the Chouf mountains. As always he's smoking a cigarette; his yellow scarf is wound tightly around his neck, and he's wearing his plaid-checkered suit. We bought coffee to go back in Beirut, and now the city spreads out beneath us in a haze, looking like it's yearning to push off into the Mediterranean.

The Chouf mountains have been inhabited by Druze and Maronites for four hundred years. We pass by Druze mountain villages, where old men wear fezzes and baggy pants. Shortly after we drive through Maronite towns. Originally these two ethnic groups, Druze and Maronites, made up the majority of those living here.

Raymond draws my attention to the numerous houses alongside the road. Many of them are unfinished, naked, with lifeless façades and steel rebar sticking up. These concrete skeletons have been built where centuries-old, limestone Maronite houses stood until just over thirty years ago. Today the Maronites live in Beirut, but their property has been returned to them. They want houses here, even if they'll never be able to afford or have time to finish them, much less care to live in them.

We stop in at a Druze butcher where Raymond always buys meat on Sundays. Saddles of lamb hang in the window along with sausages and offal. Raymond orders lamb liver and an especially tender cut of the upper front leg of the lamb; the young, bald butcher slices it off. He wields his knife quickly and confidently as he cuts off tendons and dices the meat, then adds a bit of fat. A picture of an ancient Druze sheikh with large ears and a snow-white beard down to his stomach hangs behind him, and beside it is a painting of St. George astride a horse, driving his lance into the belly of a dragon.

We drive farther up, around a mountain and alongside a deep valley, and finally over to the other side, where we stop at a monastery. It is among the few old buildings left in the area that were allowed to stand untouched. In a small grotto stands a plaster statue of St. Marion wearing a blue prayer shawl around his neck. He blesses visitors with the ring and middle finger of his right hand. Necklaces, armbands, and rosaries have been draped over his hand; one of them bears a picture of the pope.

Thirty years ago, thousands of people gathered here in flight. They are in our thoughts as we drop coins in a copper box, light a candle, and stick it in the sand in a stone urn.

Finally we reach Raymond's childhood town, Majd el-Meouch, population four thousand, farther up the mountain. We park at the mansion owned by his uncle, the monsignor of Beirut, whom I met at the condolence visit and later talked to in his spacious office while he played computer solitaire and smoked Davidoff cigarettes. He isn't home.

An Assyrian family that fled from Syria takes care of the mansion; Raymond greets them. The father walks up the long, winding driveway while two small boys run around, pretending to help him. Their mother is in the kitchen. Raymond gives her the meat for the lunch that we have climbed 2,500 feet to eat. Before we attend church she serves us Turkish coffee. We sit in the sunshine and drink while looking down the slopes at the peach and olive trees in the valley. Everyone in town gathered there in 1983.

Raymond was five years old back then. A month before the whole town fled, he and his family had walked all the way down into and across the valley, climbed the cliffs, and sought refuge in the town on the other side. From there they were taken to Beirut. They brought with them only what they could carry or load on the back of a donkey. They lost all the rest of their belongings, including their houses. They feared what was coming.

After finishing our coffee, we drive to the church, a small, simple limestone building with two bells in the belfry. The ancient church also survived the civil war. We sit and listen to the sermon. The church is half full, and Raymond, who believes that the Catholic Church should stop excluding non-Catholics, brings me along to take communion. I bow my head, more in shame than reverence; again I feel as if I'm committing a blasphemy.

We walk outside after the services. Some of the men are tugging on two ropes hanging alongside the church. They want me to try, too, and the church singer helps me. I pull so hard that I end up being lifted a few feet off the ground, but finally the bells ring deep and loud. It's me, the atheist, whose enthusiasm and hard work causes the well-known sound of Christianity to peal over the green hills and across the valley, all the way over to the snow-clad peaks to the east. As the bells pull us up and gravity pulls us down, as we snort like two happy, worn-out trotting horses, I try to recall whether or not I heard this sound in the churches when I was in Egypt. Were bells permitted there? I can't remember. I've never thought I would miss the sound of church bells, and retrospectively to boot.

After giving the bells a rest, Raymond drives me up to another church and cemetery at the town's highest point. From here we can gaze out over the entire region. The church and cemetery are new. A tree with a trunk several yards thick once stood here; it had been cut down in those horrible days over thirty years ago. Its stump had to be blasted out with dynamite, and you can see where it was from the newer, lighter asphalt.

We walk up to the graveyard where Raymond's family plot is located. Several small, windowless mausoleums have rusty iron doors adorned with crosses. Graves here were also smashed and desecrated, and the new mausoleums are either limestone or concrete. Burned candles and withered flowers lay beside several of them. Raymond's body will be put to rest here in the family plot. Like so many others, he will return to his hometown only after he dies.

We walk back down to the church, over to a railing from where we can look out over the mountains. Two workers in a peach grove below us are eating lunch. "They came over the hilltop," Raymond says. He points to a mound behind the town. "The Druze and Syrians."

They haven't always been on the best of terms, the Druze and Maronites, even though Raymond says that about three hundred years ago the Druze gave the Maronites permission to live in this part of the mountains. His family has lived here for all that time. But in 1860, the Druze murdered eleven thousand Christians in the Chouf mountains and destroyed 380 towns and 560 churches. They wanted to drive the Christians out and establish a region for Druze only. The Christians could live in the mountains to the north. The fighting spread to Damascus, where Druze and Sunni Muslims murdered twelve thousand more Christians. The mass murders led to what has been described as the world's first humanitarian intervention, by France.

This was the beginning of 123 years of peace. The civil war in the 1970s and 1980s brought Israel into the conflict; the Israelis took possession of the Chouf mountains, from where they could observe Beirut. In 1983 they decided to change their positions and left the mountains. By then the Druze, supported by Syria, were already at war with the Christian militias. After 145 civilian Druze were killed by the mainly Christian Lebanese army, they were bent on revenge. The Druze leader, Walid Jumblatt, controlled one of the strongest militias, which was armed by Syrians and Russians. When the Israelis pulled out, the Maronites in the Chouf mountains were no longer protected, because Lebanese forces were too weak to step in.

Raymond believes the Christian leaders of the Lebanese forces made a backroom deal with the Druze to establish a Christian region in the northern mountains, which meant that the Druze could cleanse the area of all Christians. In my research, I haven't been able to confirm this version of events at that time. The story seems to be that the Lebanese army had no chance against the superior Druze forces. True or false, Raymond's point is one I have been confronted with during my entire stay in Lebanon: that Christians were betrayed by their own.

Shortly before the attack, the Christians in the mountains were warned that an invasion was imminent, and they were told to flee. In Majd el-Meouch, Raymond's hometown, from whence he and his family had fled a month earlier, the townspeople left their houses and belongings behind and sought refuge in the monastery where we had lit a candle. Later they walked down to the valley floor. Most of them continued through the valley to the largest Christian town in the area, Deir al-Qamar, a day's journey by foot. But two hundred Christians decided to stay and hide in the toolsheds there on the valley floor; some were too old for the long journey, others hoped that the danger would pass; still others refused to cower.

"They were stubborn and proud," Raymond says. When the Kurds and Syrians found them in the toolsheds, they slaughtered them all. Some had their throats cut. In the neighboring town, which we also visit, forty of them hid in the town church. They were also found and murdered. The church is closed when Raymond and I arrive. Flowers wrapped in red foil and long since wilted are stuck between a light pole and the church wall. Trash and a few empty bottles litter the surrounding ground. A cross in relief over the front door has been hacked off.

From September 7 to September 13, 1983, sixty-two Christian towns were blown to bits and burned down—more or less destroyed, in other words. Druze moved into the few houses permitted to stand. Fifty thousand Christians were driven off, fifteen hundred were murdered. Only one Christian town survived without being attacked—Deir al-Qamar, birthplace of President Camille Chamoun, where many Christians had fled, including the survivors from Raymond's hometown.

There isn't a single memorial in Majd el-Meouch or the neighboring town. "It's still too close," Raymond explains, when I ask him why. "Some people lost their brothers and sisters. I also lost members of my family."

That strikes me as a strange logic for not erecting a memorial, but I drop the subject. Maybe no one wanted to bring attention to their loss. Maybe people just wanted, or still want, to forget about it. The way Raymond describes the whole episode reminds me of something I read about how mountain people hide their emotions. Mastering, it's called. Invisible. It's as if the whole story doesn't affect him.

On the way back to his uncle's house, we stop by his old home. He shows me a few of his pistols, one called Browning's Patent Depose from Belgium and his favorite weapon, a Pietro Beretta from Italy. You have to protect yourself when others won't. I'm allowed to hold them.

The Druze left the Christian towns after the civil war, and the Christians could return to their ruined houses. Raymond says that although Christians have been given back their towns and homes, they haven't actually returned. I sense that something has been damaged, a sense of home, of belonging, and the wounds won't heal. Most of those driven away have remained in Beirut or have moved to the West.

Lunch is ready when we return to his uncle's splendid new mansion. A columned entryway, two stories, balcony, red tile roof, Oriental windows. His uncle is still not at home, the place feels uninhabited, with not a single scratch or mark in sight. The interior is furnished with antiques that only seem old. It's like being in a museum of exquisite copies, or the sarcophagus of a dead person you visit on special occasions.

The lunch table, however, is very real; it's lavish and barbaric. The main course: raw lamb and raw lamb liver. Raymond demonstrates how to eat it. First tear off a piece of *khobez*, an Arab bread something like a pita, then cut an onion into quarters, place one on the piece of bread, and add a mint leaf. Then dip three or four small pieces of liver or meat in salt and lay on the mint leaf. Dip a bit of fat in salt and put it on top. Fold the bread around it all and eat it in one mouthful.

The taste of an entire region's wisdom, suffering, stupidity, and death. We wash it down with home-brewed arak, Lebanese ouzo. On ice.

· · ·

Running into Elias Toumeh is somewhat of a coincidence. He is staying in my hotel in Beirut, along with Danmission, a Danish Christian organization that arranges cultural meetings between Muslims and Christians. They have been active in Syria for decades. I run into the Danes at a reception and tell them what I am doing, and the next day they introduce me to the Syrian bishop. His country is in the middle of the most desperate civil war of our time, from which hundreds of thousands have fled. There are rumors of the expulsion of sectarian groups, similar to what happened in the Chouf mountains.

Among the many human tragedies, there is a war within the war that threatens to end the presence of one of the oldest religious groups in Syria—the Christians. They were in the country before Paul, himself the persecutor of Christians, had his famous vision and was baptized in Damascus.

Christians were said to have made up ten percent of the Syrian population. Several people I've met say they've been attacked because of their religion by Islamist rebel groups controlling parts of the country, but not by the Syrian regime. Christians have fled by the thousands to all of Syria's neighbors. Should the Assad regime fall, they fear that their time in the country will be over. And that's why I am eager to meet this priest with the sad, dark eyes.

We sit down in the plush chairs of my Beirut hotel lobby. The short, paunchy man wears a black mantle with a gold-embroidered medallion around his neck. His title comes from the castle that has made the entire region famous: He is the Bishop of Pyrgou, or *Qala'at al-Hosn* as it's called in Arabic—or Krak des Chevaliers, as the castle is known throughout the world. The Krak des Chevaliers is one of the best-preserved Crusader castles in existence, sitting majestically on top of a 2,130-foot hill with an open view on all sides. It was built in 1031 for the emir of Aleppo. Crusaders captured the castle in 1099, rebuilt it, then defended it until Muslim forces recaptured it in 1271.

In 2012 it was taken by rebel forces, who have fought the regime from behind its thick walls. Several missiles capable of breaching the walls have exploded a few yards from this castle which is on UNESCO's list of World Heritage Sites.

Bishop Toumeh says the Christian refugees come primarily from Aleppo to the north and Homs to the west, thirty-five miles away. Both cities are crumbling little by little from the fighting. The priest says that in Homs, the "Revolution's Capital," the previous population of fifty thousand Christians has shrunk to eighty families. Rebels captured the Christian quarters, now in ruins.

Approximately twenty thousand Sunni Muslims live in villages around the Crusader castle. Many Alawites also live nearby. But mainly it's a Christian region; between thirty and thirty-five thousand Christians live there, and tens of thousands of Christian refugees have joined them. According to the bishop, seventy thousand Christians have fled to the Valley of Christians from Aleppo and Homs in particular. Elias Toumeh says there are almost two million Christians in Syria, 70 percent of whom, like him, are Greek Orthodox.

"When the conflict began, we had no problems in my area," he says. "But when the government attacked Homs in 2011, it affected the Sunni Muslims in the valley. Many armed groups showed up, and they attacked the government forces and took over a large part of the area, including around and within the Krak des Chevaliers."

The rebels' arms come from northern Lebanon, most likely from ships docked in Tripoli, the city I visited with Raymond and his girlfriend. From there the arms are smuggled over the border and into Sunni Muslim towns.

The Christians in Syria have been allied with the Assad family and their regime. They have enjoyed special privileges; some of them have been appointed ministers and to other high public posts, some became administrators in the private sector. Many, also in the West, have described the regime as showing tolerance toward religious groups, and Damascus is often touted as a city where everyone lives in peace with one another.

Today Christians are paying the price for the imminent

collapse of a profoundly oppressive regime. From the very beginning of the uprising, Church leaders issued clear public statements of support for the regime. In that way Christians themselves are responsible for their awkward and very dangerous situation, Bishop Toumeh says. The war has become a battle between Sunni Muslims and Alawites, who make up about 60 percent and 10 percent of the population respectively. Christians have placed themselves in the line of fire; if the regime falls, they fear they will be the target of a well-nourished Sunni revenge for decades to come.

It's difficult to find unbiased information that confirms what the Christians I meet in Beirut tell me. Obviously Christians, just like hundreds of thousands of others, can be fleeing simply because they live in a war-torn country, and not because they are being driven away.

Human Rights Watch and numerous journalists have described kidnappings, the sacking and burning of churches, and an increasing sectarian violence in the war, though it's difficult to see a definitive pattern in the expulsion of Christians. On the other hand, it should be said that the Syrian regime has an interest in depicting the reason for the flight of Christians as being worse than they really are. Assad's best card to play in avoiding Western intervention is fear of the regime that may follow.

In a country where journalists and human rights activists find it harder all the time to work and over a hundred news media workers have been killed, many can end up spreading misinformation stemming from the Syrian regime. The Vatican's official organ, *Agenzia Fides*, wrote that Islamists were committing an "ethnic cleansing" of Christians in Homs. Later it came out that the information came directly from a pro-Syrian propaganda website, SyriaTruth.

But there is no doubt that Syrian Christians find themselves in difficult and dangerous circumstances. Anxiety for the future has forced Christians to move to the Valley of Christians, where many Alawites also live, or to surrounding countries. "We are trapped between a rock and a hard place, in a war that can go on for years, and which won't end if and when the regime falls," the bishop says.

He adds that many of the tens of thousands of Christian refugees in the area have lost their homes. "They live as refugees, they receive all the emergency aid we can scrape up. But they must realize that they will never return to their homes. Their homes no longer exist. And we might as well get used to the fact that this will go on for years, that there will be no winner. Christian refugees must find work in this part of the country, they must earn their own money and pay for their food and shelter."

He believes that the war will result in well-educated Syrians leaving the country, and that Islamic fundamentalism will prevail. The fanatics aren't Syrian, he says; they come from the outside. He calls them "tourists." Al Qaeda and like-minded groups have settled in Syria, just as they have in Iraq.

The longtime alliance with Assad's regime still exists in some circles. I visit a satellite television station, SAT-7, which produces Christian programming for the entire region, where I meet a young technician who makes programs for Syrian Christians. He encourages them to keep their faith and remain in the region. He comes from a large Syrian port city, and he believes God has decided that Syria will continue to exist, that God will create a new Church in the country.

"We had the freedom to do what we wished before this war," he says. "Now it's getting ugly. The Church still proclaims publicly that it supports the government. This is why it is being attacked." According to him, all Christians support Assad. They believe mistakenly that he can protect them. It can't be done.

I ask him what he personally thinks about Assad. "Honestly, I love him. I feel that he is a good person, and that he wants to work for the country. He has done much good as a leader. I also want more democracy and freedom, but not this way."

The next day I meet George at one of Beirut's refugee camps. I can't say where, and I can't reveal his real name, just as I can't reveal the name of the young technician. George is twenty-eight years old and big and strong, a Christian Syrian musician who along with his wife has sought refuge in Beirut. He lived in a small town close to Damascus, but he fled when Druze soldiers fighting for the government set up a barricade right under their apartment. Snipers took positions on their roof. There was no electricity, no food, no heat, no security.

He also feared being kidnapped. Stories about the kidnapping of Christians and demands for enormous ransoms are heard everywhere; it's the same thing that happened in Iraq. One evening he sensed that he was being followed by a suspicious-looking man. When he went to the police, the man disappeared. His wife worked in the Ministry of Interior, she could have been assaulted while driving back and forth to work. They felt like human targets.

George believes that even though their leaders have declared loyalty to the regime, most Christians today are against Assad. Their situation is hopeless, he says.

"Whether or not the regime falls, Christians will be attacked. We will lose no matter what. I don't count on ever returning to Syria, because I'm a Christian. Life is dangerous for us in Syria. This is how many Christians like me think. We have a feeling that a much stricter regime is about to take over."

I ask George his opinion of the people presently in power. He laughs loudly and long.

"It's true that the regime in the past forty years has given us security, but it's a false security. We always had to be careful of what we say. One wrong word spoken on the phone and we disappear for ten, fifteen years. It was very seldom that Syrian Christians passed up an opportunity to leave Syria."

The regime has brainwashed its citizens, it has fooled them into thinking they are fighting for the Palestinian cause. "We've been living in a closed world," he says. "We haven't been allowed to open up to the West. We feel that we are lagging behind in every way. Sixty percent of Syria's economy is in the hands of President Assad's closest family. They raise the price of goods and lower the wages. Now the truth about Assad's regime has come out, and the next regime will only be worse. It's just like in Iran, they lived under a horrible regime before the ayatollahs came to power and made everything worse."

I ask him if he believes that the international community should come to the aid of Christians.

"Yes," he practically screams. "Christians in Syria feel more and more like strangers in their own country. I feel like Muslims look at me as if I don't belong anymore. Sooner or later we will be thrown out. The West should help us to get out of the country." George is unable to obtain a visa to leave Lebanon. He's stranded in Beirut.

I ask if he thinks the Church was mistaken to ally itself with Assad.

"The mistake was the Church even taking a political position. But their hands have been tied. The Church had to ally itself with someone, for the sake of protection.

Pastor Shadi Saad grants me an audience at a Starbucks a few days later. He is Lebanese, but for many years he worked in Syria. I want to know why Christians have allied themselves with a regime that everyone could see was brutal and oppressive.

"You have to remember that the Assad regime is built on an extensive network of agents," he explains. "Secret agents have attended services and taken notes on the sermons given by priests. One wrong word and a priest can end up in prison. Many people I know are aware of who the agents are in the congregation."

But the agreement between the Church and Assad was that as long as the Church didn't speak out about politics, a relative freedom would be granted. "And yet the regime interfered in everything the Church did. Also in Church politics. They decided who would be given the most influential positions. Assad's people elected church leaders. Naturally none of them have opposed the regime."

Now after the civil war, they're paying the price. Saad knows of two priests who have been liquidated. He knows of an entire family who were taken out and shot by Islamists and many others who have been kidnapped, especially in Aleppo. "This is definitely the greatest fear of Christians. Greater than the fear of not being able to provide for their families."

Saad has felt the oppression in Lebanon. "We have been occupied by Syria for thirty years. We know how it feels. We know what it feels like to have to whisper to each other. We have been raised to not say certain things publicly, to not write these things in letters or emails, not to speak about certain issues on the telephone. We know how it is to never be able to speak positively of the West. We know because of our Syrian friends how it feels to never be free to walk down the street and tell others what we believe. We know all about the constant fear of being thrown in prison because someone doesn't like you and has spread lies about you. We know the fear of disappearing forever, without our families ever finding out what happened to us."

The pastor says that the Syrian regime has planted a deep fear in the population, so deep that they have begun thinking the way the government wants them to. I ask how this fits with the image of a Syrian state tolerant to Christians. "Tolerant? What do you mean? Of course, the regime has given the Christian certain advantages, but if a Muslim converts to Christianity he will be killed, and the priest who performs the conversion will come under attack. What sort of tolerance is that?"

All the Syrian Christians I speak with are in Beirut. I want to meet a Christian living in Syria. From my Beirut hotel room I call Archbishop Yohanna Ibrahim in Aleppo, one of the cities hardest hit by the war, but he doesn't answer. After several days of trying to contact him, I give up. A few weeks later, while in Denmark, I find out that he is in Cyprus, and I call him again. We talk for a half hour. He tells me that Aleppo is a "dead city. Everyone is afraid. There is no work, no school, no gasoline." A third of the city's Christians have left, he says. "They have fled to Lebanon, Armenia, Europe."

He also says that he knows of more than 120 Christians who have been kidnapped, but he assures me that the Free Syrian Army, a group fighting Assad, isn't responsible. The kidnappers are Islamists from Pakistan and Afghanistan. They have also murdered Christians, some just because they are Christian.

Archbishop Ibrahim doesn't support Western military intervention. Nor does he think the West should arm the rebels. "It will only prolong the war," he says. "The only thing that can stop a bloodbath is peace negotiations."

I ask him what the future holds if Assad falls. He believes that if the rebels win, the Islamists will not take power. On that modestly optimistic note, I thank him for his time. He says I'm welcome to contact him whenever I wish.

On April 22, 2013, a month after we spoke, the archbishop and Bishop Paul Yazigi were kidnapped outside of Aleppo. Some reports claim they were doing humanitarian work in a town near the Turkish border, others have reported that they were trying to secure the release of two priests kidnapped two months earlier. For whatever reason, they were stopped by armed men who killed their driver. They are still missing.

Is this what is in store for Syrian and other Middle Eastern Christians? A new Iraq?

CHAPTER 4

Iraq

Why was Abdul Jabar killed? Why was he shot by masked men as he got out of his car at his home in Mosul, on a Sunday evening in April 2013?

Abdul Jabar, fifty-six years old at his death, is just another in a long line of Christians who either have been kidnapped or murdered in Mosul since 2003. But was he murdered because he was a Christian, or was he just in the wrong place at the wrong time? We will probably never know; these types of cases are rarely solved. Most people view the murder as a bloody prelude to the local elections held in Iraq a few weeks later. Since the war in 2003, it's been open season on Christians and many, many others around the country in the time leading up to an election. Several murders of politicians and innocent civilians took place in the weeks following Jabar's death. In April 2013 alone, 561 people died in terrorist attacks.

The day after the murder, I drive to Bakhdida, a large Christian town twenty miles outside Mosul, to attend Abdul Jabar's funeral. Here I find myself among those who have been considered outcasts during the past ten years of civil war. Of all the Arab countries I've visited, the persecution of Christians is without a doubt worst in Iraq, and as a result there's only one thing Christians in the country want: out. Mosul, the large city where Jabar grew up, has seen some of the most horrible murders of Christians. The situation is the same in Baghdad.

The church is only half full, and I sit on the aisle halfway to the front to be able to see Archbishop Nicodemus Daoud Matti Sharaf. The red-bearded, overweight man is holding a gold scepter, the top of which ends in two gilded rattlesnake heads. The open mouthed snakes are leaning away from a cross. A photo of Jabar has been placed on the lid of his coffin.

"The murderer is not the one who actually murdered Abdul Jabar," the bishop says in his funeral sermon. "The murderer is all those who convinced him to do it." He is sweating from the spring heat in this spacious marble church, and his voice is emphatic. "In five to ten years there will no longer be Christians in Iraq for them to murder, and when that happens they will begin murdering each other."

I'm embarrassed about intruding on this family's most private ceremony, and I recall the words often said about 9/11: Al Qaeda's act of terror changed the world. It's true, but the change happened first and foremost among the guests in this church who lived and are living in this country. Because for most people in the Western world, the change largely amounts to annoyances we have to endure when flying.

September 11, 2001 led to the invasion of Iraq in 2003, which in turn incited the country's motley uprisings and reduced the Christian population to an alarming level. No one knows exactly how many Christians lived here before the war, but estimates range from 1.2 to 1.5 million, approximately 4 percent of the total population. At present it's estimated that there are less than three hundred thousand Christians left, or 0.9 percent. This is nothing less than catastrophic.

After having spoken with countless Christian Iraqis, I understand why so many are leaving the country. I want to join them on the first flight home, even though I've never experienced such genuine hospitality and warmth as from the Christians I meet here.

While sitting in the church pew, I also take a good look at my own prior self-assuredness. I supported the Iraqi war, as I did the participation of my own country, Denmark, in the fighting that started ten years ago. A sectarian orgy of violence broke out after the collapse of the Iraqi regime; Sunnis and Shiites murdered each other, sometimes with the help of the country's ministries. And both groups hunted Christians, who were accused of being allied with the United States.

The past ten years have been chaotic for Arab countries, and if we use Christians as a seismograph for the rumblings these radical changes have caused, there isn't much reason for optimism. For those in this funeral procession, in this church, where a few mourners keep a suspicious eye on the foreign guest seated halfway down the aisle, the consequences of the war ten years ago might be the end of a two-thousand year Christian presence in this country.

During the worst period of attacks, the percentage of Christians fleeing was several times higher than that of Muslims. According to a 2008 report from the United Nations High Commissioner for Refugees, over 40 percent of all Iraqi refugees were Christians. That's an enormous percentage, considering that only 4 percent of the Iraqi population before the war was Christian—as mentioned; today it is closer to 1 percent.

The archbishop finishes his sermon and calls the family up to the coffin. The women shriek in agony. From the modest size of the wooden box, it's evident that the murdered man was small and thin. The lid rests a few inches above the lower portion of the coffin, held up by four nails pounded halfway into each corner. His closest relatives stick their hands in the gap to touch him one last time before the nails are hammered down.

A tearful young woman asks me to leave. I walk out the side

door and to the front of the church, from where I watch Abdul Jabar's coffin being borne on the shoulders of his three sons and three older men. They load it onto the back of a pickup, and it is driven through the potholed streets of the town to the cemetery.

• • •

On this trip to Iraq I have once more allied myself with a native of sorts. Amir Almaleh and his family have lived in Norrtälje, a town north of Stockholm, Sweden, since the early 1990s. He travels back and forth with me and accompanies me nearly everywhere I go in Iraq.

I met him through the helpful people involved with a Danish-sponsored project, International Media Support in Iraq. Amir runs one of the most popular websites for news about Christians in the Middle East, ankawa.com. He doesn't shy away from claiming it's not only the most popular, but the best. This trip convinces me that his confidence in the website is justified. He has connections in all the towns we visit, and he provides reliable information concerning everything I ask him about.

It's no coincidence that so much interest in Iraqi Christianity comes from Sweden. The country has taken in at least fifty thousand Iraqi Christians, Amir says, which is one of the largest concentrations outside of Iraq. The Swedish border is temporarily closed. Of all the Scandinavian countries, Sweden is currently the most restrictive in accepting Iraqi Christians.

Several days before Jabar's murder and funeral, I rented a hotel room in Amir's quarter, Ankawa, for which his website is named. Many exiled Iraqi Christians had returned home to participate in Amir's wife's sister's wedding, to which about a thousand people were invited. The entire quarter was filled with Swedish-speaking Iraqis. I've never spoken so much Swedish in my life; Amir laughed and said that I sounded like an immigrant. Finally we gave up on the Scandinavian languages and spoke English.

Ankawa is a Christian quarter in Erbil, a large Kurdish town in northern Iraq—or Kurdistan, as it's also called. Forty years ago, seven thousand people lived in the area, but today there are over thirty thousand, many of them refugees from Mosul and Baghdad. Several restaurants, hotels, clubs, etc., have opened in Ankawa within the past ten years. Numerous churches have also been established.

The same development is seen throughout Erbil. It's bursting at the seams; it's like a poor teenager who suddenly comes into money, with cranes everywhere, new malls, large gas-guzzling SUVs, hotels with reflective glass in strange forms.

Erbil's new airport also looks extravagant, even though the café there sells six-month-old copies of *The Economist*, with concise analyses of the Obama-Romney election of 2012. Kurdistan, which has enjoyed a form of autonomy since international forces established a no-fly zone there in 1991, obviously wants to become a new Dubai. And there is money to be made in this region. As Amir told me when we landed, there's so much oil underground that people hit pay dirt when burying the dead.

The archenemy to the north, Turkey, has invested significantly here. The only obstacle is the government in Baghdad, which won't let the Kurds get too many independent ideas; it demands that no new oil wells be drilled without its express permission. That doesn't seem to be holding the Kurds back. They have begun exporting oil, and Turkey is a willing buyer. A dangerously carefree and strong Kurdish nationalism is in the air, the type of self-confidence that has led to war in the past.

Amir tells me that almost everyone in Ankawa was communist when he was a boy. One of his brothers was arrested by Saddam's police in the 1980s during a demonstration, and he was executed shortly after. Amir himself belonged to a communist partisan organization for five years. Back then Kurdish rebels fought the Iraqi regime, and Amir was exposed to chemical weapons that killed thousands of people in the region. He remembers the yellow clouds hanging in the valley, how everyone covered their mouths with wet cloths and sought shelter in the mountains because the gas was heavier than air.

When the war against Iran ended in 1988, Saddam's forces were free to fight the decisive battle against the rebel groups to the north. Amir fled for his life, through the mountains and across the border to Iran. He waited there for a year and learned to speak Persian before he and a few others continued on to the Soviet Union. He spent two months in a Russian prison before being granted asylum in Sweden in 1991. Some people experience several lives in a single lifetime, and Amir is one of them. Today he calls himself a liberal, and he expects his three children to be Swedish in every respect. Immigrants must embrace their new country, he says.

I soon found out that Christians, despite feeling relatively secure in Ankawa, are uneasy about the Kurds. Erbil's airport is built on land that belonged to Christians, but Saddam confiscated it to use as a military base. After the fall of the regime, the Kurdish authorities expropriated the area; the Christians received what they considered to be extraordinarily low compensation.

After ten years of conflict, Christians mistrust their fellow Muslim citizens. Ankawa is approximately 80 percent Christian, and I'm told that Muslims are not permitted to build mosques there. This city has a large number of Christian refugees from other parts of Iraq, and little is being done to conceal the residents' disdain for Islam.

The Kurdish government has in fact supported the renovation of churches and permitted children to be educated in Syriac, the mother tongue of northern Iraqi Christians. The government even looks the other way when Muslims convert to Christianity. This hasn't created a sense of fraternity. Later I discover part of the reason why, though I have already detected a pang of envy: the Kurds are favored by the West at the expense of Christians, who like the Kurds consider themselves a nation. They belong to the Chaldean, Syriac, and Assyrian Church, also known as the Assyrian Church of the East. Throughout history their missionaries have been decisive in spreading Christianity to faraway parts of the Asian world.

Iraqi Christians don't think of themselves as Arabs or Kurds. They do consider themselves a nation and a religion, and many Christians want to be the boss in their own house. They dream of having their own country in the half-moon shaped area on the Nineveh plains northeast of Mosul, where a large number of Christian villages are located.

Such a development is nowhere on the horizon. On the contrary, the question is whether there will be enough Christians left for an autonomous region, and I'm interested in hearing why. What happened when Saddam Hussein was defeated? Why do Christians in other countries I have visited point to Iraqi Christians as an example of what could happen to them?

Amir takes me to see the newly elected young Archbishop Bashar Warda in his Ankawa church. We sit in the waiting room of his office until he receives us. He wears a black V-neck sweater over a white shirt with a mandarin collar. His pastoral staff rests against a dehumidifier, Easter eggs lay in a bowl on the coffee table. After the battles in the spring of 2003 ended, he says, a free market and a free press blossomed for a short while. In July 2003, however, the first terrorist attacks began. Christians were among those murdered in several Iraqi towns, almost always by unidentified killers.

The worst period began on August 1, 2004. During Sunday services that day, six churches were hit by coordinated attacks, five in Baghdad and one in Mosul. Bashar Warda's church was one of them. Twelve people were killed, seventy injured by car bombs in front of the churches, set to explode just as church-goers were leaving. This attack was condemned by everyone, including the most prominent Muslim leaders among Sunnis and Shiites, but the religious admonishments changed nothing. Kidnappings and murders increased.

Some church attacks came about because Christians were considered allies of Western forces. A few attacks can be traced to the fact that some Christians were rich, or at least thought to be rich, and others were simple robberies, committed by groups of thieves claiming to be Al Qaeda.

I learn quickly that the identities of these groups are a tangled web. It can be difficult to separate religious persecution from attempts at economic gain amid the tragic welter of cross-fire casualties, suicide bombings, spontaneous shootings, and massacres. This has been everyday life for Iraqis for over a decade, though persecution has fallen the past several years. It's certain, however, that one reason Christians are being kidnapped and murdered is because of their faith, and no matter what the motive behind their suffering, they are fleeing in great numbers. Much greater numbers than others, relatively speaking.

"It was a nightmare," Archbishop Warda says about the aftermath of the 2004 church bombings. "I watched my congregation fall apart. Every week I was visited by a Christian with a family member who had been kidnapped or killed. I was powerless. I couldn't give them work, I couldn't give them security. Everything got worse and worse."

In the ensuing civil war between Shiites and Sunnis, Christians were caught in the middle. In the Assyrian Church's Baghdad congregation alone, three thousand families dwindled to four hundred. Where previously the archbishop might perform three services on Sundays, barely enough Christians were living there for a single service.

"We didn't expect that Americans came to Iraq to protect the Christians," the archbishop says. "We're Christians, but we think of ourselves as Iraqis. We never asked for special treatment from the Americans. We just expected that the changes would be good for all Iraq. No one had foreseen that all this would happen."

He managed to handle life in Baghdad for almost two years after his church was bombed before fleeing north to Erbil and Ankawa. "A series of kidnappings took place in 2006, and one of the people whose ransom was paid and then was released told me that the kidnappers had mentioned my name. So I asked to be transferred."

His concern is understandable. Seventeen priests were murdered in Iraq from 2005 to 2008. From the summer of 2004 to the spring of 2013, seventy-two churches were attacked or bombed: forty-four in Baghdad, nineteen in Mosul, eight in Kirkuk, and one in Ramadi. Christians all over the country began receiving letters containing bullets. There was no mistaking the message. Others were threatened directly on the street, sometimes by police or soldiers. Graffiti on the walls of Baghdad and Mosul demanded that Christians leave.

"Today we still feel we can be attacked anywhere, any time," the archbishop says. All the Christians I meet say the same. This fear also explains the results of a survey published by International Media Support in the summer of 2013: 87 percent of the one thousand Christian Iraqis polled said they "always or sometimes" consider seeking exile. 40 percent of them want to leave Iraq because they feel "marginalized," 29 percent because of the lack of security. Only 11 percent answered that they wanted to leave for economic reasons. The survey also shows that 91 percent of them believe the Iraqi government is unable to protect them. 84 percent of them believe that it's either possible or certain that no Christians will be living in Iraq in ten years. 84 percent!

Were things better under Saddam Hussein?

"We learned to keep quiet," Archbishop Warda says. "Saying that life was better for us under Saddam would be naïve. He closed Christian schools and threw the Jesuit teachers out of the universities in the 1970s."

All schools were nationalized under the Baathist regime, which was a blow to the Christian churches that have existed for several centuries. The regime felt that Christian education was incompatible with Arab nationalism and also was a type of Western imperialism. Sectarian differences were to be erased; there would be no more Kurdish, Christian, Shiite Muslim identities. Education would form the Iraqi citizen in the fight against Zionism and imperialism.

After the first Gulf War in 1991, Saddam began ruling more from an Islamist perspective; at the end of the 1990s, for example, he banned the giving of Christian names to newborns.

"We felt like prisoners in this country," the archbishop says.

Christians like the notorious Foreign Minister Tariq Aziz were allowed in the Baath party only because of their complete loyalty to Saddam. "It was totally different in Syria, where Christians were a part of the regime as Christians," he explains. They were appointed to high posts in the military and management positions in the private sector. This didn't happen in Iraq.

But as in Syria, agents noted what priests said in church. After Saddam's removal, Bashar Warda found copies of several of his sermons in the intelligence service's archives, which were opened in the chaos after the war. He is pleased to say that he never paid lip service to the regime.

• • •

Amir takes me to his older brother's office. Dr. Saadi Al Malih is the Kurdish government's managing director for Syriac culture, a type of minister of culture for Christians in Kurdistan. He has written twenty-six books, both novels and nonfiction, and has translated books from Russian to Arabic. He became a writer at the age of seventeen. Like his brother, he speaks several languages and has moved back from Canada to establish a museum for Assyrian culture. Iraqi, Kurdish, and Assyrian flags stand on his desk.

When his brother leaves the office, a small man enters. I'm not allowed to reveal his name. He tells me about a "near relative," the Syrian Orthodox priest Paulus Iskander. It's one thing to read about how many Christians are killed or kidnapped, it's another to meet the people who live with the consequences. The crimes are given a face—one with a wild, wronged expression. It oozes permanent disgrace.

That we never learn the identities of the killers and kidnappers is part of these nerve-shattering years of mass murder. We don't know who they are or what they look like, these masked perpetrators; they slide messages under doors and send threats by SMS, and they are almost never arrested. We know only the victims; it seems as though Ankawa is brimming with them. One of these victims is sitting here in the office.

The sofa almost swallows the small man up. He explains that many of Saddam's former allies took up with Al Qaeda groups and headed for Mosul. In 2006 they wanted to rid the old Assyrian city of Christians, who were assumed to be an American fifth column. This is why they decided to kill the city's three most well-known priests. The effects of a few targeted assassinations would be maximal.

Six months before the murder of Paulus Iskander, he was told to close his church if he valued his life. He refused. On October 9, 2006 he was kidnapped. His family was told that it was revenge for Pope Benedict XVI's speech in Regensburg several weeks previous, construed as criticizing Islam for recruiting followers by violent means, which the pope contrasted to Christianity's use of words and common sense to persuade people to convert.

The kidnappers ordered the small man to make thirty posters with a message condemning the papal speech, and to put them up around Mosul. While he's telling me his story, I imagine him desperately pasting them on city walls, these posters denying his own church leader's words—words that the actions of the kidnappers confirm. This scene, this perverse irony, encapsulates the conflict between the West and Islamism.

When he hears that I am from Denmark, he asks me to tell my country to stop drawing caricatures of Mohammed. He says that it is hurting Christians in the Middle East. I've heard the same plea from people in Gaza, Egypt, and Lebanon. There is public sentiment among Middle Eastern Christians for outlawing it in the West.

It's hard to react in any meaningful way to this call for Western self-censorship while talking to the completely innocent victims of an act of revenge committed several thousand miles from illustrators in Denmark or the pope in Italy. It strikes me, however, that in addition to the priest in Mosul, the man across from me who ran around the city in panic, slapping up posters, was also a hostage during this terrible ordeal. Other Christians in the Middle East are hostages, too, when threatened and persecuted because of a drawing, a film, or a speech in a Western country. Stop criticizing Islam, or else the Christians will suffer, is the message to the West. I tell him this, but he doesn't understand. I don't want to spell it out for him. It's difficult to persuade people living with a pistol pointed at their heads.

He put up nineteen posters that day before being told it was enough. Then they demanded that the kidnapped priest convert to Islam. He refused. On October 12, they beheaded him. His arms and legs were also dismembered. The police found his body that evening on a street in an industrial area outside Mosul, with his head, legs, and arms arranged on his body. No one was ever arrested for his murder. No one knows who killed him. A large burial was held in Mosul despite threats that the church would be bombed if the family attended, but nothing happened. Christians were meant to be so scared that they wouldn't even dare attend the funerals of their own relatives.

A month and a half later, on November 26, 2006, a Protestant pastor, Mundher Aldayr, was murdered. On June 3, 2007, a Chaldean priest, Ragied Aziz Gannie, three deacons, Basman Yusuf David Al-Yousef, Ghassan Isam Bidawid, Wahid Hanna, and Hanna's wife drove off after Sunday services. Five hundred yards down the street, armed men stopped them and pulled them out of the car. They shot the men with machine guns. The wife was "allowed" to watch. Then they placed bombs around the bodies to prevent anyone from approaching. Explosives experts had to be called in to deactivate the bombs. As a consequence of these murderers and the gruesome attendant display, over half of Mosul's Christians fled, either to poorer Christian cities to the north or east or out of the country altogether.

And what about those who remained in the city? The small man reports that to avoid having their churches bombed the congregations began paying jizya, the Muslim head tax. "This means that the Church in Mosul has helped finance terrorism. Now the city's Muslims also pay protection money to the terrorists. They are a mafia. One Muslim told me that the terrorists take in six million dollars a month."

He himself ran an auto garage on a street with several other garages. They were told to pay jizya. They all refused. The garages were bombed soon after. "We condemn all Western countries for not helping us and not putting pressure on the Iraqi government to rescue us. We can't get asylum in Europe. This is disappointing."

That evening Amir and I meet another man with a story to tell. Rafi Dahan's mother serves us Turkish coffee and water at his home in Ankawa. His new home. In 2005, his family lived in Mosul on a street leading up to one of Saddam's palaces. That street was bombed incessantly.

We're here to talk about his father, Adnan Dahan, who earned a living selling automotive parts. One day he received a text threatening the entire family, and they moved to one of the neighboring villages. Every day Rafi rode the bus past their empty house on his way to the city's university.

Six months later they thought the situation had improved, and they moved back to Mosul. They were wrong. Adnan Dahan was kidnapped from their home in July 2007. He was released eight days later after the family paid five thousand dollars in ransom.

Three years later, on February 2010, he was taken again. This time no one called to demand a ransom. Seven days later he was found, shot in the stomach and face. Rafi had to be called to identify his father at the morgue.

After the first kidnapping he asked his father why they shouldn't seek asylum abroad. His father answered that Christians had built the civilization of this country. "The churches are here to serve us. We can't just abandon them. Who will keep them going?" No one was arrested for that murder, either. Rafi says that the first time his father was kidnapped, he was driven through a checkpoint manned by an Iraqi policeman.

"Look what we've got in the back seat, a Christian dog," one of the kidnappers said.

"God bless you," the policeman answered.

Rafi says that the second kidnapping of his father was also close to a checkpoint. The kidnappers fired guns in the air to celebrate their catch. The policemen did nothing. He has seen bombings, kidnappings, and murders out on the streets of Mosul every day. I ask him how this has affected him. "I know now that we are going to die a hard death," he answers.

The situation in Mosul improved for a brief spell, though even then, the quiet was relative: Fewer Christians were killed, fewer churches were bombed in Iraq. From 2003 to 2011, 841 Christians were reported killed, about 75 percent of them by unknown perpetrators. The worst years were 2004, 2007, and 2010. Estimates put the number of kidnappings in Iraq since 2003 at two thousand, though the majority of cases are never reported for fear of reprisals. Now of course, things are worse than even the most pessimistic Christians could have imagined.

As we are about to leave, Rafi predicts the murder of Christians will resume soon. With every approaching election Christians are killed, politicians are murdered, bombs explode everywhere, sectarian conflict is stirred up. Five minutes after his prediction, a text comes in on Amir's cell phone: a Christian has been shot in Mosul.

We attend the funeral the next day, a Sunday morning. The funeral of Abdul Jabar, in Bakhadi, about twenty miles southeast of Mosul, about an hour's drive west from Ankawa. I feel like an unwelcome guest as I listen to the archbishop speak about the forthcoming emigration of the entire Christian Iraqi population.

· · ·

To enter Bakhadi you have to pass both an Iraqi and, a few yards farther on, a Kurdish checkpoint. It takes an eternity to enter the town; suspicious but lazy officers flip through my passport before I'm allowed to pass through. The sun is shining. It's spring, it's dusty, and the town looks dirty and unkempt. The streets are in horrible shape.

This large village is officially outside the area of Kurdish autonomy, but Kurdish soldiers are stationed in many of the towns I visit on the Nineveh plains, Kurdish flags flying on their outskirts. The small autonomous region is experiencing growing pains, and the flailing Iraqi government has much to think about besides putting greedy Kurds in their place. I am told that the Kurds are financing the building of churches here and in the surrounding villages, thereby buying the loyalty of the Christians when the showdown comes.

Louis Markos Aube from the Iraq-based Hammurabi Human Rights Organization is a large man with a walrus mustache. We meet him in the church. He tells us that the Iraqi government is trying to force all Christians north, to the Nineveh region east of

Mosul and Kurdistan. They want all Christians out of Baghdad and Mosul. He explains that the poorest Christians can't afford to move, and many publicly employed Christians in the two cities feel unsuited for life in these villages, where there is very little work, life is primitive, and the economy is terrible.

After the funeral we visit an elderly lady from Mosul. She is wearing a black dress, worn by women who have lost those closest to them. We sit on plush sofas. The room is bare except for a photo on the wall of her husband and son. "Martyrs," they are called, and the photo shows them as such. In the background behind them is a dying Jesus wearing a crown of thorns, looking up plaintively at the sky. She has placed an olive branch on top of the frame.

Except for Jesus, the picture reminds me of my time in Nablus in the Palestinian Territories. I saw similar glorified portraits of dead sons and husbands—suicide bombers—in the homes of Palestinian Muslim families. Islamism has affected Christianity; it can be seen in the region's aesthetics.

The word "martyr" is used both in Islam and Christianity, but in different ways. The men in Muslim homes often have sacrificed themselves through violence for an Islamist or nationalist cause, sometimes taking others, including civilians, along with them into death. It's seldom that Christians do the same; their martyrs have been killed by others, they weren't murderers themselves. On the other hand, in homes like the one of this woman, there is an attempt to regard those murdered from a religious perspective: Her son and husband were sacrificed for their faith. They not only died because they were Christians; they died for Christianity. From the picture in her living room it seems as if she is comforted by this thought.

The woman's husband died first. He planned to rent out the shop he owned, and he went there for a few hours to take care of something. He never came home. Two days later his wife was told that she could pick up his body at the hospital. Nine days later her son went to the shop to see if he could learn anything about who murdered his father. He was shot there also.

"When my son died, no one came to the church," the mother sobs. "No one dared."

She moved to Bakhida, though she had no money and no job. The Christians in large Iraqi cities speak Arabic; in villages such as this they speak Syriac. She lived in a two thousand square foot house in Mosul, but this dilapidated concrete apartment is a fourth that size. The killing of her husband and son put an end to her prosperity and welfare. Moving from the big city of Mosul to this tiny, poverty-stricken village was like traveling back in time.

"They were killed because they were Christians," she says. "I know this because the only thing they took from them were their ID cards. That is how they proved it was Christians they murdered." It's well-known that Al Qaeda groups have paid for the murder of Christians.

The human rights activist with the walrus mustache takes us to an elderly couple in the village. The man, Taleh Matti, is wearing a green jogging suit; the woman, Nasran Aziz, a black skirt and brown-striped blouse. Two of their grandchildren, a boy and a girl, are visiting them.

Their loss is not only a story about them as Christians, but as Iraqis as well. If it were possible to distill all the past decades of misery into one family, this would be it. The first casualty was the oldest son. In 2004, at the age of twenty-one, he joined the Iraqi police force. He was killed when his squad ran into an ambush. After the war, insurgents began targeting national security forces, which have suffered enormous losses. "I told him he was an idiot to join the police, but he didn't listen," his mother says. Her son died for this country.

The next to be killed was the son's widow. Like tens of thousands of other Iraqis, she died because she was in the wrong place at the wrong time. She lived beside a police station that was attacked by insurgents in May 2005. A grenade meant for the station landed on her house.

The third, fourth, fifth, and sixth to be killed presumably died because they were Christians; the case has never been solved, therefore no one can be sure of the motive. They were the elderly couple's second-oldest son's wife, his mother-in-law and brother-in-law, and a female guest. While they were eating dinner at the mother-in-law's house, a group of terrorists broke in and shot them all. The two-year-old daughter of the guest crawled around among the bodies for several hours before a neighbor discovered the mass murder.

The bodies lay in the hospital morgue for three days. No one dared pick them up. Nor was anyone willing to risk their life by showing up at a funeral. Finally the son, now a widower, bought four coffins and drove to the hospital with a friend, picked up the bodies, and buried them.

The family left Mosul.

Two years ago the son, who had become a soldier and had been the target of a kidnapping attempt, was threatened with the extermination of the rest of his family if he didn't cough up twenty thousand dollars. He paid. Now this family, a synopsis of modern Iraqi life, has finally been left in peace.

• • •

We say goodbye to the family, and they wave to us from their house as we drive up the muddy street. The mother, who had done all the talking (the father in the jogging suit didn't speak a word), has her arms around her grandchildren. She looks animated; some people can survive anything without being defeated. We also part with the human rights activist and drive north out of the village, through the flat, fertile, green Nineveh region along the eastern side of the Tigris River. This is the original home of Iraq's Christians.

We arrive at a small monastery, Mar Oraha, which on this day happens to be holding its annual festival. The monastery is surrounded by Christian families sitting in plastic chairs on the grass, eating food they've brought along. They light candles in a side room of the church and place them against the sooty wall under a portrait of the Virgin Mary. Outside they dance in rows to music from a shrill trumpet, buy Christian knickknacks, plastic figurines, and other trinkets in the ramshackle booths.

Men and women walk hand in hand along the road. People are drinking beer and wine. After several days of hearing one gruesome story after another, I feel like lying down and dozing in the tall grass, listening to the buzz of happy people. It's a beautiful spring evening, the air is thick with pollen. We crawl up on the roof of the monastery and watch the sun go down in a yellow haze. A few kids have climbed all the way up on the cupola, a red cross looks down on the grounds as if it owns the entire area.

After we climb down, we meet a liquor store owner from the neighboring town. Someone had thrown a stun grenade against the wall of his store and shattered a window. He is certain it was a warning. "A yellow card," he says. He is thinking about heeding the warning and closing his store. He laughs nervously. "The Muslims in my town want to drink my alcohol, but they don't want me to sell it."

We drive in and out of villages where Kurdish soldiers are at their posts, even though the area isn't Kurdish. Soldiers are also standing at the outskirts of a large Christian village, Alqosh.

It's dark when we enter the town. We make our way to a large house and are invited inside by a writer, Yousif Zara. Several of his friends are there; many people mill around, it's as if we're in a train station. Zara is wearing large brown glasses and a blue suit and tie, his white hair is combed back. I sit down with him.

"For a thousand years there were no problems between Christianity and Islam," he says. "Then the war came along. Now Muslims want to throw Christians out of Iraq, and the government does nothing to stop them." He lived with his family in Baghdad until 2004, when his son was killed in a terrorist attack. Today there are several wars going on across the country, wars between Sunnis and Shiites, Kurds and Arabs, Christians and Muslims.

"There's an enormous amount of racism in these groups," he explains. He emphasizes that not all Arabs are evil, just as not all Christians are good, and that there's no sense in becoming a racist.

Zara asks if I'd noticed who was standing at the edge of town. He answers himself. "We are under Kurdish rule. Baghdad is our government in name only. But we are not free, no matter whether it's the Kurds or the Arabs in power." Nevertheless, this elderly writer believes the situation has improved in the past few years, and he is convinced everything will be better in another two or three years.

I sit beside his daughter, Sharara Yousif Zara. She's wearing a blue T-shirt and sandals. Besides being a politician, she holds an influential position in the Iraqi Ministry of Education. I relate to her what I was told in Egypt, that for several decades history books in schools mentioned nothing about Christians.

"It's the same situation in Iraq," she says. "There's almost nothing about us in our history books, and what there is, is totally wrong. There's nothing about us being here before Islam. The only Christians mentioned are from the West. Many Iraqis believe we moved here. From the West. That we are guests in this country."

The archbishop in Erbil, Bashar Warda, told me the same thing. He believes the hatred of Christians that has arisen in much of the Arab world has been nourished by this ignorance, and from the Christian perspective it has caused a split with the Muslims. Christians have no idea if they can be part of a country where the majority doesn't want them.

• • •

We walk around among the guests and say our goodbyes, then we drive out of Alqosh past the Kurdish guards and head north. Finally we reach the official border of Kurdistan. We look up one of the journalists who works for Amir's website. He has recently built a house in Dohuk, a Kurdish city in the mountains close to the Turkish border. The air is cooler here, the stars are out. A significant number of those living in this town of five hundred thousand are Christian. If Christians have a future in Iraq, it's here in Kurdistan. The Kurdish government apparently bends over backward to accommodate the needs of Christians.

The next morning, Amir's journalist takes us to the outskirts of the city, where several pink buildings have been built on the slope of a mountain. Many Christian refugees who have fled from the insanity of Baghdad and Mosul live here. Immediately we are surrounded by people who want to know if we can get them a job. A few of the women have put on an extra layer of makeup and are wearing their best clothes.

There's no way we can help them, so we duck into a small,

tin-roofed kiosk built from concrete blocks. The one-armed owner wears jogging clothes and sandals. He lost his arm in 2004 while buying a pistol in a market. Many markets with guns for sale popped up after the Americans disbanded Saddam's security forces; suddenly weapons were available everywhere. Beside him at the market, a man who had just bought a gun fired it in the air. A nearby U.S. Army patrol took it to be enemy fire, and they sent a barrage of bullets directly into the crowd. Many people died; the kiosk owner's arm was hit and had to be amputated. He believes there must have been poison in the bullet for it to go so badly. His sister was hit in the knee.

It only got worse for his family. Two of his brothers supplied fresh drinking water to the American forces for two years, until in 2007 insurgents captured them, drove them out of town, and killed them with electric drills. Six masked Islamists tossed their bodies in front of their houses. A note attached to the bodies claimed they were spies.

The one-armed man got out of Baghdad alive. He has much to thank the Kurds for. They gave him and his family a place to live. What is the problem? Should Christians not show gratitude? Is Kurdistan not a safe place for them?

We drive into the center of Dohuk to seek an answer to these questions. The city is overcrowded and ugly. A large, round Kurdish flag has been painted near the top of the highest mountain overlooking the city to show everyone who is in charge. Our plan is to have a look at a clubhouse for Christians that had been burned down. A metal door lying in the grass near the front lawn entrance looks as if it has been kicked down. We walk over it.

On December 2, 2011, hundreds of youths attacked liquor stores, tourist shops, hotels, casinos, hair salons, businesses, clubs, churches, and massage clinics. Common for all these targets is that they were considered to be part of a modern, decadent culture belonging to Christians or Yezidis, another religious group living in the region. Once probably as many Yezidis lived here as Christians, and they are every bit as tormented by religious intolerance.

The attacks began after prayers one Friday in the Al-Rashid mosque in a neighboring town, Zakho. The mosque's imam railed against the "un-Islamic" businesses in the Kurdish towns, and afterward he drove around in a car with a loudspeaker on the roof, inciting hundreds of youths in the streets. Everyone describes what followed as a well-planned and coordinated attack: businesses in six different cities were burned down that day. Two other towns came under attack, but local armed Christians managed to fight them off. The hundreds of rioters knew precisely which places to burn down. They were well-supplied along the way with Molotov cocktails and other weapons they could throw.

Had this happened in Europe, it would have been deemed a pogrom. I'm thinking about this as we walk through the yard and up the steps to the clubhouse. Broken glass from Molotov cocktails thrown through windows crunches under our shoes. Everything has been left as it was when the building was ruined a year and a half ago. Untouched, a mausoleum commemorating that day.

A trace of the social life here is still evident in the many blackened rooms. Playing cards, beer cans, political pamphlets, and soccer posters (FC Barcelona, of course) litter the floor, typical of male paraphernalia the world over. I spot an ash-covered shoe on a step, perhaps abandoned in haste.

We walk over to a nearby house where the former manager of the Christian clubhouse is sitting. Raid Jarvis, a big man wearing a black shirt and jeans, his hair combed back, tells us that when the demonstrations in the neighboring town of Zakho began, several hundred youths had already gathered. By the time the riots ended that night, the number had grown to several thousand. I recall the many towns in Egypt and Taybeh, the brewery town in the West Bank, and once more I wonder how anyone can round up so many and incite them to go amok.

"Obviously they knew their targets," Jarvis says. "Two beauty parlors next to each other, for example. One of them owned by a Christian, the other by a Muslim. Only the Christian's shop was destroyed." They also tried to attack churches in some towns, but both Christians and Muslims warded off the mob.

No one knows who was responsible, and that's odd when you think about the number of people involved. Radical Kurdish Muslims in Kurdistan's Islamic Union have been blamed, but no one I speak to is convinced. Many people noticed that the youths looked like most kids do, that they had no long beards like the Islamists. They also saw a Kurdish flag and a picture of the Kurdish president, Massoud Barzani, hanging on the wall of the only room in the clubhouse left untouched. Apparently something here wasn't to be destroyed.

"I don't know where this group comes from," Jarvis says. "But I do know they were organized. They shouted Islamic slogans. Some of them wore cloths around their heads with Islamic slogans written on them, but I'm still not sure who organized it all."

At one in the morning they arrived in Dohuk, where many Kurdish soldiers had taken positions. Raid Jarvis called the club's guard, who told him to leave. He wouldn't stand a chance against the mob. Later the club was attacked from all sides and set on fire. The firemen who arrived to put out the fire were also attacked. The police could do nothing.

"Many were arrested later on," he says. "Most of them were teenagers. No one was punished." He adds that the Kurdish government subsequently compensated the Christians. The amount was a fourth of the clubhouse's value. The Kurdish Islamist headquarters was also burned down that evening; no one knows who did it, though the authorities accused young Christians bent on revenge. The Christians I talk to say the same crowd who had burned down all the Christian businesses was responsible.

The theory is that the Kurdish government needed a reason to punish and thereby get rid of the Kurdish Islamists, who were considered a threat to Kurdistan's stability. The leaders of the Kurdish government organized the attacks, using Christians as an excuse to come down hard on the radical Muslims. Three days before the attack, Kurdish security forces supposedly had tracked down the addresses of all the businesses that were victimized. Whether that's true, whether it's just another of the conspiracy theories rampant in the Middle East, we will probably never know, Jarvis says. "This is Iraq, not Denmark."

I say that this explanation sounds grotesque to me.

"What is grotesque to you and your country is not grotesque here."

The explanation is supported by the Iraqi human rights organization, Hammurabi, which has investigated the episode. According to them, the imam whose sermons set the wheels in motion belonged to the Kurdistan Democratic Party, led by President Barzani. According to people I spoke with, his regime uses methods differing only slightly from those used by Saddam Hussein.

True or false, this explanation shows how suspicious Christians are of the Kurds, who claim to be protecting them. And it does seem odd that no one has been arrested and tried, given that over one thousand people took part in the riots and that the imam and his aides are on YouTube. Barzani has formed a committee to get to the bottom of what happened. Christians and Yezidis are still awaiting the results.

We leave Dohuk and drive on to the entirely Christian town of Shioz to meet Thamir Marogi. He wears a short-sleeve purple shirt, his black hair is well groomed. We meet him in front of the church just inside the village. He points back at the long, straight stretch of road we have just driven. On that December day in 2011, he says, seven hundred cars came down that road with enraged teenagers screaming "Allahu Akbar."

"We heard what had happened in the other towns, so we hid in our houses. A few Kurdish politicians came earlier and said they would protect us, but people here didn't believe them. People believe these politicians are on the side of those who attacked us." He points at a big barn with a large store of alcohol; the rioters had burned a previous barn on the site to the ground. They also tried to attack the church, but the village had placed guards at its entrance. The church was saved.

"The kids were armed, and police cars were following along, but our guards held them off. We called the Kurdish police, but they didn't show up for four hours. By that time the kids had left."

We follow him back to his small house and are invited into his living room. His wife serves us orange-flavored water, and his two daughters come in and sit on his lap.

"Two days later," he says, "the village decided that all the men must buy illegal weapons, so we can protect ourselves if this happens again. Before there were maybe ten people in the village with such weapons. Now there are hundreds. All Christian towns have done the same. We don't trust the government to protect us."

He lowers his daughters off his lap and walks out. He brings back his Kalashnikov, which he loads and hands over to us. "We bought this without a license. It cost three hundred dollars, but now the price is double because so many people want to buy them."

I ask him to come outside with me so I can photograph him in front of their clothesline. Children's pajamas, bras, dish towels, underwear, and a father holding a loaded Kalashnikov. Carrying the gun seems to have changed him; at first his expression is ironic, as if he can't take the role of middle-aged village warrior seriously, but then he straightens up. His posture is erect, his demeanor serious.

Back in the living room, he lays the gun down beside him on the sofa. He laughs apologetically and lets his girls crawl up onto his lap again. "Ten families or so in our village left the country after the riots. I thought about doing the same with my family."

Before we leave, he says that no Muslims live in the village, that the villagers have an agreement to never sell land or houses to Muslims. This isn't the first time I hear about such an arrangement. Keep Muslims out of the village; don't sell property to them; never trust authorities; Christians themselves must protect their villages. Christians in Iraqi Kurdistan feel strongly that the Muslims around them, the people they have lived with for generations—that includes the youths with Molotov cocktails, the Kurdish police, even President Barzani—are all in cahoots with each other. Christians regard them as enemies, to be kept out at all costs.

• • •

We drive back to Alqosh. Before sundown we want to take a look at a certain building, evidence of a people who once lived in this country. Their presence ended abruptly sixty-five years ago.

Nahum, an Old Testament prophet, is said to be buried here. A synagogue has been built around the grave. The Jews of the town attended the synagogue for centuries—and Jews from all over the country made pilgrimages here—before being driven out in 1948.

The grave still exists; it's covered by a green cloth. But the synagogue building is falling apart. Parts of the roof have collapsed, and walls are piled up in corners illuminated by sharp sunlight. An iron cage is all that keeps the stone and chunks of roof away from the grave. Old oil lamps hang from rusty hooks on columns, and fading Hebrew texts are etched on plates set into the wall. Biblical messages for a congregation long since gone.

First the Assyrians forced Jews out of Israel in the eighth century B.C. into what today is Iraq, then the Babylonians did the same two centuries later. It is believed that Jews have lived in Alqosh and the rest of the country since then. Around the time of World War One, a third of the population of Baghdad was estimated to be Jewish. The first Iraqi minister of finance was Jewish. It is believed that the first Christians in the region came from among the Jews.

I see traces of blue paint on the portal leading to the garden surrounding the synagogue. Its form looks like the azure-blue impression of a hand; I've seen many of these— *hamsas*, they're called, meaning five, for the fingers of the hand—on limestone doorways in the Jewish quarters of the Jerusalem. They are meant to ward off evil spirits. It didn't work here.

After the birth of Israel in 1948, Iraq entered the war against the new country. Zionism was forbidden, all Jews employed in the public sector were fired, and a number of anti-Semitic laws were passed. The Iraqi prime minister announced: "The Jews have always been a source of evil and harm to Iraq. They are spies." About 120,000 Iraqi Jews fled the country in those years; everything they owned was confiscated by the state. Whereas Jewish persecution more or less ended in Western Europe after World War Two, it continued in the Middle East and is still evident today.

Before we leave I am asked to sign the guest book kept by the man with the key to the synagogue. The book contains messages written in various languages, including Hebrew. In Danish I write that this synagogue should be taken care of, that it represents several thousand years of Jewish presence. I don't write what I'm actually thinking: that anti-Semitism is widespread in the Arab world, also among the Christians I've met there, and that Christians in this village should restore the synagogue in consideration of what might happen to them.

• • •

On the evening before I leave for Baghdad, I'm invited to the wedding of Amir's wife's sister. His cousin Khaldo, who besides enjoying Cuban cigars and Chivas Regal owns an exclusive Lebanese restaurant in Erbil, has loaned me a pin-striped black suit jacket so I don't show up in my dusty journalist outfit.

A grouchy Chaldean priest scolds the bride; for several years she belonged to the Evangelical Church in Iraq, which is involved in converting Muslims to Christianity. They are despised for this, also by Christians in the Arab countries, some of whom compare what the evangelicals do to what Al Qaeda groups have done to Iraqis the past decade, as if terror and religious freedom are in the same category. They are accused of upsetting the delicate balance between Muslims and Christians.

When the ceremony is over, several men in Amir's family

want to beat up the priest. The bride looks unhappy as she and her impractical white silk gown are helped outside into the rain, then over to several parked cars. We are driven a short distance to the enormous hall where hundreds of invited guests gather. The tables are decorated with Jack Daniels Black distilled in Jordan; all my Ankawa friends ignore the whiskey and make some calls for better quality Western wares. A DJ plays "I Will Always Love You," filtered through a confused, sobbing synthesizer before a power failure cuts off the lights and music. The generator is soon up and running, and it all starts up again. The electricity continues to go out, to the guests' somewhat bored, here-we-go-again amusement. When it happens, we turn on the flashlights on our cell phones and continue our conversations in the glow until the generator kicks on again.

Hundreds of entangled wires dangle threateningly from telephone poles near pedestrians on the sidewalks. The government of this oil-rich country can't seem to maintain a steady supply of electricity; in some places it's interrupted several times a day. Every district has a generator that all houses are allowed to plug into, if they're willing to pay for it. The electrical infrastructure is like everything else in Iraq: No one trusts the authorities, and if you want service, you have to arrange for it yourself. This has become so common that no one lets it annoy them.

I sit beside a businessman I met the day before. I told him I was going to Baghdad, and he replied half-jokingly that he would make sure my ransom was paid if I was kidnapped. Everyone I talk to thinks I'm crazy to go there. They try to scare me away from it. And even though I know very well that more people are killed in the daredevil Arab traffic than by terrorism, I punch in the businessman's number on my cell phone, just in case.

Solaqa Polis is aristocratic and relaxed. He lived in Baghdad for over thirty years, and he believes that Iraqi corruption is one of the major reasons why no one can stand living in the country. In 2012, Iraq was number 169 out of 176 countries on Transparency International's annual list of corrupt countries. The Iraqi government has been called an "institutionalized kleptocracy."

I hear about prisoners who are found not guilty, and yet they have to pay to get out of prison. I hear of government ministers who set up dummy corporations abroad and arrange to receive enormous orders from the government worth billions of dollars. Since 2003, seven billion dollars should have been spent on Baghdad sewers that either don't work or don't exist.

"The Baath party corrupted Iraqis," Polis says, "but American actions provoked the corruption. When they disbanded the security forces after the war, Iraqis were free to plunder and kidnap people. It hasn't been possible to do anything about this mentality."

The businessman also explains that this—together with American-approved Article 2 of the Iraqi Constitution of 2005 stating that Sharia law forms the Constitution's foundation—makes it difficult to imagine that genuine democracy and human rights will ever be established in Iraq.

"Democracy can't be based on Islam or corruption," he says.

Besides, Iraqis vote for politicians who belong to their own group. That goes for Christians, too. "If faced with choosing between a corrupt Christian and an honorable Muslim politician, Christians will vote for the Christian. Everyone thinks in a sectarian way." The same sort of corruption and sectarian mentality exists in Kurdistan, he explains. It can't be called democracy.

He was kidnapped in Baghdad in 2005 and held captive for five days. The people holding him demanded 1 million dollars, but the amount was negotiated down to 170 thousand. "I wouldn't wish that on my worst enemy," he says. "They kidnapped me in the name of God. What kind of God is that?"

The wedding guests have begun dancing. Many people stand in a long row, holding each other's pinkies as they move around in a circle to Iraqi music. I want to get in on it, but a man sits down beside me.

Fawzy also doesn't understand why I'm going to Baghdad. His face is craggy and his eyes penetrating, and he grabs my arm and tells me how horrible the Islamists have been. He nearly laughs as he tells about the assault on his own family, as if they were the victims of some crazy joke.

Fawzy comes from the capital, but he had to flee with his family after a long period of constant anonymous threats. He left his house in the care of a Muslim neighbor he considered an old friend. The house is on Palestine Street in one of Baghdad's better districts; he says the house is worth nine hundred thousand dollars.

The friendship wasn't as genuine as Fawzy and his family believed. His neighbor moved into the empty house and has no intention of giving it back. He warned Fawzy that he would be killed if he returned to Baghdad to sell the house. That threat had to be taken seriously. Many people have lost their lives in efforts to keep their fortunes intact. I'm told about an elderly couple who returned to Baghdad from Kurdistan to sell their house; they were found inside on the floor, murdered. The killers had carved crosses on their bodies with a knife.

Fawzy's neighbor offered to buy the house for two hundred thousand dollars, seven hundred thousand less than its value. Fawzy refused the offer. Now he is convinced that his ex-neighbor is the one who made the threats. He grabs my arm again to help me understand what this type of experience does to people like him. "What sort of person steals his neighbor's house? How do you think this makes me feel about Muslims?"

His two daughters, aged fourteen and sixteen, come over and try to teach me the Apostles' Creed, which I'd never bothered to learn in Danish. They go over it with me word by word in Aramaic, the language Jesus spoke. If I'm going to recite this creed, it will be in this country in this language among these people.

Then I manage to free myself from the horror stories of a decade of Christian persecution and dive into a night of dancing with Amir's family and all the hundreds of others in the ocean of the dance floor. The Arabic music is circular, it comes in wave after wave, and I gladly lay aside my plans for tomorrow. It's as if all of Ankawa is here in the circle, like a giant throbbing jellyfish, zooming into the center and out again.

• • •

The next morning I rise early, drive to Erbil Airport, and fly to Baghdad. It's a short flight to another world. Christians in the Arab world consider Baghdad to be the modern epicenter of persecution; it's estimated that as many as 75 percent of the Christian population has left the city. It also happens to be ground zero for all other Iraqis, though no other group can match the extent of Christian flight. Over one hundred and twelve thousand civilians are thought to have lost their lives in Iraq since 2003, half of them in Baghdad.

On the plane, I sit beside a woman wearing a veil who works in the Ministry of Construction and Housing. She tells me that while foreign investment is helping rebuild and modernize other cities, currently no one dares invest in the capital. For over a decade, Baghdad has been collapsing.

I'm here to meet a man who fascinated me the very first time I heard about him. Andrew White has been a priest in the Anglican Church in Baghdad since 2002, and he has written several books about his life in this maelstrom. One of the book covers shows him smiling beatifically while wearing a bulletproof vest. There is something death-defying, moving, and crazy about this man, and I want to meet him and find out just what it is.

Andrew White promised to have me picked up at the airport and taken to his residence in the middle of Baghdad. He has spoken to authorities to expedite my path through the endless bureaucracy, and I have no problems at the airport. Obviously he can pull strings.

A car picks me up outside the terminal and drives the three miles to a checkpoint, the actual entrance to the airport. For security reasons you must have a special permit to drive all the way up to the airport, which means that most people get out here and are fleeced by the security guards before being allowed to enter or leave—Iraqi corruption begins at the airport.

I'm met there by Daoud, White's adopted son; the priest found the then-ten-year-old runaway behind an American tank. When the American soldiers learned that Daoud was Christian, they handed him over to White, who has taken care of him ever since.

Daoud sits in the spacious car's front seat beside the driver, and I'm alone in back. A large white Toyota pickup is parked in front of us with four Iraqi soldiers inside, while two more wearing orange sunglasses sit in the back to keep watch on the road behind us. All of them are heavily armed; I notice SWAT is written above their bulletproof vests. They are my escort into Baghdad. The drivers floor it, and quickly we're racing one hundred mph down the freeway. The soldiers in the Toyota wave all other cars aside with their guns. I leave my seat belt unbuckled in case I need to get out of the car fast. I lean over toward the middle of the back seat, as if that would help if something happened. Will our formidable protection stop an attack or attract one? I'm not certain.

American forces call the road to the airport "RPG Alley," because driving on it during the first years of the war was extremely dangerous. Today large concrete plates alongside the road absorb the brunt of attacks, which on this stretch are rare nowadays. On the way I wonder if the priest, who is aware of the media's attraction to the dramatic, has staged this arrival.

Ten days later, two car bombs kill three people at the airport checkpoint. The bombs are part of several simultaneous coordinated attacks throughout the country that kill sixty-two people. It's another sign of an upcoming election. Clearly this route is still dangerous.

We enter the narrower streets of the city, and we fly through red lights and past all the many checkpoints in the city. It's Friday, the Muslim holy day, and traffic is sparse; what on any other day would have taken us an eternity goes quickly. At last we reach the center of Baghdad, which is practically deserted. We turn off on a street and stop in front of a large security checkpoint. The soldiers in the Toyota leave us, and a few other soldiers check our car. Then we drive behind the building and in through an iron gate to the Anglican church.

The military calls this area the Red Zone, the part of the city outside the four-square-mile Green Zone where the Iraqi government and the U.S. embassy are located. The Green Zone is also where most non-Iraqis live; as a rule, most people there don't stray outside the zone's barriers.

This church in the Red Zone is also completely surrounded

by protective walls. Probably no other church in the world is so well-guarded. Andrew White steps out and greets us heartily.

"So ... now ... you ... are ... in ... Baghdad," he says, tasting every word, with a teasing undertone of British sarcasm. He knows what effect this type of military escort can have on travelers.

Beside the church fortress are the ruins of the Iraqi National Theater, a skeleton of rusty iron and crumbling walls. It's been this way since 2003. After greeting him, I ask if the theater was bombed by Americans.

"It ... was ... bombed ... by ... us, my Danish friend. Ussss!"

He glares at me, then breaks out laughing.

Andrew White is a giant of a man. Enormous and round in every way. His face is like a globe, his glasses are round, his nose round, his cheeks round when he smiles. He has the biggest feet I've ever seen. He looks like an overgrown child. He also has a loose-jointed appearance, which stems from multiple sclerosis. He uses a cane to walk and prefers sitting down. Here in Baghdad he is like a Gulliver in an evil version of Lilliput.

Immediately he steers me to a modest monument in a small garden alcove fronting the church. It's the only monument there. At the top is a quote from John the Baptist inscribed in marble: "Jesus said: I am the resurrection and the life. He who believes in me will live, even though he dies; and whoever lives and believes in me will never die."

Underneath is the name, rank, unit, age, and date of death of the eight Danish soldiers who fell during the war in Iraq:

Pfc. Preben Pedersen, Jutland Dragon Regiment, 34, Killed in action, 16 AUG, 2003

1LT Bjarke Olsen, Jutland Dragon Regiment, 22, Killed in action, 1 OCT, 2005

PVT Jesper Nielsen, Royal Life Guards, 20, Killed in action, 23 MAR, 2006

Pfc. Dennis Ove Hansen, Signal Regiment, 23, Killed in operations, 6 JUN, 2006

FLSP Kim Wadim, Air Force, 36, Killed in action, 23 SEP, 2006

PVT Martin Hjorth, Jutland Dragon Regiment, 20, Killed in action, 5 OCT, 2006

PVT Henrik Nøbbe, Jutland Dragon Regiment, 20, Killed in action, 14 MAY, 2007

OF-3 Johnny Mikkelsen, Naval Operations Command, 51, Killed in operations, 22 JAN, 2008

The memorial was dedicated in May 2008. The Danish ambassador at the time, Bo Erik Weber, participated in the ceremony. Three wreaths from the Royal Danish Embassy, Defence Command Denmark, and the Danish Defence Protection Team in Baghdad were placed in front of the monument. White's Iraqi church choir had learned the Danish national anthem, "There Is a Lovely Country"—in Danish, of course. He can still remember some of the first verse, which he sings for me. I ask why there isn't a monument honoring the British soldiers who were killed. Andrew White has a special fondness for Denmark. And that's why.

He follows me into the wing of the church where I am to spend the night. We sit down on a large leather sofa. An elderly woman in the kitchen is preparing lunch. Daoud, the boy who picked me up at the airport, would like time off to buy shoes for his sister. He is given permission.

White says he has been in Iraq since 1998. The church congregation back then was exclusively Westerners living in Baghdad. After the war, it quickly became too dangerous for Brits and other foreigners to leave the Green Zone. "They stopped coming," he says. "Instead, Iraqis began to show up."

He discovered that they needed food, medical care, and a decent education. He began distributing food once a week, and he has built a modest-sized dental/medical clinic, not only for Christians but for everyone. He has also built a modest school; he shows me the small, colorful chairs.

He began establishing connections to all the leading figures in Iraq, including those with blood on their hands. Former Iraqi Foreign Minister Tariq Aziz, for example, who was then on death row in prison—though his sentence was commuted to life without parole, essentially. Andrew White visited him the week before I arrived. The priest also met with Saddam Hussein twice. And he is in contact with some of the most brutal Muslim leaders on both sides of the conflict; he does this, he says, to try to convince them to leave Christians alone.

While walking back inside, we pass by a man with a crew cut watering the lawn. He's wearing a Danish national soccer team jersey. "No one has saved as many lives as Denmark," White says, when we return to the church annex. The British priest is talking about two conferences held in Copenhagen in 2008 and 2011, to which both Sunni and Shiite Muslim leaders were invited. The latter meeting occurred after the most violent of all terrorist attacks on Christians, at the Syriac Cathedral in Baghdad on October 31, 2010. Fifty-eight people lost their lives, over one hundred were taken as hostages.

"After this act of terrorism in the church, there was really only one country who helped—Denmark," he says. White believes the meetings were a breakthrough. For the first time, a joint Shiite and Sunni Muslim fatwa was formulated, forbidding the murder of minorities. He claims that after the conference, Christians were murdered less frequently. "It was a momentous event. It worked immediately. The murder of our people ended that day because of the fatwa and the Danish people. At the risk of sounding pathetic, it was a question of life and death. Your country saved us. We will never forget that."

I quickly discover that Andrew White is a man who believes that exaggeration promotes understanding, and that's probably the case concerning the Danish efforts to help Christians in Iraq. I've asked Christian Iraqis such as the archbishop in Erbil, Bashar Warda, and Amir, who writes daily about events in the country, if they have heard anything about the conferences in Copenhagen and the joint fatwa having major consequences. They haven't. On the contrary, they dismiss the contention that these conferences promoting dialogue between Christians and Muslim leaders have had any effect on what's happening on the streets.

"It's always Christians who must take the initiative, never Muslims," the archbishop said when we spoke in Ankawa. "And should I arrange such a conference, I would also invite my Muslim friends, the ones I know will be friendly to me. The imams who show up at these conferences aren't the ones we need to convince."

I give White the archbishop's answer.

"There are some people who can't be engaged," he says. "Al Qaeda isn't interested in reconciliation. But we might be able to engage the Sunnis who otherwise would support Al Qaeda. We stopped the major terrorist attacks, but the murders and kidnappings continue. We bus most Christians to our church. They are still being assaulted."

We eat lunch. He nibbles on some overcooked vegetables and bread. He says he eats only one small meal a day, but he's big anyway, possibly because of the tea biscuits served to him all day long. Even though there's a slight air of megalomania about him, I can't help being moved by the fact he is even here in this city. After lunch I fall into conversation with his twenty-year-old assistant, Lina. Even though she calls the priest "Daddy," she is a surrogate mother to him. She makes sure he gets enough rest, arranges his schedule, serves him tea and biscuits, teases him about being so messy.

"I've seen nothing but war in Baghdad," she says, as we sit in the priest's office. "As Christians we live under the constant threat of attack, even when it comes to the smallest things. Just going out requires three days of preparation. In school my Muslim teachers and classmates often ask me why I stay in the country. I tell them that we are the roots of this country. 'Not any longer,' they say."

To her it feels as if the Christians are strangers in their own country. I hear these words again and again during my travels: strangers in their own country.

"We've received so very many threats. I know life shouldn't be like this, because I've traveled abroad and I know how people live in other places. But here in Baghdad I've seen all the horrible things a person can see."

After a massive bomb exploded by the wall surrounding the church, she went outside and helped the wounded. One hundred and sixty-three people died, including a few churchgoers.

The bomb was most likely meant for a member of the government about to drive by, not for the church. Back then Andrew White lived in the Green Zone; it was too dangerous to be close to the church.

"When I see someone get killed, it doesn't affect me anymore," Lina says. "My heart is used to it. I'm not afraid to die." She has worked for the priest for several years, but now she is in doubt as to why she stays.

"I said to Daddy, 'You always want people to stay in Iraq, and I also want to give people a reason to stay, but I can't find that reason any more.' Daddy says we have to stay because God wants us to. But I stay because my family is here. If Daddy leaves, I will leave, too."

White, who is listening to the conversation, says that it's not only Christian Iraqis leaving Baghdad. The coalition, the countries that took part in the war in 2003, is on its way out. That includes Denmark. "The Western world is in the process of abandoning us. The Danish embassy has moved. There will still be a Danish embassy for Iraq, but it will be located in Copenhagen."

The Danish embassy was in fact closed in July 2012, and has been replaced by a so-called "traveling ambassador." The American government pulled its troops out in December 2011.

"There is no coalition, not any longer, " White says. "Their influence on the events in Iraq is insignificant. If you had asked me four years ago about the future of Iraq, I would have been optimistic. No more. It's unlikely there will be any Christians in this country in ten years. They will all be gone."

He says that Denmark did the right thing during the war, but they should stay. Otherwise things will just get worse, not only for Christians but for all minorities.

"The only country that has done something for us is Denmark. That's why it is very sad that you have abandoned us. Now it's getting worse again. We need a new Denmark."

After our conversation, the soldiers in the Toyota are summoned. We are going to visit a poor Christian family on the other side of the river. As before, the pickup with six soldiers leads the way. They are wearing balaclavas now, they don't want to be recognized.

Again we drive at breakneck speed, this time through the center of the city, past the outer walls of the Green Zone and several checkpoints, then across the Tigris. Concrete walls line the streets here, too, to prevent roadside bombs and rocket attacks. In the rearview mirror I notice our driver's eyes darting around, he's sweaty and nervous and enraged that his car can't keep up with the soldiers. He is trembling. Often there's enough space between us and the soldiers for other cars to squeeze in. A few pointed gestures by the soldiers with their guns is enough to drive them off.

Baghdad has been split into sectarian districts, which also are divided by concrete barriers to prevent militant Sunnis and Shiites from going at each other's throats. Though sectarian violence has fallen in the past few years, dozens of Iraqis are still killed every day from roadside bombs, terrorist attacks in cafés and markets, random shootings, and assassinations attempts often directed at politicians, police, and soldiers. And now in the spring of 2012, the violence is beginning to mount again.

A website, www.iraqbodycount.org, calculates the number of daily murders in Iraq, as if it were the pollen count. A random week in April 2013 looks like this: Monday—three; Tuesday—seventy-one; Wednesday—thirty-two; Thursday—eighteen; Friday—twenty-eight; Saturday—eleven; Sunday—twelve. Forty of these 175 murders happened in Baghdad.

Peace has yet to come to Baghdad, to say the least. The major city of Iraq is splintered, damaged, weakened, unable to exercise authority. The country's head has been separated from its body, but we don't hear so much about that nowadays. It's as if the Western media has given up on any comprehensive reporting in this country that for many years divided the general public throughout the world, cost thousands of Western soldiers their lives, and spawned many large demonstrations. Vicious, traumatic debates have taken place, nationally as well as within families, while presidents and prime ministers have been praised, reviled, and removed from office. It feels like all this happened a long time ago. Leaving Baghdad seems to have been easier for the West than being abandoned has been for Iraqis.

We arrive in the district where the family lives. Goats and sheep are grazing and eating garbage on the streets. One of the leading oil producing countries in the world has done nothing to alleviate the conditions in this slum. And it wasn't ruined during the war. Both vehicles drive down a narrow alleyway; a gutter in the middle of the road acts as an open sewer. We stop outside a small building. The soldiers hop out holding their guns and peer anxiously in all directions before we enter the family's home.

A cheerful, toothless old woman with gray hair bristling in every direction greets us. An overweight woman lies on the floor in front of the television; she rolls over and gets to her knees, takes Andrew White's hand, and kisses it. A few chickens scratch around in the kitchen. A skinny old man sits expressionless on a wooden bench, his cap pulled down over his half-closed eyes. The television blares. The place is small, dirty, and messy. We could almost be in the lobby of a mental hospital from days gone by; the six or seven people living here seem somewhat intellectu- ally challenged. They tell him they are doing fine, the neighbors are helping them. They are obviously deeply honored to be visited by the priest.

He wants to pray with them, so they all stand up and hold hands as he recites a prayer in Arabic. When he finishes, he gives them two hundred dollars and we leave; the entire visit took ten minutes. A Christian family has received economic and spiritual aid, and we have been escorted by soldiers as if we were visiting an important minister or arresting terrorists.

We drive by several Iraqis playing soccer behind a barbed wire fence, past garbage-strewn squares and churches hidden behind barriers, then across the Al Jumariyah Bridge, where we can see the English church's neighbor, the big, ugly Al Mansour Hotel. We follow the Tigris.

In the car, the priest asks me which faith I belong to. None, I answer.

"I've never met a totally secular person, someone unaffiliated with a religion. That's a Western thing. It doesn't exist here."

An odd silence follows, as if he doesn't quite know what to do with me. "You can see the enormous amount of damage religion has done in this region," he finally says. "When religion goes wrong, it goes very wrong. But if religion is the problem, it must follow that religion can solve it."

Church services for a few dozen Iraqi children take place when we get back. White announces that they have a guest from Denmark.

"We like people from Denmark, don't we?"

"Yes," they answer in unison.

I feel obliged to stand up from the pew and bow on behalf of my country. In his sermon he says, "We have lost everything, but not Jesus."

After the services, sandwiches and soda are served in front of the church. Darkness has fallen. A small fountain sprays water over the Danish monument; water runs down over the names of the fallen soldiers. Lights from the church reflect off the wet marble. The only sound is the running water; the city is silent. Nothing like the normal buzz you expect to hear in a metropolis of some seven million people.

The English priest finally gets to sit down in a chair. Three soldiers stand behind him, but they disappear when I take photos. I begin speaking with an elderly Iraqi man, Ra'at, who is wearing a burgundy-colored shirt. Because St. George's Episcopal Anglican Church itself has no bells, it is Ra'at's job to call churchgoers to services. I sit down in the doorway with him. He says he has lived in Baghdad his entire life, and it has never been as bad as in the past ten years.

"Everyone has left to get away from this terrible life. We are killed and persecuted, and our churches are being attacked. We feel they don't want us here." He tells about the events of March 18, 2004. He was sitting at home with his children, two sons and three daughters, watching TV in his living room. A volley of bullets burst through the window. Two of his children sitting by the window, a son and a daughter, were hit in the neck and died instantly. He explains in detail how his daughter looked as she collapsed onto the coffee table. The back of her head was split open. "There are still bullet holes in the wall. I can't seem to make myself repair them."

Ra'at believes a Shiite militia, the Mahdi Army, was responsible. The militia was formed in 2003 by an Iraqi political leader, Muqtada al-Sadr. "They shot us because we are Christians," he says. The family first fled to Jordan, but life in the UN refugee camp was horrible, so they returned to Baghdad. "I would leave again if I could," he says. White looked up Ra'at after the murders and offered to help him and his family if they needed it.

They have attended church here since then.

I also talk to one of the soldiers, a short young man in civilian clothes. He's a Christian, but because he's a soldier he is not permitted to leave the country. Though he has nothing against living in Baghdad, he says. "You can do anything you want in the city," he says. He sounds euphoric. "Corruption is wonderful. You can buy anything."

He travels anyway, and he tells how he recently bribed some Iraqi border guards to let him enter Syria. A Muslim friend told him that Islamist groups paid three hundred dollars for each Christian murdered.

After the worshipers leave, I follow White into his office, where he lies flat on his back in bed, his head on a pillow. It's a small room with a desk, a sofa, and a bed. Several tacky trinkets, gifts he has received throughout the years, hang on the wall. I sit on the same sofa as earlier that day. I'm served coffee in a cup bearing the emblem of the U.S. Department of State, accompanied by "International Zone Baghdad, 2009." That was back when the Americans weren't ashamed of advertising their presence.

"I didn't expect that I would still be handing out food to the poor ten years after the war started," he says. He fingers a red rosary and lays a pillow on his stomach. I ask him about conversions. My experience in the Muslim world is that it is extremely controversial to convert Muslims, and many people despise the priests—often from the West—who do so.

"It's difficult," he says. "One time we converted thirteen Muslims. Eleven of them were killed within a week, a family who all converted at the same time. But I don't try to convince people to convert, I'm not actively involved in this. If I am asked, I have to do it."

His most recent conversion, a woman, took place two weeks

ago. "I asked her why she was doing this. She wanted to become a Christian and marry a Christian man. The day after I baptized her, she moved to Turkey."

He assures me that he doesn't try to recruit the Iraqi Christians who attend services here for the Anglican Church. They are allowed to continue being whatever they are: Assyrians, Chaldeans, etc. I ask him if he doesn't feel responsible for those who convert, given the mortal danger they are in.

"That's why I try to avoid it. We do nothing to encourage the Muslims who use our clinics and schools to convert. But once in a while, if they ask me and I see they're serious, I have to do it. I tell them they can't let anyone know about it, not even their spouses."

He explains that his church is under special protection, the reason being that it's an English church. Another reason is Andrew White himself. But this protection doesn't mean he is completely safe. He says that in 2006, hundreds of notes were put up all over the city, declaring that he was wanted, dead or alive. "So I left the church for two weeks, but then I came back."

I ask if it's possible to get used to living this way. "I can't imagine anything else. It's strange. Unfortunately I'm not the type of person who gets scared. It's the honest-to-God truth. It's very, very seldom that I'm really nervous."

Only once, when he was kidnapped, did he seriously fear for his life. He was thrown into a basement with chopped-off fingers and toes littering the floor. He was carrying a considerable amount of cash, and he was able to buy his freedom the same day he was captured.

I ask him if he supported the war in 2003. "Yes. There was no freedom in Iraq. Everyone lived in fear. It had proved to be impossible for Iraqis themselves to remove Saddam from power."

He still believes that getting rid of him was the right thing to do. "But what we did immediately following the war was completely wrong. The coalition forces didn't foresee what the war would result in. They had no sense for religion."

Andrew White says he personally told Paul Bremer, the American diplomat who after the war became civil governor of Iraq, that a civil war would break out if Americans didn't take the religious aspects of the country seriously. According to the priest, Bremer said his government was convinced that religion and politics should be separated. Bremer, who in those years was referred to as the "King of Iraq," believed that restoring electricity and clean water were the highest priorities.

"What he didn't understand was that in the Middle East, religion and politics are bound together. Terrorism came into play because the Sunnis felt they had lost their political power."

I ask him if it makes any sense at all to stay here. "It's important that we Christians in the West show our support for these persecuted Christians. For me that means living here among them. I feel strongly that I need to be here. This church is like a family to me. We belong together in a way I have never experienced anywhere else. They've lost everything."

But is it only idealism that has caused him to seek this place out? "I have to admit that the dynamics here, the danger suits me well. I love it." Isn't he afraid of being killed? "Truthfully, it doesn't worry me one bit. I've been shot at and all that, so it's not because they haven't tried. Many of my closest aides have been killed. In fact, it's probably most likely that one day I'll be killed, too. I'm one of the few people from the West living and working in the Red Zone. At least I don't know of any others. The people who come here live in secure housing or in the Green Zone, and they return home quickly. I'm here, and I've been here a very long time."

Western human rights organizations no longer report from

Baghdad. They write about what's happening but are unwilling to live here, the priest explains. "The only ones I really respect are those who come here to live among Iraqis in Baghdad."

A number of Western journalists returned to Baghdad in the spring of 2013 for the tenth anniversary of the war. Many barely left their hotels, and they caught a flight home as soon as they could. Westerners are now a rare sight in Baghdad's streets. Without the presence of the international media, the attention of Europe and the United States is flagging. Recently five bombs exploded in one day here, killing many people. Reports about it were brief and succinct.

"Many journalists lived here for several years. Their lives were in danger every single day. But their employers either didn't have the means or the will to maintain a presence here, so they were sent elsewhere."

It's ten p.m., the priest looks tired, and I decide to let him rest. I return to the annex, which I have all to myself, and I lock all the doors and go to bed. On the wall is a large painting of a Jewish patriarch who lived in Iraq in the 1800s. One of White's special interests is Orthodox Judaism, which he studied in Jerusalem. For a time he lived in Mea Shearim, the Orthodox Jewish quarter in the city. A book about Hasidic Judaism lies on his night table. You won't find this book on many other tables in Baghdad.

Earlier he told me how much he loved Israel. The Arab countries have forgotten why they hate the country so much, he said. It's become instinct. There are only six Jews left in Baghdad. He named them all for me.

I turn off the light and gaze out the window at a streetlamp beyond the protective wall. It's still unearthly quiet outside. I strain to hear cars honking, ambulance sirens, people shouting, the waters of the Tigris flowing—any sign of life. But there's nothing. I could just as well be the only one in the city.

The silence is disturbing, and I can't sleep. I turn the night lamp back on. All there is to read is a Bible. One side is in English, the other side in Arabic. When he preached for the children earlier that day, White read aloud from the crucifixion and resurrection scenes in Mark. Therefore I read Mark's Easter passages about Jesus, who is betrayed by his own disciple with a kiss, and who allows himself to be whipped, scorned, and spit upon before dying, lonesome and naked on the cross.

More than anything, I'm struck by the story of Peter, who is closest to Jesus. "Even though all may fall away, yet I will not," Peter announces during the Last Supper, after Jesus says that one of his twelve disciples at the table will betray him. The day after, Peter denies his master three times before the rooster crows twice, as Jesus foretold.

I have to leave early the next morning. For breakfast I eat a fried egg and bread; I tear off pieces of the bread and soak them in the yolk. I drink tea with the priest in his office, then I say goodbye and walk out in front of the church. The morning sun blazes down. I want to take a final look at the monument commemorating the Danish soldiers.

Roses and newly mown grass surround the monument. This peaceful sight before me seems so unnatural. This memorial for the eight soldiers would never be allowed to stand in Baghdad if it were not for this priest. And without extensive protection the church couldn't be active. There's something backward about this entire setup, some inverted illustration, an uplifting, moving, and sad exception in a city of failure, flight, and decay. Denmark has abandoned the country we sacrificed eight soldiers' lives to help. The Western world is leaving Baghdad. As are the city's Christians. The powers-that-be have been unable to protect them.

The driver calls me over, and I sit in the backseat. The gate opens, and we stop behind the pickup with the six Iraqi soldiers ready to escort me to the airport.

Instinctively I lean over toward the middle of the seat to protect myself against whatever may come. I look at the driver's face in the rearview mirror and see the same sweaty nervous wreck who drove me around yesterday. He makes the sign of the cross.

EPILOGUE

Today it's clear that the majority of Christian Iraqis who in 2013 believed there would be no Christians left in Iraq within ten years were too optimistic.

Christians have disappeared from Mosul, former home to the largest number of Christians in Iraq. For the first time in two thousand years, no sermons are being preached there; in some of the abandoned churches, ISIS is selling war booty and other goods. In Bakhdida, one of the stops on my travels, Christians fled after being told they would be killed unless they converted to Islam or left. They abandoned all their belongings. Since last hearing from Nasran Aziz, the elderly woman I visited in Bakhdida who lost a son and two daughters-in-law, she has fled with her family, first to Dohuk, then to Ankawa, the Assyrian quarter in Erbil, where they were living in a refugee camp, hungry, cold, and sick, with no roof over their heads. The family is in dire economic straits, and she has gone through major surgery, a hysterectomy. In November 2014, Andrew White, the vicar of St. George's Church, left Baghdad on what he says were the orders of the Archbishop of Canterbury. It was simply too dangerous to remain. Even the Lord's work has its limits.

Apart from a few in Baghdad, the only Christians left in Iraq are in the areas controlled by Kurds. What happened to the Jews after World War Two has happened, *is happening*, to Christians. Ethnic cleansing is a reality.

Perhaps the reason no Western leaders seem much affected by

what is going on lies in relativizing the suffering of Christians versus the dangers of Islamism. Several researchers and some media were far too optimistic during the so-called Arab Spring; they described the Muslim Brotherhood, for example, as moderate. The Copts I met didn't share this analysis. To them the pressure from Islamists was the major reason why so many Christians have emigrated in the past several years. It made little difference to them whether movements such as the Brotherhood came to power by democratic means or by violence, when the end result was the institution of Sharia law. They wouldn't dream of underestimating the threat from Islamists, whether they be mild or unyielding.

We must acknowledge that developments in Egypt, Libya, Gaza, Syria, and Iraq have proven these concerned Christians right. When they lost the protection that rulers such as Mubarak, Qaddafi, Assad, and Saddam Hussein gave them, they were damned. They were linked with the hated former regimes and the West.

A third of the six hundred thousand Christians in Syria are thought to have fled the country since the uprising began in the spring of 2011. They have been targeted and chased out by movements such as ISIS and the al-Nusra Front. One of the worst attacks on Christians in centuries occurred in August 2013, while the Muslim Brotherhood in Egypt was in power: more than forty-two churches across the country were burned, with numerous deaths. The situation for Egyptian Christians under the heavy-handed, undemocratic leadership of president Abdel Fattah el-Sisi has, however, improved.

I have met several people who believe that Christians are the most persecuted group in the world. Among others, the pope stated this at the United Nations in 2011. In the fall of 2012,

German Chancellor Angela Merkel echoed exactly these sentiments. According to the international Christian organization Open Doors, one hundred million Christians across the globe are being persecuted. According to a 2011 report from the PEW Research Center, 130 of the world's 191 countries have reported that Christians are being harassed. PEW believes this makes Christians the world's most vulnerable religious group.

During the writing of this book, all this seemed to have little effect on the Danish Foreign Minister at the time, Villy Søvndal. At a conference in Kolding, Denmark in the fall of 2012, he said, "It's unwise to enter into a conflict on behalf of a single group."

His colleagues in the United States seem to share his viewpoint. In an article in *The New York Times Magazine* in July 2015, Eliza Griswold wrote: "It has been nearly impossible for two U.S. presidents—Bush, a conservative evangelical; and Obama, a progressive liberal—to address the plight of Christians explicitly for fear of appearing to play into the crusader and 'clash of civilizations' narratives the West is accused of embracing." Condoleezza Rice, the Secretary of State in the Bush administration, is said to have stated that the United States doesn't intervene in "sectarian" issues.

This fear of being looked upon as Islamophobic can be detected in the U.S. government's rhetoric. During Obama's presidency, he and his administration have consciously avoided the use of words such as Muslims, Islam, and Islamism in connection with the abuses and terrorism committed by violent Muslim groups in the Middle East. When twenty-one Egyptian Copts were beheaded in February 2015 by ISIS on a Libyan beach, the U.S. State Department referred to those executed as "Egyptian citizens." As if the faiths of the executioners and victims played no role in this barbaric act. This cleansing of language leads to confusion, distortion, and dissimulation.

In this book I have limited my focus to "one single group." I hope it's clear why I've done so. Rarely do we solve grave problems by avoiding them, by not shedding light on them. At the same time, our supposed fellowship with Christians has been weakened by the divergent paths of, and increasing distance between, the West and the Middle East. Christians in the Middle East find themselves in a desperate, lonely place, stuck between secular apathy in the West and a religion-based contempt by an increasing number of Islamists in their own lands.

Tribal mentality may be on the retreat in the West, but it is gaining strength in the Middle East. We can ill afford the luxury of not treating this matter seriously. These Christians need our attention; they are being persecuted because they are Christians.

Change is on the horizon, however. In June 2015, a center-right government was elected in Denmark. As part of its platform, the government states that "in several of the world's flashpoints, a systematic persecution of Christian minorities is taking place. This government will put a special focus on strengthening international efforts to protect these minorities." The same stance has been taken by the German government under Chancellor Angela Merkel. An important recognition of the ISIS atrocities against Yezidis and Christians has also taken place. In February 2016 the European Parliament voted in favor of calling these crimes a genocide.

This book hasn't dealt with the worst countries. Every year Open Doors, which concerns itself with persecuted Christians, compiles a list of the fifty countries where faith spawns the most dire consequences. Of the four countries my research led me to (and a fifth, Syria, which I have written about), one—Lebanon—is not even on the list. In 2016 Open Doors places The Palestinian Territories as #24, Syria as #5, and Iraq as #2.

North Korea tops the list. According to Open Doors, tens of thousands of Christians have been sent to refugee camps because of their faith. Of course I don't need to mention that Muslim countries are far from the only ones who have mistreated minorities; we have a strong tradition of doing that in European Christian countries. Currently, however, it appears to be communist, former communist, and Muslim countries that top the ignominious list. And persecution seems to be worst in Africa, Asia, and the Middle East.

What should we call the treatment that these Christians are being subjected to? We know what anti-Semitism is. We also understand what racism means. The fight against these criminal mentalities has changed our part of the world.

But the abuse of Christians in the Middle East belongs to the same categories as racism and anti-Semitism, and the longer the cruelty remains unnamed, the more difficult it is to do something about it. We can't call it racism; Middle Eastern Christians aren't a race, they speak and look like others in their societies. Xenophobia doesn't work either, because these Christians aren't strangers—on the contrary, they have lived there for two thousand years.

The term "Christianophobia" is being used increasingly, but I don't care for it since it indicates a "morbid fear" of Christians. Discrimination and persecution of Christians in the Middle East is not a clinical, irrational sickness. It is not a phobia. It is a deeply-rooted judicial and administrative discrimination that Christians have been subjected to for centuries. It also comes from an educational system that for decades has avoided informing Muslim students about who these Christians really are. This is the source of the contempt that regularly evolves into violence.

While we wait for the correct term, the governments of the West—the United States, the European Union, my own native Denmark—would do well to listen to the warnings of Christians like those whose voices have been conveyed in these pages. Too many times in modern history have we ignored such voices, resulting in terrible death and destruction. Let us not make the same mistake again.

ACKNOWLEDGMENTS

First and foremost, I wish to thank Allan Sørensen, my best friend in the Middle East, who has helped me with practically everything the past fifteen years. Also, thanks go out to Arne Hardis, who battled through earlier versions of this book and as punishment has plagued me with his merciless but usually spot-on corrections. Likewise I want to thank my first-rate editor, Johannes Baun, for insisting that I carry out my travels. I am indebted to Raymond Merhej and Amir Almaleh, who followed me around and gave me exclusive access to the most hair-raising stories in Lebanon and Iraq. In the United States, I'm grateful to my American publishers, Ross Ufberg and Michael Wise, who have taken a chance on this book, and for the thorough and precise translation performed by Mark Kline, as well as to Eamon Moynihan, who read the book in Danish and has been supportive of its American publication. Thanks to my generous sponsors: Consul George Jorck and Wife Emma Jorck's Foundation, Lademann's Foundation, Ellen and Carl Tafdrup's Memorial Trust, and the Danish Arts Foundation. I owe a debt of gratitude to *Weekendavisen*, to my bosses Ole Nyeng, foreign editor, and Anne Knudsen, editor in chief, for giving me the time, resources, and newspaper space for this project. And of course I wish to thank Margrethe Wivel, my beautiful wife, who in spite of two full-time jobs has been amazingly patient with all my traveling and writing.

Thanks also to:

Dr. Saadi Almalah, may he rest in peace, and all of Amir's

family in Ankawa, Louis Markos Aube, Taher Bahoo, Pernille Bramming, Nik Bredholt, Hani Danial, Naji Daoud, Jakob Erle, Hamdy (my Egyptian driver), Hanne Foighel, Garth Hewitt, Dr. Cornelis Hulsman, Anita Baun Hørdum, Isaac Ibrahim, Steffen Jensen, Kurt Johansen, Yoram Kaniuk who will be greatly missed, Habib Malik, Nabil Melki, Monsignor Joseph Merhej, Mogens S. Mogensen, Bishop Moussa, Maikel Nabil, Birger Nygaard, Jens Juul Petersen, Herbert Pundik, George Qamawaty, Samir Qumsieh, Henrik Ertner Rasmussen, Danny Rubenstein, Antoine Saad, Dr. Bernard Sabella, Nasim Sadeq, Waleed Safi, Sirine Saghira, Youssef Sidhom, Jakob Skovgaard-Petersen, Frederik Stjernfelt, Samuel Tadros, Khaled Abu Toameh, Andrew White, Peter Wivel, Hanna Ziadeh, Zoughbi Zoughbi, Lone Østerlind, and two courageous women, one Egyptian and the other Palestinian, whose help was invaluable but whose names I've promised not to reveal.

NOTES

2   *We are only now beginning*: For a statistical overview of the displaced Christians from the Mosul and Nineveh regions, see: http://english.ankawa.com/?p=13134

4   *Two stories illustrate*: Much of the information that follows comes from a lengthy article by Kirsten Powers called "The Muslim Brotherhood's War on Coptic Christians," August 22, 2013: http://www.thedailybeast.com/articles/2013/08/22/the-muslim-brotherhood-s-war-on-coptic-christians.html

5   *They witnessed how*: Lorenzo Cremonesi, "I cristiani rifugiati in Kurdistan 'Il mondo ci ha abbandonati,'" *Corriere della Sera*, August 26, 2014: http://www.corriere.it/esteri/14_agosto_26/i-cristiani-rifugiati-kurdistan-il-mondo-ci-ha-abbandonati-07a9ec12-2ce3-11e4-b2cb-83c2802e5fb4.shtml

6   *As a Christian refugee in Erbil*: From an article by Daniel Williams, "Christianity in Iraq is Finished," *The Washington Post*, September 19, 2014. Williams is the author of *Forsaken*, one of the few recent books on the subject of the persecution of Christians in the Middle East, published by OR Books in March 2016. https://www.washingtonpost.com/opinions/christianity-in-iraq-is-finished/2014/09/19/21feaa7c-3f2f-11e4-b0ea-8141703bbf6f_story.html

10 *About seven thousand Christians*: For more on this subject see Mitri Raheb, ed., *Palestinian Christians in the West Bank, Facts, Figures and Trends*, 2nd Revised Edition, Bethlehem: Diyar Consortium, 2012.

In Latin America alone: See Viola Raheb, ed., *Latin Americans with Palestinian Roots*, Bethlehem: Diyar Publisher, 2012.

At that time some of the citizens: Many of the statistics in this chapter dealing with the population of Palestinian Christians have been taken from two papers by Dr. Bernard Sabella:

"Palestinian Christians: Population, Interreligious Relations and the Second Intifada," Unpublished paper, 2001; and

"Palestinian Christians: Historical Demographic Developments, Current Politics and Attitudes toward Church, Society and Human Rights. The Sabeel Survey on Palestinian Christians in the West Bank and Israel—Summer 2006," Jerusalem: Sabeel Ecumenical Liberation Theology Center, 2007: http://www.sabeel.org/pdfs/the sabeel survey - english 2008.pdf

For more on the rights on Non-Muslims in Muslim societies, see Kasja Ahlstand and Göran Gunner, *Non-Muslims In Muslim Majority Societies. With Focus on the Middle East and Pakistan*, Cambridge: The Lutterworth Press, 2011.

11 *No population in the world*: See Toni O'Laughlin, "Census finds Palestinian population up by 30%," *The Guardian*, February 2, 2008: http://www.guardian.co.uk/world/2008/feb/11/israelandthepalestinians.population

Before I see a word: See Mitri Raheb, *Palestinian Christians in the West Bank, Facts, Figures and Trends*, as mentioned above.

17 *Mitri Raheb rebuilt it*: To read more about Raheb's personal story, see his book, *Bethlehem Besieged: Stories of Hope in Times of Trouble*, published by Fortress Press in 2004. Raheb also wrote a memoir, *I Am a Palestinian Christian*, Minneapolis: Fortress Press, 1995.

19 *Once I met the man*: Over the past two decades, I have written extensively about the Middle East for the Danish newspaper *Weekendavisen*, and many of the incidents recounted in this book, including this one, were first reported there, and can be read (in Danish) for greater detail.

21   *But such harassment is well-documented*: The executive summary
      of the U.S. State Department 2013 Report on International Reli-
      gious Freedom: Israel and The Occupied Territories can be viewed
      here: http://www.state.gov/j/drl/rls/irf/2013/nea/222295.htm

22   *Ten years ago, Israeli tanks*: Charles Sennott, the European bureau
      chief of *The Boston Globe*, surveyed the situation in 2002 in his
      book *The Body and the Blood: The Middle East's Vanishing Chris-
      tians and the Possibility for Peace*, which was published by Public
      Affairs Books.

32   *The report states directly*: The full report can be accessed here:
      http://www.state.gov/j/drl/rls/irf/2007/90212.htm

41   *It was built from 1929*: One can read more about the town of Tay-
      beh in a July 2011 article by Hanne Foighel in *ONE Magazine*
      the publication of the Pontifical Mission Jerusalem, accessible
      here: http://www.pontificalmission-jerusalem.org/default.aspx?
      ID=3558&pagetypeID=4&sitecode=JER&pageno=1

57   *The Gaza imams*: For more on this topic, see the 2010 article
      by Itamar Marcus and Barbara Crook, "Hamas video: Allah, kill
      Christians and Jews 'to the last one,'" *Palestinian Media Watch*:
      palwatch.org/main.aspx?fi=157&doc_id=3895

70   *In a country where 95 percent*: The Pew Research Center released a
      report in 2010 that can be accessed here: http://www.pewglobal.
      org/files/2010/12/Pew-Global-Attitudes-Muslim-Report-FI-
      NAL-December-2-2010.pdf

71   *Others have been prosecuted*: Human Rights Watch and The Egyp-
      tian Initiative for Personal Rights released a report on personal
      religious freedom in 2012, accessible here: http://www.hrw.org/
      sites/default/files/reports/egypt1107webwcover.pdf

72   *In Coptic Egypt*: For a further discussion of Copts in Egypt, see
      John H. Watson's book *Among the Copts*, originally published by
      Sussex Academic Press in 2000.

75   *It was a death blow to Alexandria*: Philip Mansel discusses the cosmopolitan and varied histories of Alexandria, Smyrna, and Beirut in his 2001 book, published by Yale University Press, *Levant – Splendor and Catastrophe on the Mediterranean*.

77   *Others say there are under*: Pew estimated that in December 2011, 5.3% of the Egyptian population and 4% of the entire Middle East population was Christian. For the full report see: http://www.pewforum.org/Christian/Global-Christianity-middle-east-north-africa.aspx

   This follows a pattern: Further analysis of the statistics, and information about the difficulty in capturing accurate numbers, can be found in an article by Cornelis Hulsman, "Discrepancies Between Coptic Statistics in the Egyptian Census and Estimates Provided by the Coptic Orthodox Church," *Mideo*, vol. 29, 2012.

80   *The enormously popular television cleric*: Clips of Qaradawi's segments, including those discussed here, can be viewed at: *http://www.memritv.org/clip/en/3287.htm*

87   *He mentions that American foundations*: When I later asked Dr. Hulsman to send me a source, he emailed me a link to a report from the left-leaning think tank Center for American Progress.
       The report tracks an alleged spreading of "hate and misinformation" in the United States to five key persons: Frank Gaffney of the Center For Security Policy, David Yerushalmi of the Society of Americans for National Existence, Robert Spencer of Jihad Watch and Stop Islamization of America, Daniel Pipes of the Middle East Forum, and Steven Emerson of Investigative Project on Terrorism. These five men funded by several donors organize campaigns that "reach out to millions of Americans."
       The report can be viewed here: https://www.american-progress.org/wp-content/uploads/issues/2011/08/pdf/islamophobia.pdf

95   *There is no end to the subjects addressed*: Many of Dr. Muhammad Salah's videos can be seen on YouTube and on Facebook: https://www.youtube.com/watch?v=w1ls9eA5RCE; https://www.facebook.com/YT.CallToIslam1/

97   *He believes that Jews control*: Some of Naik's speeches on 9/11 can be seen here: http://navedz.com/zakir-naik-the-open-hypocricy-of-west/

    The New York Times reported that King Salman of Saudia Arabia awarded Naik one of the country's highest honors, for "service to Islam," in 2015: http://www.nytimes.com/2015/03/03/world/middleeast/saudi-award-goes-to-dr-zakir-naik-a-muslim-televangelist-who-harshly-criticizes-us.html?_r=1

101   *When I finished Goddard's book*: This led to an exchange of opinions in *Weekendavisen* with one of the book's Danish publishers. First article: Klaus Wivel, "Saudi Arabia's Western Face," *Weekendavisen*, December 2, 2011; Response: Jakob Skovgaard-Petersen, "Feature: The Prince, the Saudi Casanova, and Bigotry," *Weekendavisen*, December 9, 2011; Counter-response: Klaus Wivel, "The Racism of Low Expectations," *Weekendavisen*, December 16, 2011.

103   *My search bears very little fruit*: For example: Rubert Shortt's 2012 book *Christianophobia: A Faith under Attack*, published by Rider & Co.; or the informative *Persecuted: The Global Assault on Christians*, by Paul Marshall, Lela Gilbert and Nina Shea, published by Thomas Nelson in 2013. By far the best book I've read on the topic is the beautiful road trip, *From the Holy Mountain: A Journey in the Shadow of Byzantium*, by William Dalrymple, published by HarperCollins in 1997.

106   *Earlier that day*: Samuel Tadros, *Motherland Lost*, Stanford: Hoover Institution Press, 2013.

110   *In Egypt in 2010*: The Pew Global Attitudes Report for 2010 can be accessed at: http://www.pewglobal.org/files/2010/12/Pew-Global-Attitudes-Muslim-Report-FINAL-December-2-2010.pdf

111 *Video clips show the attackers*: https://www.youtube.com/watch?v=ejnU4ErmwMk

A little over a week later: The following paragraph makes use of a report from Maspiro Youth Movement concerning sectarian violence in 2011. The collection of articles refers to several human rights organizations, and has links to dozens of disturbing videos: http://sectarianviolenceegypt2011.blogspot.dk/

112 *The list of attacks against Copts*: Here are more examples: on April 7, 2011, a network of Arab human rights organizations sent an open letter to the then-leader of the Egyptian forces, Gen. Mohammed Hussein Tantawi. They wanted the attacks on Christians ended, and they named episodes where Copts had been attacked, often by groups with Salafist connections. They reported, for example, an attack on a young Copt in the city of Abu el-Matameer and the burning of his shop. He had been accused of harassing a neighbor's daughter. After a so-called dispute resolution meeting, the young Copt's family was told to pay a fine of approximately $17,000 and leave the town. The network also told about a group of Islamists who were terrorizing Copts in the towns of Albderman and Nazlet Albderman; the Islamists demanded that the Copts pay a head tax, and they also stole Copts' land. The burning of a house owned by Ayman Anwar Mitri, a Copt, on March 20, 2011 in the city of Qena was also mentioned. Three women were living with the forty-five-year-old schoolteacher, and three Salafists in the town claimed that the women were prostitutes. First Mitri's house was set on fire; the fire department put the fire out. Later he was standing guard himself when twenty men overpowered him, beat him up, and cut off one of his ears. The schoolteacher told the police what happened and who was responsible, but according to his lawyer, none of these men were arrested. On the contrary, a meeting was set up between Coptic priests and representatives of the men who had attacked Mitri. "The meeting was only to get me to drop all charges without getting any compensation," the earless man told Human Rights Watch. A week later, the Grand Imam of al-Azhar Mosque, Ahmed El-Tayeb, offered to pay for an ear operation. Mitri met with the imam but declined the offer.

113 *Video clips show armored military vehicles*: The disturbing clip can be seen here: http://www.jadaliyya.com/pages/index/3103/ the-maspero-massacre_what-really-happened-%28video%29

133 *According to a census in 1932*: For more on the census and the history of Lebanon, see Kamal Salibi's *A House of Many Mansions: The History of Lebanon Reconsidered*, Oakland: University of California Press, 1989.

134 *Charles Malik played a decisive role*: Much of the research from this section is based on Harvard law professor and author Mary Ann Glendon's book, *A World Made New: Eleanor Roosevelt And the Universal Declaration of Human Rights*, New York: Random House 2001.

138 *They enjoyed no political rights*: Habik Malik, *Islamism and the future of the Christians of the Middle East*, Stanford: Hoover Institution Press, 2010.

144 *When Lebanon achieved full independence*: Based on a report by the Lebanese Information Center, a nonprofit research group in Alexandria, Virginia. Accessible here: https://www.google.com/ url?sa=t&rct=j&q=&esrc=s&source=web&cd=1&ved=0ahUKE wiv9Yibg-nKAhVHXD4KHV7DBbwQFgggMAA&url= http%3A%2F%2Fwww.lstatic.org%2FPDF%2Fdemographen- glish.pdf&usg=AFQjCNFI9iRSNbe7gy3X1NcF9D-NZHM _FA&sig2=AGPDJBdfQAUE7FuRUUcwVg&cad=rja

168 *Is it a type of cultural chauvinism*: See the full Pew Research Center Report from 2011 here: http://www.pewforum.org/2011/08/09/ rising-restrictions-on-religion2/

191 *In April 2013 alone*: The Iraq Body Count project keeps meticulous data here: https://www.iraqbodycount.org/database/recent/

192 *At present it's estimated*: More statistics available here, in the 2011 report on Global Christianity by the Pew Research Center: http://www.pewforum.org/2011/12/19/global-christianity-exec/

193 *According to a 2008 report*: http://www.refworld.org/cgi-bin/
texis/vtx/rwmain?page=country&category=&publisher=&
type=COUNTRYPROF&coi=IRQ&rid=&docid=4954
ce672&skip=0

196 *After the fall of the regime*: The theft of Christians' land is confirmed in this 2011 report by the Hammurabi Human Rights
Organization: https://www.google.com/url?sa=t&rct=j&q=&es-
rc=s&source=web&cd=2&ved=0ahUKEwigncWihunKAhVL-
Gj4KHYo0BbwQFggkMAE&url=http%3A%2F%2Fwww.
hhro.org%2Fhhro%2Ffile_art%2Fhhro_report_2011_
english%2Fhhro_report_2011_en.pdf&usg=AFQjCN-
EqhUCq_C2-ABKFoxLw4BicuDbOkw&sig2=LkyVvQ9kH-
DZalRaqN5HSLQ

199 *Seventeen priests were murdered*: See Suha Rassam, *Christianity
in Iraq*, Bayswater: Freedom Publishing, 2010; and the Assyrian
International News Agency's regularly updated website for more
news and statistics: http://www.aina.org/index.html

222 *In 2012, Iraq was number 169*: http://www.transparency.org/
country - IRQ

246 *Open Doors*: That list is downloadable in full here: https://www.
opendoorsusa.org/christian-persecution/world-watch-list/

INDEX

New Vessel Press

For more information on other New Vessel Press titles
please visit newvesselpress.com.